PENGUIN BOOKS

US GUYS

As a former national correspondent for *The New York Times* Charlie LeDuff has covered the war in Iraq, crossed the desert with Mexican migrants, and written about work and race in a North Carolina slaughterhouse for which he was co-awarded the Pulitzer Prize. In 2006 LeDuff produced a 10-part television show of participatory journalism, *Only in America*. He is the author of *Work and Other Sins: Life in New York City and Thereabouts*. He has contributed to *Vanity Fair* and *Rolling Stone*, among other places.

Tulsa, Oklahoma

Oklahoma City, Oklahoma

Amarillo, Texas

Oakland, California

Black Rock City, Nevada

US

Coos Bay, Oregon

Crow Agency, Montana

Detroit, Michigan

New York City, New York

Cleveland, Tennessee

Miami, Florida

Guys

The true and
twisted mind
of the
American man

Charlie LeDuff

PENGUIN BOOKS

PENGUIN BOOKS

Published by the Penguin Group

Penguin Group (USA) Inc., 375 Hudson Street, New York, New York 10014, U.S.A.
Penguin Group (Canada), 90 Eglinton Avenue East, Suite 700, Toronto, Ontario, Canada M4P 2Y3,
(a division of Pearson Penguin Canada Inc.)
Penguin Books Ltd, 80 Strand, London WC2R 0RL, England
Penguin Ireland, 25 St Stephen's Green, Dublin 2, Ireland (a division of Penguin Books Ltd)
Penguin Group (Australia), 250 Camberwell Road, Camberwell, Victoria 3124, Australia
(a division of Pearson Australia Group Pty Ltd)
Penguin Books India Pvt Ltd, 11 Community Centre, Panchsheel Park, New Delhi – 110 017, India
Penguin Group (NZ), 67 Apollo Drive, Rosedale, North Shore 0632, New Zealand
(a division of Pearson New Zealand Ltd)
Penguin Books (South Africa) (Pty) Ltd, 24 Sturdee Avenue, Rosebank,
Johannesburg 2196, South Africa

Penguin Books Ltd, Registered Offices:
80 Strand, London WC2R 0RL, England

First published in the United States of America by The Penguin Press,
a member of Penguin Group (USA) Inc. 2006
Published in Penguin Books 2008

10 9 8 7 6 5 4 3 2 1

THE LIBRARY OF CONGRESS HAS CATALOGED THE HARDCOVER EDITION AS FOLLOWS:
LeDuff, Charlie.
US guys : the true and twisted mind of the American man/Charlie LeDuff.
p.   cm.
ISBN 1-59420-106-4 (hc.)
ISBN 978-0-14-311306-5 (pbk.)
1. Men—United States.   2. Men—United States—Psychology.
3. Masculinity—United States.   I. Title.
HQ1090.3.L43 2006
305.310973—dc22   2006042179

Printed in the United States of America
Designed by Stephanie Huntwork

In memory of Nicole LeDuff

CONTENTS

PREFACE

There are certain things an American man should know. And if he does not know them, he at least has been convinced that he should somehow know them, even if they are a detriment to him.

The American man has been taught that while it is better to avoid a fight, he should have been in a fight; that honor cannot always be defended with reason. He should never admit fear. He should strive to put the blade in his adversary's chest, not his back. An American man should know how to load and fire a gun. He should know how to ride a horse, bet on a horse, bet on the stock market and bet on the cards. A good man should know a woman's body and know how to please her. His woman, in turn, should never speak anything but well of him in public. An American man should have been raised in church, rejected the church and eventually found virtue in the church.

The American man should be educated. He should work. He should honor his debts and live within his means. He should be able to recite poetry and have bits of true philosophy at his fingertips. He should be able to play an instrument and know how to help a rose grow. An American man should dress and speak his language well. He should be handy and mechanically inclined and yet his nails must be clean. A man should have children, and at some point his children should reject him. And in the course of his life, a man's children should return and find virtue in him.

This is what an American man should be. Of course, no such man has ever existed and no man probably ever will. It may be that he prefers men. It may be that he was born weak-bodied. He may have been abandoned. He may be dull-witted. He may live in a trailer, or a ranch house, or a squat city apartment. Men crave dignity and fulfillment, and when they cannot attain those, they become unhappy, quarrelsome, small-minded, blowhards, overintellectuals, chauvinists, cowards, dopers, abstainers, aesthetes, racists, talk show know-it-alls and critics.

Some men are strong despite their shortcomings and are able to get on with the dreary business of living. This sort of man is at ease with the idea that in the great scheme of things, he means absolutely nothing.

And then there are the American men who, unable to grasp the Ideal, begin to call themselves a minority, a victim . . . they pine for those good old days that were never very good. They fall back on bromides and empty slogans; they demand action that they are not willing to take themselves. They are anxious and so they make excuses and tell lies. They criticize leadership because they can never lead. They take pills that give them feelings of enlargement but lack the abilities to sustain it. Still, these men are important. As they go, the world goes, and they are ensnared in a disorienting swirl of change.

This book is not a sociological study. It offers no solutions to the problems of crime, immigration, the economy, spiritual bankruptcy or other maladies afflicting the male citizen of the United States of America. It does not suppose to crawl into his brain. It is simply intended to be a conversation with him, a participatory look into his world, an attempt to feel what he feels. While this is not a memoir, there are personal bits of my history here; after all, I am one of these men. In that sense, looking back, this was a search for the angry, forgotten middling America from where I come.

US Guys, as the title implies, has a personal point of view: my subjects' and mine. It is an American travelogue, a year spent on the road crisscrossing this great nation. What I found were the same worries and uncertainties, the same preoccupations in the minds of virtually every American man I spoke with—namely, race, sexuality, God, ambition, isolation, misunderstanding, fear.

You may notice some references in these stories to a camera, a crew, a producer. This book was born out of a television show, the name of which I am contractually obligated to withhold. The program, in my mind, was designed to seek out the American man at a profound time of war and debt and extravagance and sexual dysfunction and digitization and globalization and mass migration and so many other -ations that the people of this nation no longer understand what it is to be an American. And so I struck out with a camera and a notebook to explore certain ideas that consume the public conversation.

I hung with a biker club in Oakland, California, and brawled at one of their fight parties to find out why the American man is so aggressive and angry. I went to a gay rodeo in Oklahoma City and rode a bull to explore the notion of virility and manhood. I went to Oregon and became a trapeze clown with a one-ring circus because I wanted to talk with immigrants about what America looks like from their eyes. I went to Texas to play professional football to speak with men about race and prowess. I went to the Burning Man festival in the desert of Nevada to romp in the sandbox of counterculture. And so on.

You will find no stories of rich people in this book, nor will you find stories about the executive washroom. Why should you? You can find those in any respectable newspaper or magazine. The stories in this book are about average Americans, the majority of Americans.

A man, a journalist, recently wrote a popular book that discusses the interconnectedness of the new world and how in the face of global competition, American ambition has gone flat. He describes the average American as lazy, profligate, fat. The American lacks gumption, he wrote.

I doubt it. Consider that while our factories have moved to Mexico, the Mexicans still come north where wages are twenty times higher. If I could go to Canada and make $200 an hour, I'd shovel horseshit with my bare hands. Most of us would. Somewhere in there lies the root of ambition.

In any case, sweeping people into the ash can of history is dangerous. Polemics about the future are of little use to those struggling today. To disregard these anxieties is to be unaware of the future that children of privilege face. Violence is my guess. Poverty breeds resentment. The rich cannot survive behind the gates.

You will also find little talk about the American woman. She is in this book, but hardly. Someday, someone, some woman most likely, with some ambition will write *US Gals*. It won't be me. I hardly understand women. I do know that women still judge themselves against man, still demand entrance into his clubhouse, still write and whisper silly little things to irritate his ego. I know they still play the carnal office games: stuffing their aging legs into stockings and half skirts, clucking pleasantly to their male colleagues while lying in wait to slit the throat of any other hen with the audacity to enter the barnyard. Do women still need men? Yes. Men are still necessary.

They say the American man is falling to pieces; that he is spooked, spiritually deadened, disassociated, infantilized. That's just the television talking. There's nothing wrong with us guys, except everything. But that's the way it's always been.

US Guys

klahoma City, Oklahoma

Amarillo, Texas

Tulsa, Oklahoma

Oakland, California

Black Rock City, Nevada

Coos Bay, Oregon

Crow Agency, Montana

Detroit, Michigan

New York City, New York

Cleveland, Tennessee

Miami, Florida

The poems and stories of Charley W. Murphy are aided and abetted by vodka. The vodka, like the poetry, is cheap stuff. Neither should be savored, but rather consumed quickly in a single sitting. The vodka is sold for $13 in shatterproof half-gallon bottles so that when an asshole trips over himself, he doesn't sever an artery.

Charley has scars, about nine of them, and shows them proudly as though they were antique foil paper and he a sturdy wall. There is one that runs from his testicles to his sternum from a bayonet wound and another that stretches from ear to ear and was inflicted by a sword, injuries Charlie suffered, he says, as a twelve-year-old enlistee in the Korean War. Charley tells stories. That's what he does. He tells stories and writes poems and drinks himself to dust.

Charley is a walking coat rack with hair the color of nicotine, skin the color and texture of wax paper. He is sixty-five, has a voice ruined by cheap cigarettes, dentures rubbed smooth and a dignity that even the cheap booze cannot wash out. His stories are tall tales, mostly, but as it goes with most tall tales, Charley's germinate from a kernel of truth. And one story currently consuming him is the ballad of Elmer Steele, former getaway driver for Pretty Boy Floyd.

Elmer Steele, Charley says, died ten days ago. And though Charley was both too busy and not invited to the funeral, Charley says he knew the old highwayman and the highwayman had bequeathed a secret unto him.

It seems that Elmer Steele buried a considerable amount of money in some old whiskey jugs, money from the old bank jobs with Pretty Boy. Charley claims to know near exactly where the money's stashed.

"I know, but I ain't telling," Charley says dubiously to the beaten-down denizens of his bungalow motel who have gathered around the table to hear the story about the buried treasure. "No matter how much people around here might need the money, I ain't telling. It don't belong to them."

Charley doesn't need the money. He writes checks. Charley Murphy is the cowboy poet laureate of the Shady Rest Court in Tulsa, Oklahoma, one of the old motor lodges along Route 66 on the westbound side of the highway, the side pointing toward the better days of California. It is in a highly unrecommended corner of Tulsa, on the west bank of the Arkansas River, a place of grift and destitution and deceit.

The Tulsa on the east bank was built by two businesses: oil and Jesus. There they have country club weddings, Oral Roberts University and blond women in tight sweaters. On the west bank the people are ridden hard and hung up wet to dry. They sleep on their left sides to wear their hearts out a little faster. But without the west side, you could not have an east side.

The north side of town used to be the most affluent black community in the United States until 1921, when a mob of whites burned thirty-five square blocks to the ground, shooting, lynching and drag-ging to death perhaps three hundred people and dumping many of them into the river. Tulsa has yet to come to terms with this nightmar-ish and shameful history. The north-side district is charmingly referred to today as "Niggertown."

Everywhere in America there is a west side and a north side, though sometimes they are called the east side and the south side, but there is always the other side where the other half lives. I was hanging out at the Shady Rest around the time of the 2004 election, when John Edwards, the Tom-Thumbed vice presidential candidate for the Democrats, was barnstorming around the country jabbering about the two Americas: the haves and have-nots. For the record there is at least a third America, the have somewhats, and a fourth, the self-defeated, the people who fell off the table and are never getting up to the supper plate. There are more and more of them out there. The country's adrift. Uneasy. Broke. Making less. I got myself a weekly room for sixty-five bucks, the last room available.

The Shady Rest is a peeling, run-down place of thirteen unlucky bungalows, and for God's sakes would somebody get a shovel and a broom and get rid of the dog shit and maybe then the flies would go away. Charley drinks too much, spends too much time underneath the shadow of the paper-shell pecan trees, bitching about the flies, talking about those old Oklahoma days when outlaws ran the highways and his own mother gave him three fingers of liquor and a $10 bill before dumping him on Georgia Street.

"I was only six years old," Charley croaks.

The people of the Shady Rest are much like the buildings. Slapdash. Falling down. Holding on. The Shady Rest is a place where people on the drift stick to the tar paper for a few weeks, maybe a few months, before blowing on or blowing themselves away. They usually move to nowhere, maybe somewhere around Tulsa. They talk incessant bullshit about the score they will never hit, a two-bedroom apartment they will never see. Their lives one lousy episode after the next. Charley is their model of responsibility and consistency, their anchor. They call him Dad, Grandpa, Pops.

There are at the moment four Indians living here, four lesbians, two carnies. There are two old women without teeth who cut their meat into tiny cubes before sucking the pieces down into sinew. There is an old man with an oxygen tank, another with a walker, a few kids who somehow belong to Stan the Can, a large, violent-looking man with a round rugged face currently on a three-day binge of inhaling paint and automobile solvents. Stan the Can used to be married to Charley's daughter, Lori, the manager of the Shady Rest who turned lesbian, though in between she found a second husband who is currently residing in the state penitentiary for kiting checks.

When Stan got out of the can for armed robbery, he dreamed of killing Lori. He let the moment pass, however, and now stands in the doorway tonight, the bugs crawling on his ears, staring over her way, menacing-like, sucking fumes from an empty beer can.

Stan Strome is the son of a bootlegger who died from smoking and drinking too much. Stan didn't learn anything much from him except how to fight, sell dope, smoke and drink too much. Stan, naturally, went to the pen himself. Stan's son went to the pen and Stan's grandson will probably follow in the family business. Stan's old girl is about to lose her leg from too much sugar. Stan needs a score.

"A paycheck, a beer and a two-bedroom apartment," he says. "I need a way to get some easy money." Stan found himself a part-time job fixing a two-bedroom apartment in exchange for three months' rent. It seemed like a good deal. Shut the door, spread the paint on the walls and inhale. Stan likes the smell of paint. But the apartment didn't work out.

"I gotta find some money, but jobs is hard to come by," Stan says. "Maybe Charley'll tell us where that money's at. Wouldn't that be something? *Finding* money?"

These Americans have no place left to drift. Okies don't go to California anymore because there are too many Mexicans who by way of their cheap labor denigrate the work. No way for an uneducated natural-born American to make it by his muscle anymore. So, he spins circle upon circle upon circle—from the penitentiary to a tent on the Arkansas River to the filth of the Shady Rest.

Some people on the east side of town say it's easier getting a job for $8 an hour at the dry-cleaning shop than living the way they do on the west bank. But working's not easier. Standing there, sucking fumes, face to face with the fact that you've got nothing and that's the way it's always going to be.

Scheming a big score is better. Scheming, at least, rhymes with dreaming.

And so the dream of the bank robber's money casts itself over the Shady Rest when a tall, weedy-looking guy came around a couple of months ago. He wasn't bad-looking and had booze on his breath and a history of driving while boiled. It was a hot, muggy, rotten day when he pulled into the gravel lot of the Shady Rest. He wore dark clothes and drove a dark car, one of those big old eighties-style boats like a Riviera or a Catalina. He talked about a transmission job he owed Charley, and according to Charley he owes half of Tulsa a transmission job. Anyhow . . .

The man's name was Larry, and Larry was claiming to be the grandson of one of the last bank robbers of the old Depression-era High Plains gangster days. The grandfather's name, according to Larry, was Elmer Butch Steele, an old getaway driver on a couple of bank runs for Pretty Boy Floyd, who hailed from rural Oklahoma.

Charley said he too knew the old highwayman, was a good friend of his, even hid him out in the old days when things were too hot. Charley seemed to accept the grandson's claim, and the grandson accepted Charley's. There's not much else the men had, it seemed, than their stories and their habits and their dreams.

Larry, the "grandson," believed that the old man had some of the old bank loot stashed away somewhere, buried underground in old peach jars. Larry said he was trying his damnedest to pry the secret out of the old man, but the old man was playing dumb like he couldn't remember or like it never happened or like he spent it or like he was going senile.

Larry and Charley soon forgot the transmission job and talked about how Butch was ninety-one-years old, had taken up with a young girl, a red-headed, blue-eyed diner waitress named Dixie who wouldn't let anyone go near the old man because she was fixing to dig up the money as soon as he walked on to meet his Maker.

In the few months that have passed, the "grandson" was picked up for drinking while driving and resisting arrest and was kicked out of the house by Dixie. And Elmer Butch Steele, highwayman, preacher, murderer and messenger of God, passed away about ten days ago, said Charley. The cause was brain cancer. The money is in old ceramic whiskey jugs. Charley wrote a poem extemporaneously as his liver blazed away in the afternoon sun.

Elmer Steele of Oklahoma
He was a bank robber, a killer.
He was on death row.
He was a friend of mine.
I watched him walk
Until it was time for him to go.
May God have mercy on his soul.

It is a beautiful ode to a not-so-dead man. To set the record straight, Elmer Steele is alive and unwell in west Tulsa. I tracked him down only a mile or two from the Shady Rest. Elmer has a four-bedroom house done up in shaggy carpet and butterfly cutouts on the walls and cats and spends his days in a BarcaLounger trying to piece together his memory and make peace with the Maker for having done the bad things he's done.

His wife Dixie is seventy years old and cuts a pretty figure with a slender, top-heavy build. She keeps a derringer loaded with hollow-point bullets in her brassiere and has a pretty smile. Contrary to rumor swirling around the west bank, Dixie seems less motivated in hoarding her husband's buried treasure than in protecting his twisted and contradictory legacy.

It is believed that Elmer Steele is the last living member of the short-lived midwestern crime wave that included Dust Bowl Oklahoma as a central character. Pretty Boy Floyd and Machine Gun Kelly made homes in Tulsa. Ma Barker raised her boys here. Bonnie Parker and Clyde Barrow did a lot of work in Oklahoma, and just six weeks before they were killed in a police ambush in Louisiana, Barrow purportedly wrote a letter to Henry Ford postmarked from Tulsa telling the manufacturing giant how speedy and reliable he thought the new V-8s were. The mythology of the outlaw runs deep in the Oklahoman heart.

To this effect, Mrs. Steele taped her husband's oral history and compiled the transcripts in a spiral-bound book called *The Rebel Prophet*.

Among the more interesting information gleaned from the book is that Elmer Steele has a conduit directly to Almighty God Himself by way of a mysterious figure known only to him as the Messenger. The Messenger is always dressed in white and has dark brown hair. Not only did the Messenger teach Elmer Steele to read, he continues to deliver divine revelations to him—in verse.

For instance, this from August 4, 1989, concerning Armageddon:

And it isn't going to be good.
Some of it is going to be really bad,
But it is all coming from me,
And it is all, some of it, going to be sad.
But it is because of the wicked, because of their ways,
And their ungodly things that they do and they say,
And when I tell you that I am going to destroy them,
That do these things,
You will see it happen, right at your hand.

And there won't be many, but there will be plenty
When it is all said and done.

From Elmer Steele's early age, the Messenger rode on his shoulder, according to the old Elmer Steele. Born in 1913 and orphaned young, Steele lived with a string of relatives and strangers in and around the town of Sallisaw, the same hometown as Pretty Boy Floyd and the fictitious Joad family of Steinbeck's *Grapes of Wrath*. The only two who loved the boy, it seemed, were this mysterious Messenger and a man named Noah Whinrey, who had a farm not too far away from Sallisaw on the other side of the Arkansas border. It was the Messenger who led Steele to the Whinrey farm, apparently.

Old Mr. Whinrey put the young orphan to work, fed him, taught him to drive fast, and, most important to our story, paid young Elmer Steele in coins for the work he did. It was here that the buried money myth takes its root. Young Elmer Steele took the pennies, nickels and dimes and buried them in old fruit jars at the Whinrey farm, under some young sapling. When old Mr. Whinrey died, his son Junior ran Elmer off the farm and the fruit jars went forgotten. The Whinrey son later went crazy and had to be committed to a sanatorium. Steele attributes this restitution to the divine intervention of the Messenger.

As life went on and times got tough and Oklahoma withered into burnt grass, Steele ignored the Messenger's admonishments and turned to a life of crime. It was natural that Steele would hook up with Charles Arthur "Pretty Boy" Floyd. They came from the same hardscrabble background and disdained work. The dream was to lie around in silk underwear and smoke good cigars.

Pretty Boy Floyd and the other outlaws lived on the cusp between the pony and the automobile, overalls and haberdashery. Their method was simple and always the same: Floyd and George Birdwell, an Indian man who read biblical passages on the way to the stickup jobs, would walk into the bank in broad daylight and announce the place was being robbed. Floyd wore suits and his hair slicked down. Birdwell wore a cowboy hat. They preferred Ford V-8s for their power and a younger man like Elmer Steele or Aussie Elliot was hired to drive the getaway car. Steele says he drove on three occasions in 1931 at the age of eighteen, all of them Oklahoma jobs. His job was to fill the tank, check the tires and hoses and fluids and idle outside the bank until Floyd and Birdwell came walking out with a hostage or two. The hostages were made to ride on the running boards to be sure the police wouldn't shoot up the car. Once outside the city limits, the hostages were released.

"They would go back to the hideaway and divvy it up," says Dixie, who knows her husband's stories better than he does anymore. "Those were tough days, the Depression, they spent it as soon as they got it."

The Depression had a demoralizing effect on the workingman, and those who suffered the worst made heroes of these farm boys who walked in and relieved bankers of their money. They became famous, filling the East Coast papers with their exploits and their comic-book nicknames. Floyd came to be known as the sagebrush Robin Hood for buying people groceries and destroying the land deeds of struggling Dust Bowl farmers.

Their exploits led to the rise of J. Edgar Hoover and the founding of the FBI in 1935 after the Kansas City Massacre of June 16, 1933, where four lawmen including a federal agent were murdered at the Union Station. Floyd was charged with the ambush, but evidence points to his innocence. John Dillinger was named the first Public Enemy Number One. Floyd was named the second. By 1936, the principal characters of the outlaw era were either dead or in prison. Steele did two separate bids for burglary between 1932 and 1942, according to old state prison records.

Looking at the old photographs, it's evident Elmer was never a handsome man, and today he is a hunched, moist, speckle-headed old man. He speaks in a meek whisper and tends to drift away in midconversation.

He wears brown-framed bifocals and white stockings and has hands nearly the size of his feet.

Steele says the main regret he has in life is a murder he alleges to have committed on a holdup partner named Jack Kensley, though I have found no record of such a murder.

"I was standing outside the bank door in the alley, when that son of a gun come out with that sack of money," he recalls, sitting in his BarcaLounger, drifting in and out of lucidity. "I said, 'How much we get?' and he said, '*We* didn't get nothing. You didn't walk in those doors with me.' Well, I got white-hot at that son of a gun, so I shot him in the back and took that bag of money. It was seven hundred dollars."

He pauses for a long spell. "Cheaters get buried," he says clearly.

He has since gone on to lead a good Christian life. He was a welder and was ordained as a Pentecostal minister in 1974 at the Rays of Faith Tabernacle, Inc., in Tulsa. His ordination certificate was signed by Dr. A. D. Marney, the stepfather of the shrieking, raunchy-mouthed preacher-turned-comedian Sam Kinison, who died in a car crash in 1992.

"My life, I don't say it was all good," Steele says to me. "But I've preached to people, prayed for them. They got well. I hope God forgives me for some of the things I've done."

He and Dixie have spent their golden years trying to do right by those with troubles. They've got a big house, so they took in children who weren't their own. They took in strangers, young men with allergies to work. Men from the Shady Rest. These men started calling Steele Grandpa. They stole from him. The old man put up with it since he couldn't manage his affairs on his own. "When you get old you just worry 'bout dying," he explains.

And to this end, the drifters and tramps helped themselves. The Steeles remember two men especially, who took most anything not bolted down, Dixie says. They took checks and tools and dug up the yard. They heard about the fruit jars from Elmer. But in their greed, they balled it all up, twisted it around like taffy, until an innocent little story of an orphan's piggy bank became a Tommy gun legend in west Tulsa.

"Now that I come to think about it, they sure did ask an awful lot about that money," Dixie says.

Back at the last-chance motel, everyone is getting on with the boring business of dying. The night is quiet except for the cicadas and the frogs in the swamp and a little whimper that wafts out of bungalow Number 8. Stan the Can is out late and his old woman Sandy is left to her monsters. Sandy is scheduled to have her right leg amputated the following week. She is lying on the love seat, clucking sort of, when Stan the Can walks in.

"Honey, I know you going to leave me when I lose this leg."

Stan has hardly been good to her, but he's trying now. He found love somewhere inside himself.

"What the hell you talking about?" he says with real pity. A movie about space aliens is playing on the TV.

"I think you're gonna leave me. A broke-down, one-legged old woman." Sandy Prichard isn't much to look at, short, squat, toothless, fifty-two years old, with stringy hair and a bloated leg that hurts to stand on. But she is good for Stan. She is a decent person; their bunga-low is clean and smells good. There is no dog shit and there are no flies and there is good food on the hot plate. She taught Stan things about living when nobody never taught him nothing before. Stan is thirty-eight, big arms, big chest, bad teeth and a blue heart tattooed over his real heart.

"Don't worry, baby, I'll be with you to the end, whose ever's end comes first." Stan is high on paint fumes, but he means it. He goes out-side the torn screen door and lights himself a cigarette.

"She don't think I love her," Stan says. "I wish I had things to give her. Her own private place to get better. She deserves that."

Stan goes back to the Sonic Burger the next morning and begs for another chance. The pay is $5.45 an hour. Stan takes it and tries to kick the can. "I'm gonna try. I can be a good man."

The news that Elmer is alive starts Charley to buzzing. A little bit of news, a little bit of excitement, starts a little bit of dreaming, which kick-starts a little bit of drinking, which carries on for the entire afternoon.

"Did he give a location?" Lori wants to know, because even if there isn't much money in the jars, those coins have to be collector's pieces.

"Do they got metal lids 'cause a metal detector will pick that up," she says. Lori gets it most of all. She said she'd done time for welfare fraud and selling drugs, anything to keep nine children fed, she says. This is it, not much chance for much else. And it takes strength to admit that when you're clean and not leaning on a crutch.

"Nope, it ain't in jars," Charley says. "But I know where it is."

"Yeah?" snarls Johnny Pierce, who lives in Number 3 with his young girlfriend Vicki. His tone is kind of menacing. His bad teeth are showing. "Then where the fuck is it?" I had read somewhere that the most itinerant person living in the United States is a native-born man with less than a high school education. And Johnny fits the bill. He's on the drift because the only thing he has to offer anymore is manual labor, and since the flood of illegal immigrants has dropped his wage, he finds himself perpetually on the move. Johnny drifts, gets high, works bit jobs and screws his fat girlfriend. I can hear them through the wall of the moldy little room that I share with the roaches.

When he is out hustling in the afternoon, Vicki will come sit on my bed in a half T-shirt and I'll stand in the doorway so as not to get caught in there with big mama. Carnies, after all, are known to go crazy.

Inside the traveling carnival, Johnny was a king. He worked kiddies' rides and he was important. But he got caught doing stuff he wasn't supposed to be doing. Blowing in the wind, on the outside, he says, he's nothing, just another asshole looking for a break.

"It's in jars buried somewhere," Lori tells him.

"Shit," says Johnny. "Let's go git it."

"No, it ain't in a jar, it's in an old whiskey jug," Charley interrupts again. "And I know where it's at. Everybody thinks it's in Arkansas. Well, you're a thousand miles off. Elmer didn't tell you and I ain't gonna tell you 'cause it ain't your money."

"It's stole money, innit? So it ain't his money," Lori reasonably considers.

"Yep, he stole it from the bank jobs," Charley says. "With Pretty Boy. Real bank robbers."

"Well, I'm a relation of Jesse James," she reminds her father.

"Jesse James?" her father says, incredulous. "You not related to no Jesse James. You related to Billy the Kid."

"Forget it," Lori says. "We got to figure this out. Now, when you're treasure hunting—I'm from the hills, so I know something about it— you got to rough it, 'cause you looking for money, so you can't spend money 'cause you'll be broke and probably in jail. You need a tent, sleeping bag, backpack, canned food, boot knife, canteen, metal detector, some sensible shoes, rolling papers and tobacco."

It's unclear who among them has any of these things except the inspiration. They all have the dream, if only for a fleeting moment in a humid afternoon.

"The only dream we all have here, the old people, the drug addicts, the poor people, is to have a chance to be rich," Lori says. "To have a comfortable life. A two-bedroomed house. Maybe go to McDonald's once a day and have Marlboro cigarettes. We don't want much.

"Sure would be nice to find that money. Maybe we'll go on Saturday."

Later, Charley gets in a fistfight with Kenda Harris, one of the lesbians living in Number 7, who has to report to jail this evening for stabbing her girlfriend with a nail file when Kenda caught her with another girl, a cousin. All the lesbians here have at least one kid, though none of them have their kids with them and they all try to live with that. Kenda's girlfriend has been out on a bender for a few days and isn't there to see her off. Kenda has no ride to the jailhouse and she is an agitated wildcat and Charley calls her darling one too many times and he asks her to bed down with him one too many times. Kenda doesn't want to be part of no cowboy poem or cold shower fantasies. Not today.

The old man and the wildcat hiss and spit and claw and scratch. Her insults and her fists leave Charley sullen and near tears. Here, Charley comes up with his own sad ending to his own sad life. "Okay, you want to know something from my heart? I'm dying. Not from no disease. I'm dying from loneliness. Nobody really cares about me no more."

It's true. Even the door-to-door canvasser wouldn't bother to register Charley with the Democratic Party, even though Charley was wanting to join. Charley scared him. Nobody wants the lowlifes. They smell. They dress badly. They're bigoted. They are the third America who make it work by helping each other, seeing as no one else gives a shit.

Stan the Can and my friend Eddie and I give Kenda a ride to the jailhouse, because there is no one else who will. We eat hamburgers in the parking lot, give Kenda $10 for the cantina so she can buy envelopes and stamps. We tell her not to eat the sausage or sit directly on the toilet seat and wish her good luck. As we pull out of the parking lot, Kenda the wildcat waves and shouts to us strange men. "I love you."

We stop at Orpha's, a local bar downtown just a few hundred yards away from the jailhouse where Stan likes to drink. Kenda's girlfriend is in there, reeking of paint fumes. Stan just shakes his head because the girlfriend is waiting for a liver transplant.

Saturday arrives and no one goes looking for treasure. Kenda is in jail. Her girlfriend is home in bungalow Number 7 coughing blood. Sandy lies on the couch. Stan goes to see about his dead-end job. Charley is fighting the shakes, his mouth twisted and his eyes popping like a spawning salmon. Elmer Steele is home clinging to life. Everybody on the west side of Tulsa, the other side of town, knows what it is to have to crawl in through a window and steal a peanut butter sandwich, and that can't be considered a sin, can it?

"It's hunger," Charlie says. "No one's proud of being hungry."

And as the cicadas screech and Charley nurses a couple of pity beers, I read him my own ode to Elmer Steele.

Elmer is a living man.
Done as best he can.
Done some dirty tricks.
Kissed hisself three women.
Killed hisself a man.

Elmer loved no mother.
Made a little girl his wife.
Lost hisself that wife.
Got hisself another.
Then lost that second wife.

Elmer robbed a bank.
Shot ol' Kensley in the back.
Talked to the Messenger 'bout it
who said God'll take him back.

When they dig his resting hole
And put him down to sleep
He'll take along his money
in an old peach jar
Much too far to reach.

"Shoot, that's a good one, son," Charley says sickly. "Life ain't worth living without a good story."

Oklahoma City, Oklahoma

The Reverend was awake when the door cracked open, casting a crescent of gray light into the cheap motel room. The wind was coming off cold from the plains. Baby Boy stood gripping the threshold, slightly bowlegged, his Stetson tipped back on his head, stinking of booze. The Reverend did not ask where he'd been. He'd never gotten more than a lie from Baby Boy or an argument, and he didn't expect any different now. Baby Boy pissed, then peeled off his blue jeans and lay on the bed facing the wall. The old man was crestfallen.

They were different men from different parts of the country, their only commonalities being that they were rural, Christian and gay. Baby Boy and the Reverend had gotten "married" a few months earlier, "married" in quotations because it is difficult to discern which parts of their stories were correct and which were counterfeit. You can't know intimate things about a man unless he tells you, just as you can't know why he told you unless he tells you why he told you.

Baby Boy was from near a big city in Tennessee, the son of a father with heavy fists. He made it to eleventh grade, couldn't see the percentages and quit. His true name was not Baby Boy Miller. That is the rodeo name I've given him in order to preserve his dignity. He was in his mid-twenties, spoke in a masculine, mumbling, huckleberry accent, made thicker by a pronounced overbite and a distant ignorance. His dark hair was closely cropped, his shoulders round and hunched, his teeth discolored from chewing tobacco. He held a mercurial, unfocused anger. He had no savings to speak of, his bankroll having been spent on good times the evening before. It was money the old man had given him. Baby Boy had twice been married to women, one wedding presided over by the man lying in his bed now, whom he began relations with sometime between the two wives—this according to the Reverend, who insisted that their relationship began only after Baby Boy had matriculated into manhood. The two had met when Baby Boy was a teenager, at a supper party of a mutual friend. It was love at first sight, the Reverend insisted.

Baby Boy, it was plain to see, was haunted by the mania of his homosexuality; told by the deep recesses of his upbringing that it was wrong and womanly. Grandmother wanted children and the relatives saw the old man as having tricked Baby Boy, turned him gay, at least hoisted him over the wall. Sometimes the Reverend wondered this himself. And in that spirit, Baby Boy embarked on his cowboy fantasy: to be a bull rider, the most potent and virile thing there is. Baby Boy was trying to prove to his straight man that his gay man was really a man. And so, just a few months before I met him, Baby Boy struck out on his rodeo-hero saga, the Reverend playing the part of the cowboy minister, the willing accomplice, the Humbert to Baby Boy's Lolita, driving across the continent in a battered car soiled with cigarette stink and coffee stains, eating out of a chicken bucket.

It was a life the Reverend, an urbanite with a taste for good sherry and opera, would otherwise have sneered at. But love and passion make a man do unusual things. Then again, the Reverend's story was like that—strange and erratic and careening between cockamamie and heartbreaking, the reek of a human being desperate for authenticity. A few things are for certain. The man knew little of hard work. He was heavy and soft, handsome in a round-faced sort of way. He wore silver swept-back hair and clipped whiskers, which gave him the look of an accomplished professor. He suffered from diabetes and walked with a cane. He was in his late fifties but looked ten years older. He smoked heavily and breathed in a puffing, laborious cadence.

The Reverend might have provided the money, but he was the submissive of the relationship. Baby Boy felt funny about the sex, behaving in much the way a young blond woman in pearls and fur takes up with a geriatric husband. He was distant and cold and carried on in the relationship with an air of entitlement. The Reverend rarely got love and when he did, Baby Boy never looked at him.

"I ain't a faggot," Baby Boy would tell him.

"You're as dumb as a goat," the Reverend would reply.

I had met the two of them in late spring at a rodeo school for homosexuals near Gettysburg, Pennsylvania. At the time, Baby Boy talked a river of bullshit, painting himself as a professional bull rider, offering tips and advice, playing the veteran cowboy to the hilt in his electric-green western shirt with sponsorship patches from Wrangler jeans and Bud Lite beer. But his practice rides gave him away. Baby Boy would've had trouble on a merry-go-round pony.

His rope and his boots were crisp and new. But he was afraid to be on an animal. He poured sweat when we were first put on steers—small, neutered bulls, lean, hard animals with protruding knotty spines and hips and shoulder bones. Riding one is much like riding a mile of dirt road on a seatless bicycle.

Baby Boy refused to rosin his rope, the mark of a rank amateur.

Rosin is critical for a successful bull ride (eight seconds in the professional rodeo, six seconds in the gay), creating a gluey bond when rubbed and allowing the rider to maintain a firm grip. When a bull first bounds out of the chute, it draws a large breath, causing its chest to expand. At this point, if the rope is not sticky, it will slip through the rider's fingers like an anchor chain, a very dangerous proposition.

Baby Boy, the store-bought cowboy, went first, and as soon as the chute opened, allowing the animal to buck free, Baby Boy took a dive into the cow pies. He picked himself up and mumbled nearly incomprehensibly through his overbite and mouthpiece, "Dang-nabbed critter's too small." You could smell the fear steaming off of him.

The cowboy students snickered and Carl, the burly owner of the ranch, growled under his breath, "I hate a mouth, especially a goddamned chickenshit."

We left the school, promising to meet in a few weeks' time at the gay rodeo in Oklahoma City. Baby Boy handed out autographed portraits of himself. I threw mine in a garbage can. At the first gas station I stopped at, in a garbage can, was an autographed portrait of Baby Boy. I imagined gas stations all the way to Oklahoma City littered with the unsolicited head shots of Baby Boy Miller, the gay buckaroo.

Oklahoma City is a sprawl of freeways and cottonwoods. McDonald's, Conoco, McDonald's, feed store, engine repair, Motel 6, honkytonk, church, McDonald's and so forth. The landscape is so flat and barren you could probably watch your dog run away all day long.

Within this deeply religious and conservative city of nine hundred thousand, there is, interestingly enough, a vibrant gay quarter frequented by many of the area's estimated forty thousand homosexuals, a surprising number to me. I had rarely heard any talk of rural homosexuality before the film Brokeback Mountain, except for the gruesome murder of Matthew Shepard in Wyoming. No mention of gays is made at the National Cowboy Museum in Oklahoma. But they do exist, and they did exist before the West was ever won.

For instance: George Custer's famed Seventh Cavalry, while stationed in Fort Lincoln, Nebraska, had a Corporal Noonan assigned to the regiment who was married to the camp's laundress. But as it happened, Noonan's wife was not a woman. This was not discovered until Noonan was away on maneuvers and his wife unexpectedly died and her body was prepared for burial. Upon his return, the corporal, in his shame, and to the relief of his fellow troopers, shot himself in the heart.

There was "One-Eyed" Charlie Parkhurst, a California stagecoach driver who was five feet tall and weighed nearly two hundred pounds. He was considered one of the finest coach drivers in the Old West. His death made headlines in 1879 when the coroner discovered that the hard-drinking, tobacco-chewing, foulmouthed Charlie was actually Charlotte. It is thought that Charlie may have been the first American woman to vote for president of the United States.

Calamity Jane Canary wore buckskin and trousers and passed as a male scout for General Custer. Skilled in the saddle and with the gun, she claimed to be the wife of Wild Bill Hickok. There are accounts, however, that Calamity Jane was actually a lesbian and served as a beard to old Wild Bill, since he, it is said, secretly preferred the company of men. There are many more such stories.

And so it was. The Wild, Wild West was settled by outcasts.

The Oklahoma City gay rodeo had drawn hundreds of competitors from across the country, the twenty-first century versions of these One-Eyed Charlies and Calamity Janes, outcast cowboys and cowgirls of varying skill levels, all competing for the respect of their peers and cash prizes of hundreds, not thousands, of dollars.

By the time Baby Boy and the Reverend rolled into town from Wichita, their money was all but gone; it had cost five grand for Baby Boy to chase his cowboy fantasy from Maryland to here. Now they were sleeping at a louse-box for $26 a night on the far side of Oklahoma

City. The men ate ninety-nine-cent baloney with white bread and bickered over mayonnaise. The jar stood open on top of the icebox with a spoon stuck in it, growing hard.

They were two men drifting across America, a scum of dishonesty layering the surface of their lives: a championship bull rider who wasn't, and a fawning old man who, in his lust, went along for the lie.

But the Reverend too told some tall tales. He said, for instance, that he'd been a prostitute in the West Village of New York City when he was thirteen and by divine grace was rescued by nuns. But he also said he grew up on the frigid lakes of Michigan. He somehow finished high school, enlisted in the Army and injured his back as a paratrooper in Vietnam. He was discharged at twenty-three. Here, he entered the seminary, attended Notre Dame and the University of Michigan. He finished seminary training in Rome and earned two doctorates, one in theology. The Holy See eventually appointed him, by his own account, as a titular bishop. What's more, the Reverend said that not one, but two of his lovers were murdered in hate crimes—one so gruesome, he had crosses and swastikas carved into his body, which was dumped in a lot in Toronto. The only problem is the Royal Canadian Mounted Police have no recollection of such a hate crime having ever occurred.

The night before the rodeo, there was a mixer of gay cowboys and cowgirls at a dump called the Finish Line. It was situated in a part of the gay quarter known as Humiliation Way, so named because those who have found nobody by the end of the night find themselves in the humbling position of walking back and forth in front of the low motel windows looking for a little companionship.

The place was awash in western shirts and starched blue jeans and pointed boots and white straw cowboy hats. There was a sing-along welcoming the rodeo. The drag-queen cowboys wore false eyelashes the size of tarantulas, pouring their tormented hearts out to the crowd horseshoed around the parquet dance floor. Neon and a mirror ball lit the place. Baby Boy was drinking the Reverend's last $20. A drag queen in an American flag dress was croaking "I'm Proud to Be an American" while stroking Baby Boy's chin and Baby Boy tipped her. The Reverend stood at the opposite side of the dance floor, his eyes steaming through his spectacles about his tormented life; this maddening, brutish, inauthentic, beautiful little boy. "To tell you the truth," he said, "I don't like this scene so much. It's his trip for him to feel macho." It came out like *match-o.* I bought him a beer.

"My biggest fear is sitting in a dark room with no windows in a chair, watching some crap show like *Wheel of Fortune,* dying, dying alone. That scares me to tears. If you don't understand that, no matter what you are, you've got no heart. You're dead, man."

Living on baloney because everybody thought Baby Boy was pretty. But it made him feel good to be on the boy's arm. Their life was more a costume ball, a masquerade, a dress-up cowboy fantasy. The money was gone. The Reverend was already making calls around the country looking for a wire loan to get home. Baby Boy hadn't worked in six months. Just said gimme, and the old man gave him. The sun went up and then the sun went down and the old man cried, knowing he was going to die in some dark room anyhow. That or in a hospital, and no one, including Baby Boy, was going to be there to hold his hand.

Baby Boy was talking nearby with a cowboy in a mushroom brim hat. "You should see me on a bull, it's real purdy," he was saying. They disappeared. The Reverend went back to the motel alone.

The next morning, before the grand entry, I went down to the city's stockyards to have a plate of breakfast. The stockyards were in the Old West part of town with the brick buildings and large plate-glass windows and wide sidewalks with men lumbering about with white straw cowboy hats. I ran into two ranch hands, straight men, sitting in a red Chevy pickup that stank to the hills of cow manure. The cab was littered with cigarette boxes and dead Keystone beer cans and a blanket of old hamburger wrappers. Jack had the bad teeth. Jay sat in the driver's seat, with his shirt off. He had bad freeway-style tattoos, one of an unfinished medicine wheel, another of a cartoon character and another of an eagle's head.

I bummed a cigarette and leaned on the running board, shooting the breeze. Jack was a pro bull rider. I said that I was in town to ride in a rodeo myself. A gay rodeo. His eyebrows arched. Any difference in the rodeos? I asked him.

"Yeah, in that gay rodeo, you better watch your ass."

I'm not gay, I told him. And at that moment I was glad I wasn't. He said if I was a queer, then that's my business, though I ought to step back and not touch him because he's got a phobia about queers. "Like some are afraid of cockroaches and rats. I just got a phobia about queers, is all."

"You know how to wink at a queer?" he asked, and then he pantomimed aiming over the barrel of a shotgun squinting his back eye. He laughed and smoke poured out of his nostrils.

I asked Jay if he ever knew a queer. "Yaw," he said, he knew a queer who lived down the way from his ranch outside Norman where the university and the football team are. He just kind of knew the guy was a queer, was all; he put two and two together. "The guy was a dairy farmer, kind of swishy, you know, *swishy*." But the farmer never touched old Jay, no sirree, the man was a good old boy. By that, Jay meant he was an honest guy, strong, a good sense of humor, a good-natured skeptic of strangers and a beer drinker. Well, this old boy was queer, all right, you just knew it, and then the queer just up and married a woman and moved away, and that's strange, innit? "You know, it was kind of sad, because the guy couldn't be happy, going against his nature like that."

To which Jack said he too was a queer. "That's right, I'm a lesbian trapped in a man's body," he said. Jay let out an exasperated gasp.

"Oh, come on, now, man."

"Think about it. I'm a lesbian trapped in a man's body."

I invited Jack and Jay to the rodeo. They said no, thank you.

Over at the rodeo grounds, Baby Boy was making a spectacle of himself. He'd already given me a cheap belt buckle stamped "*Hecho en Mexico*" that he claimed was his first bull-riding championship trophy. I later found a dozen just like it for sale at the concession stand. Now here he was, milling about the stables, his hat cocked rooster-style with a big turkey feather stuck in the hatband. "I'm here to help set up," he told the stable manager.

"Who the hell are you?" the manager asked with scorn.

"I'm a bull rider," Baby Boy half lied.

"No one asked you for help, saddle tramp. You just ride," he said with a finger. "You just ride. Git it? Good, now git."

Baby Boy stood there stinging, and would quickly forget the man's advice. The Reverend smiled behind his hand.

I walked into the arena to get a look at the bulls. Big and perspiring, large-horned and snot dripping from their snouts. Nearly a ton, and much taller than me. My nerves were jangled, mixed with the smells of hamburger and animal urine, and I wanted to throw up breakfast. First-time participants like me gathered in the bleachers where the rodeo director gave us the rules: no unnatural behavior, no rude comments, no alcohol, no drugs, no inappropriate conduct with the animals. A violation meant the first Greyhound home.

There were 120 contestants competing in a variety of events: calf-roping, pole-bending, steer-riding, breakaway team roping, bronco-busting, steer-wrestling, barrel-racing, flag-racing, and bull-riding.

It was real cowboy stuff, except for three events unique to the gay rodeo. One, goat-dressing, consisted of two contestants running across the arena, putting underpants on a goat and running back. Steer-decorating involved a two-person team trying to tie a bow on a neutered bull's tail. And wild drag was undoubtedly the crowd favorite, whereby a woman—ostensibly a lesbian—held a steer by a rope. When the gate was let open, she would run it to a line, where she would hand it off to a man—ostensibly gay. He ran to a third line, and turned the animal around. A drag queen was then required to jump on its back and ride it bareback back across the first line.

I was the drag queen. I wore a black sequin dress (size 10), auburn pigtails, a blue sequin head sash, brown boots and black leather gloves.

On my turn out, I got a nice hand, a request to hike up my dress and a compliment from the announcer, calling me out by my rodeo name.

"Buck Fiddy, looking good today, ladies and gentlemen, in a nice cocktail ensemble."

I got dragged across the dirt arena by the steer. We finished out of the money.

The next day in the *Oklahoman* newspaper, there was a solitary mention of the rodeo—a photo of a drag queen on a steer. The gays were sad and angry. Sure, the wild drag was what they did, but not all they did. The paper could have presented a deep and colorful five-thousand-word portrait about gay life in the heartland, considering the hoo-ha about gay marriage during the last election. But there was no story, no results, no schedule of events, nothing but a drag queen in a black sequin dress with spaghetti straps and pigtails.

The funny thing about the photo was that the queer on the steer was Yours Truly. And I'm straight as an arrow. Nobody bothered to ask. If the editors needed any proof of my sexual orientation, they could have easily sent me their unhappy wives and girlfriends and I would return them home with a smile. And the thing is, I don't represent gay people any more than Baby Boy and the Reverend did. In fact, their relationship, it seemed to me, was no different from that of some straight couples I know: a lonely old man and his needy, manipulative piece of ass. There is not much difference between people, in my mind.

At noon we drew for bulls. I got Powwow Walker. Baby Boy got

Lazy Boy. A third got Gravedigger. Russell, the number one rider on the gay circuit, got Boss Hogg.

There were two women riding bulls as well, Elody and Rhonda. This was unique, since women are not allowed to ride bulls or broncos in the traditional rodeo. This rodeo was different. There were no gender barriers. You didn't even have to be gay to ride in gay rodeo. Rhonda got stomped, the animal whirling around on her, throwing her against the fence, trampling her three times as she curled up with her arms over her head. She was carted off by the paramedics and I could hear her cussing over the applause, "Shit, I ain't hurt." She seemed to me to be the best this country has to offer. Tough, decent, independent, willful. A good old girl.

Baby Boy, on the other hand, wanted it without earning it. He was not willing to pay his dues, to be quiet and humble and learn. He managed in two days to alienate the entire arena, compounding his ridicule by jangling around for hours in his spurs and green chaps, an expensive costume that the old man must have paid for.

The cowboy code, according to pulp novels and Hollywood, is to never ask a man his name and always feed the help. The real-life cowboy code is simply the gentlemen's code: listen before speaking, don't talk an ass of yourself, take your hat off in a lady's home, never brag, never jangle around in spurs telling whoppers and passing out autographed pictures of yourself, especially when no one asks for them.

One thing Baby Boy did know was that bull-riding is the pinnacle of the rodeo. The most muscular, match-o occupation on the circuit. He made the intelligent supposition that if he just got on a bull, then he would vault himself to a certain level of adulation. Baby Boy's method was not uncommon. In America, we are full of emotionally arrested men who take the mythology of reinvention, the notion of the individualist, and screw it all up. They spend too much time memorizing television characters and then go down to the Wal-Mart and buy it in a box. The thing is, you can't buy courage or rough hands from a box. It takes effort.

The announcer called my name. Contestant Number 150—Buck Fiddy.

I climbed up onto the chute platform, strapped on my glove and adjusted my chaps. Before I crawled onto Powwow, I had a strange talk, considering the timing and surroundings, with a chute manager.

"You're straight. I'm not," he said. "That don't make me any more evil than you. I just like men, is all." The man was well built, erect, not the least lispy.

"Thing is, the Christians always use Leviticus."

If a man also lie with mankind, as he lieth with a woman, both of them have committed an abomination: they shall surely be put to death; their blood shall be upon them.

"That's Old Testament," he said. I stood there sweating like a beer bottle in the sun. "They also say in Leviticus that you should stone the adulterer. Never touch a woman during menstruation. That you should take your sister-in-law when your brother dies. Imagine that. Nobody but Orthodox Jews follow those rules anymore. When Christ came and fulfilled the prophecy he brought the new law. The old laws were finished. The new laws are love your neighbor, but they never talk about that.

"I'm Southern, from Tennessee. I was indoctrinated my whole life with the Bible. I went to school. It took me a long time to deprogram."

"You turned away from the Christians because they turned away from you?" I asked.

"Indeed," he said.

Indeed, the cowboy said. He smelled like animal dung.

I crawled into the chute and stood over the bull. I rubbed the rope hot with a little rosin. People were yelling all kinds of stuff and I got confused. I forgot what I was doing.

"Squeeze your ass like a dancer."

"Stay off your pockets."

"Find your spot. Stay forward. Point 'em, boy, point 'em!"

My vision went blank, white, like heat lightning. I must have said pull. The gate rattled open The beast leaped long, jumped a second time, throwing its haunches high in the air. The rope unraveled. In my confusion, I hadn't rosined it enough and I popped straight up like a cork on a fishing line. I landed on my feet, but the bull kicked me in the elbow. It later went black with necrosis. I pushed the rodeo clown down without realizing it and ran for the fence. The next ride, I did better, riding him one second short of time, which would have got me a ribbon. But it turned away from my hand and caught me leaning. As it turned out, I wouldn't lose to one gay man, but two.

I took a seat in the stands and waited to watch Baby Boy, the guy who never stuck to anything in his life: not high school, not work, not marriage.

Near me sat a man named Larry. Larry had a solid build, round face, pale blue eyes, manners in the form of "yes, ma'am," "no, ma'am" and "pardon, ma'am?" He had an authoritative voice. Like he was the one who said grace at the dinner table

Larry was a cattle rancher from Texas. He was "five years shy of fifty." He said he'd like to find a conservative, traditional man, like himself, to settle down with. He was private about his sexuality, but he was sharing it anyway. Larry had been married for seven years: he wanted kids, she didn't. He didn't come out until many years after the divorce. Larry had five brothers. Three of them gay.

"So, do you think it's genetic?"

"No . . . no, I don't," he said with a rising inflection. "I don't think it's genetic, and I don't think it's choice. I believe it's environmental."

On his way out of the closet, Larry read a lot of books, studies, etc., and said they pointed to a common theme: "distant fathers, over-bearing mothers."

"Do I want to believe it's genetic? Yes. But until there are studies that indicate a genetic link, I really see it as environmental."

Strange thing about the country gays, they tended to be non-demonstrative, family- and work-oriented, religious, by all means conservative and Republican if not for the fact that they felt abandoned by the rhetoric. Guys fucking in public parks made Larry sick. Two heteros making out at a bus stop didn't please him either.

Baby Boy was on deck now, the last bull rider. Larry turned to his buddy: "That's the guy who was in the parking lot. The one with the mouth."

Baby Boy fell off the bull right out of the gate, lasting no longer than a stack of hotel towels. He embodied fear, you could see it in the way he curled up tight and cramped and hollered when he was getting on, then off, then on again. How quickly he bailed out. The men watched and sipped beer as Baby Boy sprinted for the gate like a frightened rabbit. He jumped onto the first two rungs, stopped himself and looked to discover the bull was at a safe distance. He hopped off the gate and did the pissed-off short-guy walk back to where he came from.

Larry and his buddies joked about the fact that Baby Boy drove fifteen hundred miles out here from Maryland just to spend eight-tenths of a second on the bull. "It took him a whole lot longer to put on all that crap," Larry said of Baby Boy's cowboy regalia.

A fast-moving shadow caught Baby Boy's peripheral vision. He ran back again toward the safety of the high gate, leaping without looking.

Larry said, "No, that's not the bull, that's the medic."

Baby Boy hopped off the gate again, kicking the dirt with his heels.

"He just needs to go home, have a mani/pedi and take a long soak in the tub," Larry said.

The men laughed.

After the awards banquet hosted at a freeway hotel that night, I ran into the Reverend on the steps of the lobby as he waited for his car. He told me he'd done a lot of thinking. "It's a midlife crisis," he said. "I guess I'm just scared." He looked drawn and pinched, like he'd just swallowed a tablespoon of salt. Him standing there in his checked shirt and straw hat with the big feather in the hatband. This wasn't for him. What am I doing here? he seemed to be asking me. Hell if I know, was my unspoken answer. I figured the Reverend would leave Baby Boy, but that would never happen because Baby Boy would be leaving him first. And then again, you never know. Love is an impossible thing to anticipate. I gave him $40 for gas. He hugged me and we said good-bye.

Later that evening I saw Baby Boy at the Finish Line. He told me he had called for an official inquiry, claiming that he had called twice for his chute to be opened and his request went unheard. He had a whiskey in his hand, drinking on the money I had given the Reverend to get home.

Tulsa, Oklahoma

Oklahoma City, Oklahoma

Amarillo, Texas

"I wouldn't ever set out to hurt anyone deliberately unless it was, you know, important. . . ."

—DICK BUTKUS, former Chicago Bears linebacker

Oakland, California

Black Rock City, Nevada

Coos Bay, Oregon

Crow Agency, Montana

Detroit, Michigan

New York City, New York

Cleveland, Tennessee

Miami, Florida

In 1963, the writer George Plimpton, the participatory reporter, joined the Detroit Lions football squad. He practiced with them for a month as the last-string quarterback. He did it for the ordinary guy, to let him know what it felt like, and he wrote a good book about the experience called *Paper Lion*. He wore number 0, equaling his football ability. In his only action during an intrasquad scrimmage, Plimpton managed to lose 28 yards in five plays.

It had been more than forty years since *Paper Lion* was first published; Plimpton was dead, and football had changed so much it seemed like an altogether different sport. I wanted to see what professional football was like now, to let today's ordinary guy who does not go to church but watches football on Sundays know what it felt like.

I called the Lions to ask if I could do a follow-up to the book, seeing as Plimpton had just died and football had become a multibillion-dollar distraction.

You'll have to run it through corporate, the representative said as I sat in my underwear on a cot outside a San Fernando Valley courthouse, waiting in the shade for a Los Angeles jury to decide if the one-time actor Robert Blake had in fact murdered his wife. He was found not guilty a few days later and I was busted for urinating in the public parking garage.

Talk to corporate. I had a better chance of tracking down Plimpton. I tossed the number. Plan B. There is a lesser pro football game, a minor league called the Arena Football League, played in the spring and summer, the opposite season from NFL football. In this game the field is 50 yards long, not 100, and the boundary lines are not demarcated by chalk lines but walls, like playing tackle football in a hockey rink. The game tends to be fast, high-scoring and improvisational. The problem was, the Arena season would be over in June and I'd miss it because I was going to have to park my ass at the Michael Jackson trial for my newspaper job.

As it happens there is an even lesser league, something farthest down the totem pole of professional football, Arena Football 2. Known as the Deuce, it's a semiprofessional league where men are paid $200 a week plus a $50 bonus if they win; it is a league of has-beens, wannabes and never-weres, the league of last resort occupied by men for whom the only thing they ever truly learned in college was how to play football, dudes grasping at the frayed end of the rope of hope, a single step from obsolescence. They leave wives behind in Florida and Colorado in search of a contract that probably isn't coming. To make ends meet, they do what all Americans without realistic dreams tend to do these days: work phone banks, push paper at mortgage offices, wipe asses of the aged and mentally retarded, drive septic trucks, stock shoe stores or dick around an uncle's pizza shop. Maybe I can get on a team in the Deuce. At least it would seem more human than the NFL's million-dollar reality show.

I called one of the teams, the Amarillo Dusters. Amarillo! Bush country! The citadel of football. Surely they would let me on their squad, let me practice, socialize, bore my way into the locker room, maybe even get some playing time in a real game. Christ, they could use the publicity. Who the hell ever heard of the Deuce?

"Sure, come on down, we can pad you up, gitcha in a scrimmage, maybe even gitcha in a game. Anytime. Whatever you need," the coach said.

He said it in a thick Texas accent, the kind you never hear in New York because once there the Texan quickly realizes he is considered a dull-wit, a hayseed and so he quickly drops the Dixie for a flat nasally manner of speech common to midwesterners.

The coach wasn't there my first day of practice. Seems he had already split to take a head coaching job at a nearby university. This was my first lesson about the Deuce. Nobody wants to stay here. It's a team league that works much like a meat counter, a display table of potential talent.

The new coach was a follicle-challenged young white guy named Steve Perdue, who, unlike the rest of the coaches, had not played college ball. He got his job in part by virtue of his relationship with the general manager, Warren McCarty, an old high school football buddy.

"Gen'lemen," Perdue said, clearing his throat at the Tuesday practice, tugging down on his ball cap. He sounded different from when I had gotten the playbook from him the previous Friday. Now, surrounded by black men he was expected to lead, he was talking with a black accent. "We got a reporter from television who is gonna suit up with us."

A howl went up from the men, laughter of the sort reserved for the belligerent drunk who gets knocked flat in a parking lot, or a fresh-faced suburban kid sentenced to thirty days in the county jail. I was given a helmet that did not fit around my forehead and when I forced it on down, it compressed my spine. The face mask was loose. My tennis shoes were peeling at the toes. I wore knee-high socks and a baggy tank top and I felt thirty-nine years old. I drank too much and I smoked. I was skinny, six feet tall and 170 pounds after a big lunch and my best athletic days were years behind me.

The shoulder pads to me seemed gargantuan and I could not fully extend my arms above my ears. And while I wasn't going to play with the Detroit Lions, at least I got something of Plimpton's legacy: they gave me a white practice jersey with a big black 0 ironed on the chest and back. My shin was blue from bull riding, my ear was cauliflowered from the punches I took at a fight club, making the helmet exceedingly painful, my chest still itched from the waxing I got in New York and I think I had fractured my hip in a drunken brawl in Oakland.

We did some limited stretching and calisthenics and then lined up to catch the ball being thrown by the quarterbacks, the starter Julian Reese, black, a former college All-American with enough talent to make it to the next level. His backup was a white guy from Canada, Steve Panella.

As my turn in line got close, my stomach started going sour. I was worried about looking like a gangly pantywaist. How you feeling? asked Kert Turner, a lineman of impossible size and one of the few white men on the team. "Tell you the truth, I'm scared," I don't know why I told him. You never admit fear on a football field; I remembered that much from my high school days. Football players are like dogs, they've got a way of smelling fear.

"Aw, don't be afraid," he said in a deep Bayou drawl. "Be an American," he said. It came out *Ahmerkun*. Of course, he told the rest of the boys and the giggling began.

"Chawlie's scared. You scared, Chawlie?" I pretended I didn't hear.

I was next in line and the hooting picked up. "Here comes Chawlie Oh. Come on, now, Chawlie Oh, let's see what you got, Chawlie Oh," that sort of thing.

And before I sprinted my route, I heard one of the black men say, "I'm just glad to see another white boy in uniform," and I realized right there that the story here wasn't really about football dreams, it was about race, an interesting test tube in the fact that besides prison, the sporting field is the only place in America where the racial fraction is inverted. The black man rules and the white man is the silent and often suffering minority.

My turn came and I lined my toe to the line of scrimmage, struck up my best wide receiver pose with my arms up and my legs aligned like a sprinter's. Reese nodded and I took off down the sidelines, probably too fast, too eager, slightly out of control, spastic. The ball spiraled perfectly toward me over my inside shoulder. I lost it momentarily through the face cage, miscalculated the straitjacketlike nature of the shoulder pads. The ball struck my fingers and bounced away.

The team howled with laughter.

"OOOOOh," someone shouted out, not knowing he was calling me by my number.

"Just another white boy," another said.

"Ol' man," said another.

"You oughta stick with jerking off in the shower" was the comment I most remember.

I felt like I wanted to keep running to the other side of the rink, out the door, into the parking lot, into the car, onto the plane and home to my job as a reporter where I could criticize people who actually do things without suffering my own humiliation.

The next time up, the ball was too high. They laughed again. The next ball was thrown to the outside and I couldn't even get my hands on it. I saw the quarterbacks laughing and I realized I was being hazed. They were throwing the ball so that I *couldn't* catch it. Letting me know this wasn't going to be as easy as I expected: just call up, start catching some balls and get in a game. They were, I think, telling me this was serious to them. That it was their lives and I ought to handle them with care, their egos as fragile as two dozen eggs in a cardboard box. I was going to have to earn their respect by effort, not through the virtue of a press card.

The next ball was thrown low and behind me. I dove and caught it, though I don't remember seeing it. "Charlie OOOOOOOh," came the shouts again. It felt good. I trotted back into line and got a wink from Reese. I flipped him the ball. The next time I made a diving catch, over the shoulder. Again they called my number: "OOOOOOOOOh!" They were laughing with me now, not at me. "Come on, Chawlie," said Kendrik Walker, thirty-one, the most emotionally explosive man on the team, with a pat on my ass.

I had traveled with the team the previous Saturday, four hours on a bus to play the Oklahoma City Yard Dawgz for sole possession of first place. From the window of the bus, the Texas Panhandle appears flat and mundane, so flat that when Coronado explored it, he shot one arrow after another in order to keep a straight line.

The team sat segregated on the bus, as is the custom in American mixed company. The black men, including Walker and Reese, sat in the back, and the four white men up front, including the kicker and a wide receiver named Jarrod Rouanzoin, who had broken his arm in a previous game.

The black men played booming rap music that drowned out everything else in the bus, and the white men, being the minority, were reduced to listening to their country and rock 'n' roll on their headphones.

On the bus, I learned of an ugly little racial incident that had permeated the team. It was conspicuous but hardly talked about, pushed to the back like a can of Brussels sprouts, racial epithets being taboo on the playing field, at least within the team dynamic.

It seems that Walker had called Rouanzoin a cracker a few weeks ago. Rouanzoin was stewing about it, unable to let the slip go. Being a white man from the country, he wasn't used to taking shit like that from a black man. "I played with black guys in college and by far this is the most racist team I've ever played with," he said quietly to me. Secretly, I felt, he wished bad things for Walker, a man with the height of a jockey and the physique of a power lifter.

He got his wish as Walker blew the Oklahoma City game on two consecutive plays, fumbling a missed field goal that had fallen short of the crossbar, which the opposing team recovered for a touchdown, and then fumbling the ensuing kickoff, which the Yard Dawgz also recovered for a touchdown. The Dusters lost the battle of I-40 by a touchdown and it could be directly attributed to Walker and the placekicker Jeremy Hershey, who missed perhaps a half dozen extra points.

A little fat boy, a Dawgz fan, was most humorous. "Hey, Walker!" he shouted. "You stink." Walker, who did not see it was a kid, turned in his direction and gave him the finger. He could have caused a riot, so outrageous were his antics. He promised to bed a man's wife, rearrange the teeth of another. He called the opposing players impotent homosexuals, complained to his own quarterback that he was repeatedly open. He intimidated the referees. It would have been bad if not for his peculiar indecipherable vocabulary.

Then a woman yelled, "You stink!"

To which Walker answered, "Gusha ball al bite!"

What it meant, I have no idea, nor did the woman, but we all laughed, including Walker.

The Dusters' owner was not amused. Bob Rogers made his money in trucks and dairy farms and like all Texans he loved his football. Someone convinced him to buy the Dusters and so, being rich, he did. They became the biggest thing in a town that didn't have much. This made Rogers, fifty-one, the patriarch in a football-mad region. He was a white man, of course—all the owners are white, as are nineteen of twenty head coaches, despite the fact that the league must be, by the look of it, at least seventy-five percent black. Rogers had a coarse schoolboy haircut, a neatly cut beard, favored blue jeans and western shirts. He was boyish in stature, with a tan and freshly scrubbed face. The man loved football and he understood my dream, the Everyman dream; he had given his blessing for me to step in on a Saturday night and experience the life of a superman.

Rogers sat behind the bench and was not pleased with what he saw. His face looked like a saucer of milk gone bad. "I love football and I love watching people watching football. I believe in football," he said. "I have made money, I don't mind spending some of it if the community gets a real boost. So winning is not so important that you take people you don't want in your community. This is family entertainment. You can't bring in the wrong type of people. You can't take in punks. I'm not bringing in punks to win."

But of course in the Deuce, winning is everything. NFL scouts don't come to see losers. And losers rarely make it to the next level. Losing is a death sentence to the dream. And tonight the dream moved a little closer to the scrap heap. Nobody said much on the bus. Walker slept with a towel over his head. The driver stopped and the men bought $103 in alcohol, which I paid for.

As we were getting drunk, I made a provocative toast, I couldn't help myself. It's what I do. "Jesus, guys, I wouldn't want to be the team that loses twice on national television." They went quiet and I sensed I'd said the wrong thing. They moved an emotional seat over. Still, they seemed to get my point.

The Wednesday practice was crisp. No back talk, no lollygagging. The boys seemed to know what was at stake here. They were 6–4 with six games to go and hanging with greased fingers to a playoff spot. No playoffs, no scouts. No scouts, the next place you could be likely to see some of these men would be in a kitchen next to the deep-fat fryer. Besides, we were filming them. As Gil Hernandez, a Chicano from East L.A., said it, "Man, I can't go home and have guys see this on television and say 'Oh, man, you play for the Dusters, bro. They suck homey.'"

Gil, a former gangbanger with a torso billboarded with street tattoos, was sitting in the penalty box with Tommy Balom, a black man from Florida, and Hershey, the white placekicker from San Bernardino, California.

Curious and wanting to stir up the racial witch's brew, I asked Gil the Mexican-Spanish words for *honky* and *nigger*. I did it just because I was standing there, really. "Oh, yeah, man," he said in the citified Latino accent where the *r*'s and *a*'s are stretched out long. "*Honky* is *gabacho* and *nigger* is *mayate*. Yeah, hee hee hee. *Gabacho* and *mayate*."

Tommy laughed and I asked him what the derogatory names for whites and browns are in the black quarters of Florida. "Well," he said with a laugh, "Mexicans are *spics* and whites are *white boy* or *white trash*."

"I hate *white boy* more than *white trash*," Hershey said. "I don't mind being called trash, but I ain't a boy."

Despite Rouanzoin's and Walker's problem, I began to believe that one of the few places you could actually talk race was on the sporting field, seeing as everyone was an alpha male and dominance was proven by ability. I believed that until I asked Hershey the nasty white words for *brown* and *black*.

"Well, Mexicans are *beaners*." He chuckled. "*Wetbacks*."

"And blacks?" I asked. He paused. "And blacks?" I asked again. He looked around stealthily over his shoulder, like he was shoplifting. He stammered. He didn't want to say it. The black man and the brown man had said it in the spirit of brotherhood. But he wouldn't say it. I realized then that no, the locker room is exactly the same as the boardroom. Something has happened in this country. The white people have been told they are wrong, their ancestors were wrong, their words are wrong and they should not say them in public, should not use them in retaliation. If slurs are used against the whites, they must accept them as poetic justice and go home and grumble about it to each other.

"Come on, Hershey," I said. "You can do it. Ni . . . ni . . . ni . . . ni . . . ni . . ."

"Yeah, come on, Hershey, I know you know it," Balom said. "You've used it. Ni . . . ni . . . ni . . ."

We laughed at him and he looked around in that shoplifting way and whispered, "*Nigger.*"

"There you go, son! There you go," Balom hooted.

As though a pillow had been lifted from his air passages, Hershey inhaled.

"*Coon!*" he shouted. "*Jigaboo!*"

"There you go," Balom said, fascinated by the outburst, not laughing anymore, but stone-faced. There was the confirmation that contempt lurks under the skin of every man.

To be fair, Hershey was under a lot of pressure, as the coach had invited another kicker into camp to compete for his job, because he had missed so many extra points in the past few weeks. You had to feel bad for him. He was married, had a new kid and was making $200 a week trying to live his dream. Kick a football in the NFL. If that fell through, Hershey was looking at a job washing military airplanes in the Mojave Desert with his father.

"Fuck it," Hershey told me as he stared at the new placekicker practicing in his shorts and cleats. Another white boy. "It's not good money, but I got a dream."

There it was. There in Hershey's statement. The American is stuck, infantilized, holding on to some bullshit dream that's never going to happen. I'm going to be a pro football player, he thinks. Yeah, and my cousin's going to be a rocker. All those kids in Detroit are going to be rappers; the contract is just around the corner. The unpublished novelist. The country is full of them, these people of my generation. More and more, all there is is this cheap dream. What else is there? At least Hershey had an airplane job waiting for him. What about the rest of us? The jobs are gone, the benefits. I ask my generation and they'll tell you they don't expect to get Social Security. Who told us that? No one. They just somehow convinced us of it. No jobs and a mountain of debt left to us by the Baby Boomers. You can't go to a factory anymore and make a good life. The factory is gone. I went to the Wal-Mart with one of the players, Devin Lemons, to buy some shoes. They were all cheap and made in China. We don't make shoes or much of anything anymore. What are you going to do if you don't make it in football? I asked Lemons, who had made it all the way to the Washington Redskins' practice squad before tumbling down to the Deuce. He stood there dumbfounded. "I don't know, man." That's all he could find to say, standing like a man who returns home to find his wife has left with the children. Eight bucks an hour and no benefits. I don't know man, so keep dreaming.

The confusion and desperation of the regular man. Everyone forgets him, except him. The plump guy on the Op-Ed page says the loss of jobs is somehow good for the world. Murky arguments of comparative advantage and the American man's lack of ambition. And maybe it's true. But the world is still round, just cracked in a hundred parts. And the regular man doesn't understand it beyond the fact that he is the man stuck in the crosscurrents of history, a sacrifice to a new world order. His troubles and pain are forgotten. They come to see him every four years during the presidential elections and ask him his opinion while he eats his plate of eggs, and then thirty seconds later, he goes forgotten. Who speaks for him? What is he to do? He holds on to his cheap football dream and we all go about encouraging him. We do it as we snort coke and drink beer and watch him shatter his kneecaps.

Amarillo is one long sleeping pill of neon slapped up on the banks of the new river called the interstate. I-40 cuts straight through town like the lines on a palm. Everything seems lost here. Everything is the same here, as it is the same in Indiana or Florida or Oregon. Burger King. Sunoco. Starbucks. Strip mall architectural shit, man. The cultural, regional distinctions are getting siphoned down the drainpipe. Cajun, Crow, Creole, it's disappearing. There's something malignant and unknown about the dirty windows and cheap curtains here, they conceal something that I never quite uncovered. Beyond the city limits the land stretches out beyond empty.

I went to drink at night on old Route 66, the old river that this town once existed upon before the superhighway came. The strip is part brick, part board, dark. A couple of little sandwich shacks and watering holes and bikers. Empty, weed-choked, forgotten.

There was a roadside stop, where a broomstick of a man was drinking himself numb. On Route 66, Amarillo is where you're going to find Chaim Daniel, almost sixty, a biker Jew with a fresh tattoo in Hebrew on his right forearm, drinking from a plastic fifth. He invited me for a drink. "You a Zionist?" I asked. He was unsure how to answer me. This was the South, more or less. They didn't know the meaning of *Zionist* here. "If you're a Jew and not a Zionist, then I think you're a coward," I offered helpfully.

He was pleased by this, relieved. He poured a tumbler of vodka in a plastic cup and spilled his story. The usual bag of bullshit. Nam, faggot kid who dresses in a skirt, his cats, bar fights, football, women, dear old Mother. He had magnificent turns of speech like, "You're shitting in tall cotton now, boy."

"I got no family left," he told me after a few. "I ignore my friends. These people here hug me every night and I don't even know half the motherfuckers. Life changes in a heartbeat, a generation."

He threw a thumb toward 66, which was spitting distance from our picnic table. "We don't want to lose this. It's our past, not our future. It's the mother road."

He poured another. I drank it and then took the keys to his beat-up Harley and here I was, tearing it up and down 66, no helmet, stoned again, cackling into the night. I stopped to get him gas, but didn't turn off the bike because it was rigged weird and I didn't think I could have gotten it started again.

The cashier was a plump young woman, glasses, white teeth, friendly face. Her name tag said Kendra. She told me she was poor. "Real po'. Desperate po'."

"I'll include you in my prayers," I told her. She seemed sad to me. Stuck in the USA where the average household credit card debt is around $9,000. We might not have the jobs anymore, but we still have the habits of our grandparents. We like to live good. She gave me a free lighter because I played for the Dusters. Football players get free stuff in Texas, but no one loves an overweight cashier.

"All you kin do is pray," Kendra said. "Nothing else but pray."

Desperate po'. It kept ringing through my head. All you kin do is pray.

The local sports media were hanging around the practice facility. The game against Bakersfield was a must-win. Playoff implications were in the balance. The players gave the pat answers, the locker room bromides about hitting on all cylinders . . . if we can play like we're capable . . . I guarantee a win, that sort of junk.

Then the reporters got word of me. A stranger in their midst. An everyman trying to recapture a little of the glory days. Instantly I was surrounded by cameras. "What is it you're doing here?" they asked me. "I'm doing the same job as you," I said. "Only it's more interesting this way."

The idea captivated them. Why didn't I think of that? I know they're thinking, because what is more absurd than a reporter following a reporter following a football team? I know it captivated them because by game day I'd been featured on the local news. I imagined the assignment editors at the other stations yelling at their reporters, "Why the hell don't we have that? Get out there." And so they did. One after another, like lemmings. An Amarillo feeding frenzy.

I didn't like it, it made a spectacle of me, broke the team concept and the camaraderie I was trying to build. There was one guy in particular, a real dick reporter, a shiny-faced guy. I allowed him to follow me around, basically steal my story, and how did he repay it? By talking shit.

"Do you think Bakersfield will have their nose out of joint?" he asked the team. "You guys work hard and this reporter shows up, works out for a couple of days and thinks he can make it. Isn't it arrogant?"

Julian Reese, quarterback and team leader, did not bite. He knew I saw the men under the masks. He was from Fort Wayne, Indiana, from a family of thirteen kids. He had a real college education and his head was on straight. He knew what time it was when he said good things about my motives, about telling his story and how he respected my willingness to get hurt in pursuit of it.

Reese, an intelligent, handsome, personable man, had other opportunities. Disney had invited him down to Orlando to train in some sort of management capacity. Reese told me on the bus to Oklahoma City that he was giving his football dream until the end of the season. If he didn't get invited up to the next level—the levels go AFL2, AFL, Canadian Football League, NFL Europe and finally the top, the NFL—then he was going to Disney.

"You gotta have other plans," he said. "Football ain't the end-all, be-all."

One reporter asked Rickey Foggey, the offensive coordinator and onetime great quarterback for the University of Minnesota, if I had any athletic ability. I saw him say with a straight face on the local news, "No. Absolutely not. Charlie has no athletic ability whatsoever. But he has heart."

Foggey. Son of a bitch. He pulled my trousers down in front of the whole Texas Panhandle. It was a funny bit, I have to admit that.

Beyond a few guys like Reese, most of the men on the team had studied kinesiology at college, a fancy word for physical education. To a man I asked them what they wanted to be if football didn't work out. High school football coach, was the unwavering answer. It is important to say here that I went into the locker room with some stereo-types. Mainly, I figured they would be dumb jocks, seeing as they were playing bottom-of-the-barrel football. What else would they be? Guys who went through the great minstrel show of college athletics, men who never went to class. I was surprised to learn that most of them had finished their degrees or were only a few credits short. They were articulate, well mannered and focused. Still they grasped on to this dream. The team stacked them in apartments that were spare and had unique smells. If one smelled like an industrial zone, another stank like a cat box, the third like cheap cologne, the fourth like reefer, the fifth like mold, the sixth like soap residue. Other players lived out on the highway in a Red Roof Inn, a room with a single bed for two men. One coach was working for free and living out of his car. Why? For a chance at football or coaching football.

But how many jobs could there be for a high school football coach? I went to see Larry Dipple, coach of the local high school team, the Amarillo Sandies. Dipple, a dissipating white man with a deep drawl, had coached Texas high school football for forty years, and though he never won a state championship and only sent one man to the National Football League—a punter for the Cardinals named Birdsong—he was a legend in Texas. He was so well thought of that he was elected by his peers to head the state association of high school coaches.

No one knows why exactly football is so important to Texans, Dipple told me. Perhaps it has to do with the enormity of the state. "There's a lot of space between towns," he said. "There's not a lot to do. So football has become the focal point for the community."

Football is so much a part of one's manhood in Texas that a father recently shot a coach in the chest in the Dallas area because his son wasn't getting appropriate playing time. "The man thought his son was better'n what the coach thought, I suppose," Dipple said.

In 1996, Wanda Holloway, nicknamed the "Pom-Pom Mom," was convicted for soliciting the murder of the mother of her daughter's cheerleading rival.

Football in Texas is an identity. Football is a religion. Football is a priority.

Despite never having won a championship, despite having his twelve-year playoff streak snapped the previous year, Coach Dipple earned about three times the salary of the average teacher. There are 160,000 kids playing high school football in Texas and almost 20,000 coaches for grades 7 through 12. High school football is a $300 million industry in Texas and the city of Dallas recently spent nearly $200 million for new varsity football stadiums.

As it happens, there are, in fact, plenty of football coaching jobs. It is an industry, and men attend college to learn how to teach it.

"Aren't our priorities messed up?" I asked the coach. "Are you really more important than a science teacher? Is football more important than academics?"

The coach smiled. "People moving to Texas got different priorities. The football culture is under subtle attack. They just don't understand it, the meaning of the Texas way of life. Success is measured here by w's and l's—wins and losses. That's the way it is."

That afternoon as I drove to practice, I thought about the importance of football and the football coach to a young man. When I began playing football around the age of eleven or twelve, my family was unraveling. My mother worked sixteen-hour days in her flower shop. My stepfather, all but a stranger by this point.

Football saved me. There was a Little League coach, Mr. Bailey, a tall strong man of rectitude who took an interest in me and seemed to know my troubles at home. He took extra time with kids like me; there seemed to be so many in the late seventies. Coach Bailey was kind, asked about school, my mother, my sister and brothers. He knew all their names. He had a big laugh, I remember. I looked forward to the practices, not so much for the sport of it, but for the structure and peace of mind. If it wasn't for his steadying influence through some of my bad moments in adolescence, I'm quite sure I'd be in prison today. Through football I learned perseverance and self-confidence.

I made it to college, not prison. One evening, I was in my dorm, my lips wrapped around a bong, watching the news. It was Coach Bailey, looking gutted and pale. His own son, Ronald Bailey, had been arrested for the kidnap-slayings of two teenage boys in the Detroit area.

Only an animal could raise such an animal, the reporters intimated. I sat stoned, staring bug-eyed at a tortured man who would eventually move away and hide with his horror. Staring at that coach who helped right me. I knew he was good. And if his son killed two children, then the father surely rescued two hundred. Maybe he should have paid more attention to his own, but in my mind, Coach Bailey is on the right side of the ledger.

Practice went crisply. It went well enough that I was allowed into my first live scrimmage playing eight-on-eight, as are the rules in Arena football. It's different from the eleven-on-eleven in the traditional game. Players must play both defense and offense.

I went in motion as the Y receiver and the play called for me to do a five-yard curl to the inside. The ball was overthrown and Reese apologized. The second didn't come my way, or the third. Every time I felt it was my fault.

"Come on, Charlie, you got to speed it up, you got to turn that head," Foggey complained. I felt like a bobble-head doll, like I was running in quicksand, and I was frustrated.

"You ain't doing bad Charlie Oh," said D. J. Humpfries, who showed me the details of his position.

"I want to do it like you, Deej," I told him.

"You can't be able in a day, Charlie, we been doing this our whole lives."

There are things about the game you cannot realize watching from the couch. The receiver positions are less about speed than about body control. Precise footwork will break you free from a defender more than outrunning him will. Body control allows you to make a good break for the ball and allows you to avoid the walls that the defensive backs try to pin you against in order to seal you off. I also worked in a few snaps at defensive line, matched against a three-hundred-pound center from Indiana University. Though the men were elephantine, the line play was less about brute strength than about quickness and footwork. A slant was called as I was playing nose tackle, and I beat the big man to the gap on his right. The team howled my number again: "OOOOh." The big man gave me a loving slap on my helmet. It hurt my spine. Arthritis and whiplash, the doctor would later tell me.

At the far end of the field, Hershey was practicing his kicks with his rival. I felt bad for him. He was a tough guy, with a prizefighter's mentality. Still, he was mired in a horrible slump and he was blamed for losing the Oklahoma City game.

Airplanes in the desert. See you 'round, white boy.

White men like Hershey are an interesting breed in football, and they are increasingly rare in the game. Why this is so is unclear to me. Perhaps the racial baggage weighs the white man down so much that he feels he cannot compete with the tough-talking grandsons of slaves. Perhaps, in American society, white people have better opportunities and so their children do not commit their lives to the long-shot pursuit of a career in professional sports. Or maybe black men are simply physically superior.

Whatever it is, there is no doubt that white society not only pulls for the white player, but white people actually count the white faces on the football field and basketball court. Everybody, after all, needs a hero.

I put the question to the white men. Kert Turner, the gargantuan lineman, a white man from the bayou, said simply, "No, black men ain't superior. It's all a matter of the mind and will." Which was easy for him to say, standing six-five and weighing 275 pounds.

The second-string quarterback, Steve Panella, was not so sure. But being from Canada, he had the more sociological outlook. He believed in the racial garbage argument. In his first year in the league, Panella remembered a play in which a black player came rushing around the tackle, and as Panella got rid of the ball the black player called Panella a honky cracker.

"I didn't really understand it," Panella said. "I come from Canada and we really don't have that history. I was kind of speechless. I didn't know what to do. Should I call him a nigger? If I did that, I was pretty sure I'd turn my whole team against me. I didn't know if they heard what he said to me."

"So what did you do?" I asked.

"Nothing, I just took it," Panella said.

"I would have hit him in the mouth," I said.

"Yeah, I bet you would have," Panella said doubtfully.

"I would have," I said plaintively. "If white people got to give that shit up, then everybody's got to give that shit up. I'm sure your team would have backed you."

And then again, how could I know? I'd hung around for a week and a half. I didn't know the personalities or intricacies of the Dusters or Amarillo or Texas or football, for that matter. The Walker-and-Rouanzoin beef was still a mystery to me. I decided to go to Walker's.

He lived in one of those less-than-elegant apartment complexes that plague America: cheap walls, peeling paint, unmowed courtyard, big parking lot, that type of place. Walker had just gotten back from his night job as an orderly for mentally retarded teenagers in a halfway house, doing everything from cooking to wiping asses. This would be his career, he said, if football didn't go his way.

The game day was tomorrow and Walker was feeling agitated. He had to redeem himself for his misdeeds from the week before.

As it had for me, football had saved Walker's life. The way he described it, his dad was a broken-down alcoholic living in Washington and his mother spent her youth in prison over drugs. He bounced from sister to aunt to godparents to partial strangers. He would have ended up on the end of a crack pipe, he said, if he hadn't found self-worth in football.

I asked him if the black man in America was physically superior to all others. "Yeah," he said with a quizzical tone. It was as if I had asked him whether the world was really round.

"It goes back to slave days," he offered, standing there all of five-foot-four. "They bred black people to be bigger."

"That's interesting," I said. "You ever heard of Jimmy the Greek?"

"Who's that?"

"He was a gambling handicapper," I said. "He used to be on TV before football games. About fifteen years ago he said the same thing. Blacks were bred that way. Except he was white and they fired him for being a racist."

"I don't care," Walker said. "It's true."

"You think white men are genetically smarter?" I asked him.

"No," he said without pause.

"What do you think, Charlie?" asked his roommate Charles Davis, a black defensive back from a little town in Texas.

Like Hershey I thought for a long while, choosing my words carefully. "No, not genetically," I said. "But black society is messed up and a lot of black people make bad decisions."

"True," he said.

Comfortable that the conversation was not going to slip into a fistfight, I asked Walker why he had called Rouanzoin, his white teammate, a cracker.

"'Cause during a game I heard him call a guy a nigger. There ain't no place for that. It makes me wonder what he really thinks in his heart about me. So one day at practice the frustration came out and I called him a cracker, is all."

Later that afternoon, after the walk-through practice, I cornered Rouanzoin. "You didn't tell me you called a guy a nigger, man. That's what's eating Kendrik."

"Well, I didn't mean it." He swallowed like a goldfish. "It was the heat of the battle. I wasn't raised that way."

"Well, you could go a long way toward racial brotherhood by explaining that," I said.

"Oh, he doesn't want to hear it."

"Then why is he sitting over there in his truck pretending he's not watching us?" I said.

Rouanzoin went over. And the two men sat, black and white, explaining how each didn't have a racist bone in his body, how he hadn't been raised like that. It was a remarkable scene, a rare one in America. Maybe I did have something to contribute to the team. It ended with the men shaking hands.

I went over to the Best Western, one of the many soulless motels that line I–40, sandwiched between the chain barbecue restaurants. I had to meet the league commissioner, who was not convinced that I should be allowed to play. It was a lawyer thing. The old saying: lawyers are shit unless they're working for you. The commissioner sat there with McCarty, the general manager. The commissioner was a Napoleonic little figure, the kind who shakes your hand too tightly, staring you down by looking you up. He was short, with a bull neck, a balding Caesar-style haircut and had the deportment of a fry cook in a Greek diner.

This guy had the power to ruin my whole bit and knew so. He listed his football résumé. College football at the University of Oklahoma, coach, general manager, owner, now commissioner.

"Sir," I said. "Let's cut the crap. I want to play."

"Okay," he said. "Sell me why."

"For one, the town wants me to play. I'm all over the news, and that's good advertising."

"I get all the advertising I need, son," he said, fully in control. "Gimme a better one."

My producer piped in. "Without it," he said, "there's no film."

The commissioner gesticulated like a college physics instructor. Finger in the air. "There you go! Now I'm listening. You're going to have to sign a waiver."

"Done," I said.

"You will need a physical, by the team doctor," he added. "That way I got a Chinese wallet between me."

Right! A Chinese wallet. Whatever that meant.

I went to the doctor. "This shouldn't take five minutes," he said. He tapped my joints, had me do a push-up and a deep knee bend and pronounced me fit for combat.

Saturday came. I ate the pregame meal with the team. I had steak and chicken necks and yams and sweet iced tea. I went back to my motel, tried to nap, couldn't sleep, watched some golf, took a shit and didn't wash my hands in case I needed to poke someone in the eye tonight. I packed my helmet and shoulder pads and drove to the Civic Center in downtown Amarillo around four o'clock. One of the first guys there was Rouanzoin, who despite having a fractured forearm couldn't peel himself away from the game. He told me he felt funny about the whole racial episode with Walker. Be cool, I reassured him. It was the most honest thing I'd witnessed all year.

He changed the subject. "You ready?"

"Nervous," I told him.

"That's good. I been playing nineteen years and I'm always nervous." I looked at him like he was nuts, as clueless as a cowboy playing guitar in his underwear in Times Square.

"Jarrod, I haven't played in more than nineteen years."

He smiled and patted me on the ass. Why athletic men are so preoccupied with each other's ass, I don't know. To me, it's like kissing your sister on the lips.

My locker was next to Reese's. The equipment man had already put my gear in it. Pants two sizes too big. Frayed knee-high socks with white and black stripes. Decals on my helmet. Knee and thigh pads. A pair of secondhand rubber gloves that smelled absolutely beastly. My jersey was there, black and orange, Number 28, not 0 as I preferred in respect for Mr. Plimpton, and no name on the back. It was explained to me that the team had no Number 0 in stock and to order one would have taken in excess of two months. So I picked 28, the number of yards lost by Plimpton in his five plays with the Lions.

Life in semi-pro is like that, cheap and seat-of-the-pants. When

D. J. Humpfries broke his foot in a game, he wasn't taken for X-rays until two days later, when the doctor's rates were cheaper. You get better treatment in high school. But that was life in the Deuce. Raw.

I was trying to visualize my game, the journalism having given way to competitive juices. I wanted to perform well. I am a man, after all. I was trying to think, but I was numb from nerves and the rap beats blasting in the locker room. I looked around. The men were absolutely gargantuan, muscular. I was an interloper, a runt. Time moves ahead and leaves you imperceptibly less. Piece by piece, and you hardly notice it. One day you rise from bed and your knee hurts. You go to the park and you cannot catch. Your body does not respond to the commands. Your breath escapes you on a flight of stairs and you cannot run, catch, focus. It's gone and the regret comes and it comes harder if you never lived it. That's why so many men live vicariously through the football gladiator on Friday, Saturday, Sunday afternoon. Monday night.

"Fill it up, dat," someone shouted.

"True," someone called back.

"Fill it up, true, true," the men started chanting. I had no idea what they meant. My gloves stank and I worried about catching an infection from them. McCarty came by with a one-day contract. Name. Social Security. Cell phone number. DOB. I signed it all away for a chance. We filed out into the tunnel, prayed an Our Father, talked about no option but winning and lined up. The men were introduced with the house lights down and a spotlight illuminating the mouth of the tunnel where a smog machine was belching dry-ice vapors. They did unique little jigs. One guy moon-walked, another did push-ups. The last to come through the tunnel was me. The introduction went something like, "Wearing a special number tonight, from *The New York Times,* weighing one hundred and seventy pounds, six feet tall, the Dusters' secret weapon. Charlieeeeeeeee LeeeeeeeeDufffffffffff!" The crowd roared lustily and happily. I was them and they were me and this was for all of us. Now someone come on and smash me up!

I slapped the palms of all the little fans hanging over the sides of the tunnel and then ran into the blinding klieg lights. I was doing a sheriff-with-his-six-shooters bit. It broke into a stiff, self-conscious trot. The first teammate to greet me on the field was Walker, jumping on me, messing up my entrance. Walker screamed, "You're living every man's dream."

The crowd sat so close to the bench that before the first kickoff I was wearing the beer of a guy who was already drunk and spoke in the vocabulary of the cotton fields. The rubber gloves were making my hands itch. I absentmindedly scratched my eye and wondered if I'd contracted conjunctivitis.

The score seesawed through the first half and Hershey missed half his kicks. The Dusters messed up badly on special teams, missing field goals and fumbling snaps and giving away a touchdown on a kickoff. I got no action. I felt not like a football player, but like a man on a couch with a really good view. The players on the bench talked about whooping ass and steroid use and the cheerleaders' tits.

"Put twenty-eight in!" screamed the guy who dropped his beer down my back, the same guy whose kid called him a liar. He said he played three years of football at the University of Texas. I asked him what position and he said he got little playing time because he was "too white, too slow."

Too much mouth, I thought. Football is a thing men lie about in Texas. It provides macho bona fides, much like the old alkies who claim to have served in Nam. A never-was.

The score was tied 27–27 at the half and instead of going into the locker room with the team I went to an exit tunnel with the officials and smoked a cigarette.

An official said to me, "They're gonna cut Hershey. They're sick of him."

On the way back to the locker room, Mr. Rogers, the owner, took me by the arm and whispered, "They're playing poor. I guess they don't want to win."

The second half went much the way the first had. Sloppy. Tight.

Me watching from the bench. People screaming at the players, "I slept with your wife" and such.

On an extra point attempt, Hershey got plowed into, which he didn't like. A Hershey threw off his helmet and aped. The crowd erupted into violent delirium. Presumably Mr. Rogers was in his box frowning. The crowd started chanting for ol' Number 28.

They wanted the kid!

There were only seconds to go, perhaps forty, with the Dusters hanging on to a tenuous lead. Coach Perdue ordered Reese to take a knee and run out the clock. But Reese disobeyed, instead scrambling around and hitting Anthony Dingle for a touchdown, making the score 66–55 and the victory a certainty.

More important, Reese did it for me. With the game out of reach, I could be inserted. He trotted off the field and said to me, "Go get 'em, Charlie. You worked for it."

And so in I went.

"Welcome, Char-liiiieeee Le-Duuuuuuff!"

The crowd went bananas. The coach told me to do something, but I couldn't hear what he was saying. So I made it up. I lined up to the right of Hershey for the kickoff. He kicked and I ran as fast as I could, beating everyone down the field. The ball carrier went left, so I cut left. I never saw the 310-pound Hawaiian who knocked me flat on my ass. As I got up, another guy hit me and we both went down. I got up first and as he tried to lift his mass, I pushed him over. The Texas crowd lovingly approved. Never stop until the whistle blows, goes the old football adage.

That was it. The beginning and end of my pro career. It lasted ten seconds maximum. I'd broken my pinkie finger on the play.

"And how 'bout a big hand for Charlieeee Leeee-Duuuuuufff!"

It was short and sweet.

After the game, the Hawaiian guy came up with a laugh and an apology. "Sorry, man," he said. "We were all looking for you, we wanted to be on TV. My mother lives in Hawaii and doesn't get to see me play."

The TV reporter came up with his camera. "Was that a cheap shot?" he asked.

Absolutely, I said. Texas deserves to see it. Reporters. What dicks.

I signed some autographs, including the owner's boots, and then the team went to the players' apartments to party.

Most of the black guys had white blond trophy girls. They were drinking sweet stuff. Liquor and Gatorade, Smirnoff with juice, Zima lemonade and gin. One of the black players imitated a black woman out front in the yard. "Oh, you football players, you get a contract and then get yo'self a white woman." They laughed, but by the look of things it wasn't untrue. Most of the girls here were blondes.

I don't exactly know what it means, why it is. Maybe the white-women trophies are black men's way of saying they've made it to the good life. But I *know* white women. There's nothing special about them.

The next apartment over was where some of the white players lived, the apartment that smelled like shrimp and cat litter. Turner's people were visiting from Louisiana.

His old man started talking, which began pleasantly enough with complaints about the management at the chemical plant where he had worked his entire adult life. He was heavily union and thought the company should pay the workers a high wage and generous benefits even if the company was drowning. I'm a Northern man, I told him, a union man to the point of reasonableness. But whole companies are turning out the lights and moving overseas. When the lights get turned back on, Americans aren't standing in the parking lot of General Motors, but Colonel Sanders.

I asked the man's son, Kert, if he expected to get Social Security. No, he said in an accent so thick I wasn't sure he was saying no. It came out, *Nawp*.

The old man told me that, indeed, good white folk in his parts were frustrated. In fact, he let it be known, he lived in Klan country and his adjacent neighbor trained KKK members in the ways of paramilitary tactics.

Training to kill? I asked.

Yawp, he answered.

Have you reported your neighbors to the authorities? I asked.

Nawp, he answered. "You have to keep these people close. You have to be friendly with these people. You have to be *very* friendly with these people."

I looked over to his son, who was not looking up anymore, but spitting tobacco juice into a beer can.

The family took its leave and Turner turned to me as he waved good-bye to his parents. "You'll take care of that, right? You'll explain the right way what that means? Won't you? I might be from the sticks, but we got as much problems as people in the ghetto. Do you know eighty-five percent of all meth labs are in the country?

"No jobs and drugs, it's ruint a lot of my friends." He spat. I remembered then how he'd told me in the tunnel before the game that he had tried every drug there is and there was no drug better than adulation. He asked me for a cigarette. He didn't want his father to know he smoked. He loved the old man.

I said good night and walked to my rental car across the street. I looked back at the cheap faux-Monticello-style colonial columns of the apartment complex. The façade of the American Dream. I thought, Yes, Kert, I'll try to explain it the right way, if I ever could.

Football. The Klan. Trophy blondes. Shrimp and liquor and methamphetamine. Texas. America.

The following Monday, Hershey got cut.

Tulsa, Oklahoma

Oklahoma City, Oklahoma

Oakland, California

The basest of all things is to be afraid . . .

—WILLIAM FAULKNER

Amarillo, Texas

Black Rock City, Nevada

Coos Bay, Oregon

Crow Agency, Montana

Detroit, Michigan

New York City, New York

Cleveland, Tennessee

Miami, Florida

Just before I became a teenager, my stepbrother Terry came to live with us. Terry was five years older than me. He was short and stringy, wore his hair shaggy and had an exotic fuzz of a beard.

When Terry spoke, he mostly spoke with his fists. My stepbrother was angry. We were all angry, but Terry was really angry. I was scared of him and wanted to please him. He was my big brother, after all. For instance, we once got paid to scrape and paint a garage. In the end, I scraped and painted the garage and Terry got paid. When Terry's tomato rolled off the roof when we stopped for lunch, he snatched me by the hair and pitched me over the eaves trough as though the outrage of gravity had been my fault. When I brought his damaged tomato back up the ladder and presented it to him, Terry's tongue rolled up like a cannoli, his expression of rage, and he pitched me off the roof again. One of life's little lessons.

This was the late seventies when it seemed like every father was packing his bags and walking out the door. The fathers, of course, did not pay their child support and so the mothers dutifully went off to earn the bread. A generation of kids was left to their own. We made it up as we went along. Hot dogs were for breakfast and school was for suckers.

You knew Terry was pissed, but you couldn't hold it against him. He was the product of *two* broken households. First his mother and father divorced. Then his mother took him to a new place and that was falling to pieces too. So Terry was shipped off to his father's house, my house, on a busy street in the suburbs. What he found there was just another household on the verge of collapse. Terry was angry.

His buddies, I remember them well. Their names are not important, but they were all healthy, milk-fed white kids: big arms, cabled necks and they all wore the same mop tops and peach-fuzz beards. They wore tight blue jeans with combs shimmed into the back pockets and they did drugs in my mother's house. Usually it was a beer and a reefer and a line or two of Crystal T. Crystal T—if you do not know—is PCP. PCP—if you do not know—is the stuff they embalm cadavers with. Kids getting high on embalming dust, making it up as they were going along. It was, and remains, a bad combination.

Coming home from school for me was worse than going. Open the door and there was Terry and the shaggy T freaks with the couch and end tables and footstools and TV-dinner stands arranged in a square. It was fight club time. Surrounded by the dopers with the droopy eyes, my brothers and I—stripped to the waist—would have to punch and claw and bite each other until someone got KO'd. Usually it was a last-man-standing deal, but sometimes Terry would arrange it tournament-style, thus creating a nice afternoon of matches for the boys, along with intermissions for beer.

They bet one and five dollars, I remember. I usually won because I was the oldest of the four younger brothers and I learned one important thing about life from those fight clubs: the bigger man does not necessarily win. My brother Jim once opened my skull and knocked me unconscious with a wild haymaker. I once knocked out one of the tweakers with a similar desperate roundhouse. After a few wins you begin to enjoy the sting of a punch, the metallic taste of blood. After a few losses you either develop a sense of will or a sense of inferiority.

Terry dropped out of school. He hustled and drifted and did the best he could. The only possession he carried with him through life was resentment for a world he did not create. His escape from his anger and misery was sex and drugs. He died young. He shot himself to death with a needle. I loved him, but I have never been to his grave. One of my brothers tells me the cemetery grounds are much too nice for him.

And so when I walk into the East Bay Rats clubhouse in west Oakland and see two leather-bound bikers wrestling on the floor, some violent video games projected on a wall and enough reefer smoke to kill a goose, I know where I am. Back in the living room.

The East Bay Rats are a group of knuckleheads, motorcycle men with a clubhouse on San Pablo Avenue who like to drink, blow things up and throw parties where the central amusement is fighting. The important and interesting thing is that the violence is *organized*. Sure, sometimes there's impromptu wrestling or a spontaneous squabble between two Rats that ends with bruised ribs or a bloody nose, but it is quickly forgotten over slaps on the back and swigs from a bottle of Old Grand-Dad.

What drew me to the "club" were the fights; parties with violence as the central feature. It's a simple, somewhat ingenious formula: a punk band, bottles of whiskey and a boxing ring. Turn the violence into a virtue instead of a virus. Violence as free entertainment! Now, that's America! Violence. It's like sugar. Enough of it and you crash.

Whenever the Rats throw such a party, you can be sure a host of Hell's Angels will be there, smiling, drinking free beer as perfect strangers pummel each other in a handmade ring with naked cheerleaders and a brass band rooting them on.

The police and the fire department rarely come around because, you know, boys will be boys. The Rats are not obsequious toward the Angels or ass-kissers. They do not kiss ass. Rather, the two clubs get along well enough, much like yard dogs and housecats.

The Rats' clubhouse is a slapdash building in the black west-side section of Oakland. There are burnout patches on the sidewalk and beer cans in the gutter and a U.S. Marine Corps flag on the wall. There is a full moon, and from the front street you can hear a fight going on in the back. It's two women kicking each other in the pussies, biting, pulling hair. It's too much for the baying boy-men, who are howling. The Rats and Angels talk among themselves in hushed conspiratorial tones as though it were a military conference room.

Inside the clubhouse are a soda machine that sells beer, a punching bag, some weights and a long line of men waiting to smack the ass of a willing woman who, tail in the air, is leaning over an old barber's chair. In the closet is an arsenal of weapons belonging to the club's president, Trevor. The place is a pirate's den and if the bikers don't call themselves a gang, then I will. The place stinks like a toilet pipe since the toilet pipe is broken and running all over the floor.

It is up to the prospects—pledges, in fraternity parlance—to mop and wring the sewage and clean the clubhouse as part of a year's trial period before they are allowed as full-patch members into the club. They are indentured servants of a sort, minions who hustle beers, haul the trash, paint the walls, wash the motorcycles, whatever it is a member asks of them. Most importantly, a prospect is required to fight at all parties, usually against another prospect, sometimes a member, thus working to establish himself a place on the totem. The final ceremony for the prospect is getting his ass stomped by the entire club, after which he is allowed full membership and its privileges. There are about thirty members of the Rats, and eight prospects, ranging in age from twenty-one to thirty-eight, although there is an honorary member called One-Eyed Mike, sixty-five, whose mistaken onetime appearance on a Most Wanted poster is reason for aggrandizement among these men.

There are a few rules: no screwing another guy's chick for a year. That causes division. Women here are third. It's me first, man, my boys second and women get what's left. Never let a broad bust up the family. Then there's the cell phone; you're required to carry it, to be ready at a moment's beckoning. No hard drugs, that causes bad things. Weapons are welcome and encouraged. Then there is the beat-down as the price of admission. It is the shared experience. The guts. The proof that you will be there when the cell phone rings.

The fight club, at its root, it is a psychic stripping. Get beaten, lose, have your pants pulled down in front of the mob, stew in your own blood and humiliation. The individual is destroyed here, left in a wet lump for the whole world to see. You become less, you are nothing. Then you are rebuilt, taught how to fight, given worth by the group, worth you never got as a kid, a family to belong to. And when you get there, you are given the patch.

The Rats, I would come to find, are not your run-of-the-mill misanthropes and boneheads. They are former Marines, sharpshooters, mechanics, car salesmen, doctors of philosophy, missionaries, bureaucrats, government agents, fine painters, professional cardsharps. They're from everywhere and yet they're nowhere, a whole generation of bankrupt, forgotten children crumbling under the excess of abundance. They're physically fit, wild and on the edge of insanity.

The clubhouse smells of sweat, ink, leather, dope, tire rubber, oil, gasoline. There is an explosion in the alley that causes the windows to rattle. One of the boys is launching Molotov cocktails into the air with an air cannon. Another detonation rocks the west Oakland night. The electric guitar, whiskey getting slopped on the floor along with the blood, the females with chipped polish.

"Man, you want to take her in the dirt and fuck the shit out of her," one of the Rats is whispering to me about one cheap-looking girl. He's dressed in black leather jacket and pants and a T-shirt like everyone else belonging to the club. "Leave her there with the semen mud you made, 'cause she's meaningless, man, a can of shit."

Another explosion. The night sky flashes bright for a moment and then streetlights and shadows reassume their proper places.

The biker takes me by the collarbone and rattles me. "A can of shit, man." He means it.

There is a stoplight directly in front of the clubhouse and the eyes of the blacks inside their cars are wide and white and they see a white, skinhead-like biker doing a burnout in the clubhouse door, his bike half inside, half outside, the rear tire spinning like a sparkler wheel. It's a Mad Max meets John the Baptist apocalypse kind of thing and the whiskey is flowing straight from the bottle down the neck, like a gas can on a hot highway, gurgling down the windpipe.

Someone hands me the bottle. It burns the lips just to touch it, like kerosene. Next thing I see is some guy who's been drinking the same bourbon walking around with his nuts hanging out of his zipper and I don't know what's going on except the whole place is tight and violent and worrisome and the blacks are staring out the car window—idling.

"This time, dude, they're the ones scared shitless, in their own part of town, and they can't wait for that light to change 'cause this scene is hard," one hanger-on, some wannabe with a bad haircut, says to me with a giggle. "*They're* shitting themselves for once. Finally they gotta lock their goddamned doors. Look at 'em."

The Rats are squealing their bikes up and down San Pablo Avenue in the false light of the street. One wrong turn by somebody, and *boom* . . . shadows of men in leather, wild beasts darting in and out of the darkness . . . a hundred miles per hour—the exhilaration of the life-death line, and once you've gotten there, once you've crossed it? Nada.

Standing out front to catch a breath of air, I come across one of the lesser club members who's bleeding from his nose. He got his ass beaten not thirty minutes ago. He had slinked away after losing his fight. No congratulatory beer with the president, as seemed to be the custom. He just disappeared and I found him in the shadows of the awning.

"It doesn't matter and it does," he tells me about the fighting. His name is Matt and he's explaining why a thirty-year-old goes for this kind of thing.

"It goes back to the beginning. When did a boy come of age? His first kill? His first war? We don't have that anymore. No outlet, no expression or rituals to see if you trust the man next to you. Nothing to really show you what it is to be a man. That's what this is. It's not important. We're not going to war, but it's important anyway."

He is a strawberry-haired suburban kid in a soft sweet way. A kid, except he is thirty years old now. Blood trickling from his nose and he dabbing at it like a society matron. The urban decay of Oakland staring him in the face and he trying not to fear it but rather to eat it, digest it, build will and muscle and confidence against it.

Except he had lost something of value tonight—his pride. The stated purpose of the fights—and all members are expected to fight—is simply about doing it. Facing it. Having the balls. Win or lose was not the point. Rather—they said, at least—it is a test of ethics. If you stand up for yourself, then you will stand up for your brothers.

But that's a bunch of bullshit. It is always about the win. That's basic. That's as primordial as sweat and stink and riot and whiskers, bone, sinew, teeth. He that loses is less. Every lesser man knows it, and every greater man fears it. Fighting is elemental. This pinkish man knows it too.

He tells me that as a child his father left and his mother became a lesbian. There was no man to guide him through the intricacies of masculinity. So here he is, a load of confusion standing out in the street in a black uniform, a black jacket with a poison-bottle rat skull crossed with two wrenches, a sort of Jolly Roger, his nose ripped open, a loser, a runt, humiliated like he had been caught jacking off in a public toilet. He fumbles with his words as a woman in leather shows him photos of her ass that she carries around and this guy doesn't know what to make of her, what to make of himself. He doesn't have the sense to let the blood run down his face and congeal into war paint, his lipstick, his honor and humility. Blood doesn't hurt, but it stings. And so he fumbles, dabbing his nose effetely with a tissue paper.

Matt lays out the exhilaration of the death's-edge motorcycle-guns-and-fists thing that he's donated his manhood to. Scratching his rabbit ears, he says, "What's going on in there means nothing and then again it means everything."

> If civilization imposes such great sacrifices not only on man's sexuality but on his aggressivity, we can understand better why it is hard for him to be happy in that civilization. In fact, primitive man was better off in knowing no restrictions of instinct. To counterbalance this, his prospects of enjoying this happiness for any length of time were very slender. Civilized man has exchanged a portion of his possibilities of happiness for a portion of security.
>
> —Sigmund Freud, *Civilization and Its Discontents*

Nearly every Rat I had met came from a broken or estranged home from the suburbs. Trevor, the president, was of divorced parents. Jason, a prospect, had a father who committed suicide when he was a teenager. The most interesting and incongruous of the lot were the Fuller brothers, shortly built men who grew up in a cult until their father, by their account, snatched them away. The oldest, Aaron, thirty-one, is a former missionary who provided the father figure to his brothers. Aaron is a nonstop wall of philosophical monologue, jumpy and manic, a tattoo billboard including one in Hebrew just above the shoulder blades: *"Shomer Achi"*—Brother's Keeper.

He was his brothers' keeper, he said, ever since that day his father stole the family away from the cult in northern California. Their mother, morose and pliable, he said, had fallen under the sway of the leader, who was telling her to leave her husband. Since the old man worked and the old lady was a basket case, it fell on Aaron to become the father, the disciplinarian, the hand of punishment.

"I think to some degree the way we're living is a social rebellion against, like, not necessarily the powers that be but maybe the preconceived way that you're supposed to live in our society," Aaron says. "The way that you're supposed to fit in like a piece of the puzzle. I think most of us are guys that don't fit in that puzzle."

What is that preconceived way? It is something vague, an allergy for the cookie-cutter, conveyor-belt reality of the "square" world—go to school, get a job, get married, have kids, dress appropriately, speak appropriately, sweat and save, don't make waves, reach your shallow grave unfulfilled. Like most of the people these guys grew up around, these are things they've come to see as hollow.

The youngest brother was the proverbial child of the three-brother family. He has grown into a pretty, waifish man, angelic in disposition, soft-spoken, with eyes framed by long lashes. His name is Amariah, twenty-three, named so because the leader of the cult deemed that the boy be named so.

Dave, twenty-six, the middle brother, was the mother of the trio. He was the nurturer, he says, the one who packed the sandwiches and trimmed the hair. Three boys growing up in an era when the family was disintegrating, clinging to each other.

"We made it up as we went along," Dave says.

A bouncer at a bar, Dave was once the Marine commando who sat in church behind President Bill Clinton with a shotgun across his lap, a

top marksman in the United States military. He was so cloistered during this top-secret assignment at Camp David, he says, that he lusted
after the homely Chelsea Clinton as she came of age, her lips thicken-
ing, her nipples budding up through her shirt.

This man, rough stock, something Irish and indentured about him,
well accomplished and looking for authenticity, says his individuality
has no outlet except this club, its liquor and speed and sense of belonging. He wears his apathy toward the square world like a necktie.

I ask him how much longer he can belong to the group and not
himself. What does it take for the soldier to become the enemy, come
to the point where he is so dissatisfied that he boils over and turns on
the whole thing that created him? How long can the biker's leather
contain it?

"Dunno," he says with a smile.

Everything about him is primordial. The rough face, crocked eyes,
the thick neck and dirty nails, the leather, boots, zipper techno-
pyrrhic tattoos across the neck and arms and knuckles. In a soft, inebriated voice, he says he has some people he wants me to meet. And
growing bored after a few fights, I go to meet his people out front. But
they are gone. He apologizes with an arm around my neck. "They really wanted to meet you," he slurs. You can smell the bourbon on his
breath, like an old sock and cheap cigars.

And then he kisses me, half on the mouth, half on the cheek—a
real girl-boy kind of kiss. What the hell? Brotherhood? Well, I'm not
his fucking brother, man. I ain't shit to him.

Another explosion from the alley. The black eyes getting wider behind those windows—hurry up, motherfucking light, change. A ghost
flies by on a wheelie, tits and ass are coming out onto the street now.
Power, baby, power. The place is power.

About here the man kisses me again. Half cheek, half lip. Daddy,
are you home?

Kisses me, what the fuck? This isn't Europe. We don't kiss. No,
man, the thing is weird. The man is longing, lost maybe, found maybe,

I don't know. I'm just standing there like a whore on a pole. What can I do? What can I do?

I kiss him back. Full on the mouth, I kiss him back.

The whole East Bay Rats thing began in 1994 with a group of ten guys who hated the old fat-man Harley mentality, and felt the fancy-boy, electric-green, action-figure biker wasn't any better. This was just a bunch of hard guys who wanted to ride and drink but not rob or sell methamphetamines. They were already hanging out; all they did was pick a name and draw a logo, the rat and wrenches.

Rat bikes and rat life are a simple concept. Don't buy into the flashy society. Function over form. Forget chrome and green plastic. You crash a bike and throw it away, we garbage pick it, rebuild it, strip it, soup it up and spray-paint it flat black and sometimes bolt it together with duct tape. It doesn't matter. Odds are it will be destroyed within the year. That's what a rat does, he exists on the crumbs of society, he's got no money; none that he's willing to spend on something he's going to destroy anyway. He doesn't spend the weekend polishing metal. He's riding, man. A hundred and fifty miles an hour, trying to get the police to chase him. The acceleration toward the line.

Life becomes a statement. The club becomes more important than the family. Wives have been known to come down and complain loudly in front of the boys that the baby's diaper needs changing and it's his night to get his ass home and watch the kids. But they don't. The Rats come first. These men are educated, mechanically inclined, fantastic trick riders, rough, perhaps the most complete-incomplete men there are.

The unelected club president for life is Trevor Latham: well over two hundred pounds, shaved head, long beaver teeth, a pronounced limp caused by a titanium hip, and the skull and wrenches tattooed in thick ink across his entire back. The hip was a gift from a drunk driver, but it turned out this wasn't a completely unrewarding episode; Trevor caught a piece of the American Dream. That is, he caught a lawsuit and collected his way into the middle class. The $242,000 settlement paid for the clubhouse, in which he lives. Even though the prospects are expected to clean his home, beer cans and whiskers and rotting chicken carcasses are ubiquitous, the detritus from booze-fueled, knuckle-bashing orgies piling up faster than a broom-pushing prospect can clear it.

Because when the Rats aren't riding, they're drinking. And when they're drinking, they're fighting. Back in the beginning, the original Rats would get soused and rumble in public for the sheer joy of it, punching, wrestling, slap-boxing. In the streets, in the bars. Wherever they went, people watched. Something was going on, people watched. Then the observers started getting drunk and participating, and unwittingly Trevor had tapped into something. Soon there were thousands coming to his fight parties and drunken bacchanalias who *needed* this thing. Rat people. Children all grown up.

"You know, man, I'm living the dream," Trevor says. "I got a beer machine in my living room."

"You're like the Svengali of a lost generation, man," I tell him. He shakes his head, but I'm not sure he knows what I'm saying.

"All I know is that I throw a really good party."

I get to writing to myself near the beer machine:

The men of my generation are angry, howling, nasty, searching. A scratchy feeling that they're getting short-changed, screwed. One scheme after another falls apart. Then a man has no impulse control. The slightest whiff of disrespect is an irritation likely to end in physical harm. A girlfriend gets punched in the face because she wasn't listening. Two young men get in a car and hunt for someone to kill and call it working. These kind of men are a WASTE OF SKIN. We're in trouble.

"See, our parents, they were like the supergeneration of the fifties, the Baby Boomers, the superheroes, untouchables, and they grew up spoiled. You know . . . if it feels good, do it. And they did it," says Carl, the club's tattoo-maker, who joins me at the beer machine. "Drugs, they did it. Divorce? The wife and kids don't make him feel good and gone he goes and the whole system breaks down. Kids are left to their own while Mommy works. He's left to the television, and what? Like he sees seventeen thousand murders by the time he's eighteen and Mommy's got this new boyfriend and the guy's a prick or he rapes your sister or something. The family is broken and society's telling you to buy. And the factories start closing and moving to Asia and Mexico, and the kid, he dropped out of school. He's got no skills, he doesn't believe in people or God. That's what we've got."

I'm taken home to sleep. I am told the night ended with me scuffling with somebody and that I fell out of a truck onto my face. And apparently I called out the biggest, baddest Rat, a cat named Big Mike, to fight me at next week's party. I don't remember anything.

My cell phone rings. "The Ruby Room," the message goes. I like these guys, I think they accept me, not as one of their own, but more like a brother of the denomination, a neighbor, a kid from the block over, maybe.

The Ruby Room it is. The bar is bordello-red, the rain falling silver, the town smelling of boredom, the tires on the wet pavement making the sounds of frying meat. It is a mad, mad place. The Rats are rolling in from the rain and the place is packed full of wet leather and young breasts belonging to those certain hang-around chicks, looking for some length of cock for a certain length of time, and boom, you know they'd be off on other pursuits after they got it. Off to the pysch lab to meet an earnest young man who will take them away to the place with the good schools and the minivan and the kids and the certain misery that comes with that and somehow they'll have to hide those tattoos in the civilized society, right around the time their breasts begin to stretch and sag. Those girls with the skunk-stripe hair and the stories of Daddy or Uncle who did THE BAD THING to them and the violence is in their head and they want the edge, they want it, but they don't want to live there long, Daddy.

And it's this scene, the leather and the uniform, the patch, the same conversations about bikes and fighting, and I'm drinking boilermakers with the president and I'm starting to realize that this whole THING, man, this whole political society, this culture they're trying to propagate, is *cult-like*. Yeah, a cult. Think about it, Charlie, this THING. This code of ethics. Now you are a member of the shock troop, this band of men with an ideology of honor and brotherhood and violence should the world mess with you, this whole unspoken thing devised by this man sitting next to me drinking, this guy with the limp from a shattered pelvis and a titanium replacement hip, and when he walks it looks like the doctor gave him a leg that is two inches too short.

"You know, I live for my friends," Trevor says. "Every day, I just want to make this better. And if I had put this much time or energy to going to college or starting a business . . . I'd either have a doctorate or be rich, and I'm neither. I have this."

Here he is: self-satisfied with that long, strong body, the military crew cut, his fists wrenching his shot glass, and I'm feeling very, *very* close to this guy and I got a *feeling* here.

And that whiskey's working and, as whiskey will do, the moment of clarity comes . . . Attack him! . . .

I don't know why they follow Trevor. He isn't a deep thinker; he's not gifted with words or women. He is excitable, morbidly nervous, a large and silent presence. But he is the nucleus of the crowd, his identity their identity. To question his position is to question the concept. There can be no pack without a master. Is it a club or a gang? In a gang, a leader cannot, shall not be brought into submission.

We go straight to the floor and only after the barstools start flying, the rest of the bar notices the leader is under attack. I have the man neatly, I have turned him and I am fully in control, on top, he squirming, his tools, those fists taken away from him. This is when I notice the surge. The crowd has flipped. The faces and mouths are distorted squash. The shoulders have hunched, the fists have clenched. I notice all the details as one does in a car wreck, the way you see the windshield in freeze-frame before you puncture it with your face, and I know I've reached the *edge* with these guys, the animal is out, lips drawn back and teeth showing.

I would not win even if I brought the man to submission. And that is what I see, and so I let off, I let him beat me and twist my throat until I cannot breathe. I pat him with submission and he releases me with a laugh and the fangs go back in, the crowd barks, the jukebox winds up, you can hear the tinkle of ice cubes.

And that's when J.T., the man who opens his beer can with the sharp edge of his cane, tells me that I was close. "Had you gone on, put him in submission, embarrassed him, crossed that line, that would have been it for you. You don't embarrass the family, you just don't go there," he says with a sly smile, which means he means what he is saying. I realize here I'm losing the group. They're starting to realize a stranger has penetrated them, one who doesn't fully believe the message, who is fucking with them.

So no one will talk to me for about two beers. Then Big Mike walks into the bar, dripping wet and barefoot. I call him over and buy him a drink.

Trevor had arranged a fight for me with Jason, the prospect, but that first fight night I got so crooked on rooster bourbon that I crawled into the makeshift, plywood ring with the bungee-cord ropes and I called out Big Mike. Big Mike is 310 pounds and the only black man here, the only black Rat. One of the few men, ironically, with a normal childhood, parents still together.

Mike does not reveal much about his family history besides that he was raised in Oakland. Good family. He speaks with a white accent, has a white girlfriend, all his friends at the club are white and despite that he is still the black bogeyman. The body, the big, fearsome boy.

Never mind he is moderately sophisticated, twenty-nine, studying psychology at Berkeley. Mike plays the psychic black body with his dreadlocks and his habit of going shoeless. He wanders the city, the ghettos, the classroom without shoes like a big jungle cat or something. A little theater does wonders for one's reputation. His toenails are gnarled and black, but the soles of his feet are surprisingly supple. The Rat parties are interracial and they don't seem racist to me. They are probably fighting the racist tendencies they picked up in the suburbs, and that makes them good to me. Still, Mike is their only black member and he's the biggest, baddest dude on the block.

At the first fight party, I watched Big Mike disassemble the face of a man who outweighed him by thirty pounds—a *white* man. The crowd lustily crowed, their racial psychosis satisfied in the proof that the black body must defeat the white.

"You guys are doing this to turn on society. Is there a mission here?" I ask.

"Yeah, there is . . . just to get people out, just to get people involved in parts of their nature that they really repress a lot," Big Mike tells me. "To be able to do something that's exciting and a trial that they don't usually get to do outside of some antisocial way in the middle of a bar where they try to test themselves and they mess up everybody's night. We try to channel that into something that's more positive. It's about finding out how strong you are. Find out about how well you can do it. It's a personal thing."

I say, "You hold a very primal spot in this club, dude. You proud of that? Of course, right?" Big dog. Big black dog.

"In this arena I do," he says. "If you talk to the guys, when it comes to brawls out here in the streets, I'm the last one to get into it. I'm not really a big fighter. I'm diplomatic about dealing with people in the real world. I don't want to get into that kind of stuff. . . . Maybe it's because I can do it better than some. Maybe it's just my nature, I don't know, but I don't really like to get into it that much."

It sounded to me like Mike had had a good upbringing. I'm thinking maybe he's going to go a little easy on me.

From here, in the downpour, we drive our motorcycles across town
into the industrial wastes of Oakland, which deserves to be called
Frisco, since Frisco, once the rough-and-tumble center of the West,
has been painted over by Chablis sippers who don't like the place
being called Frisco because it reminds them of the cutthroats who
settled it. Gone are the body odors and syphilis and whiskers and
whores, the stuff that Oakland is. They might as well call Frisco the
Gingerbread House, as tough as it is anymore. It certainly isn't The
City, the way they like to call it. Everybody in the world knows where
the city is—back East, it's called New York.

At the stoplights children in station wagons get excited by the pirate men of motorcycles and wave to them, and the pirates wave back.
And the gang ends up in some industrial quarter in front of a ware-
house with silver shed doors and when the doors are pulled back I see
the whole place is built like a carnival ride, red lights and strange man-
nequins and guys wearing space helmets and Day-Glo stripes and
music is grinding from an act onstage in the back of the place and all
the Rats hold this kind of rapture over them. It's raining beer cans
from the balcony and no one believes in God here.

These cats are wearing clown costumes and death gear, there are
some girls making out on the dance floor and the Fuller brothers are
singing doo-wop onstage and Trevor is there with me, our shirts off,
on that edge again, and we're proud of ourselves. And I look around
and I see it on men's faces. They don't like me, not a bit. Who the fuck
is this guy? They would like to see me stomped at the hands of their
body: Big Mike, their black man, their outlet for their racial neurosis.

"I hope he kills you," one sullen Rat tells me by the toilet.

It is fight day and I would be matched with Big Mike, the barefoot
behemoth, the ultimate man whom nobody wanted to try.

There is a psychology to what I am trying. The quickest way to bona fides is to outcrazy the crazy. I could fight a man my own size, but what would be gained? If I beat Jason, I would make one small step toward the social hierarchy. If I lost, I would take one large step back into the pen of the runts. If I take on the biggest man, the baddest man, THE BLACKEST MAN, then, you see, I am not supposed to win, but I'd score the points for facing the beating. Little crazy man, you see. And on the outside chance that I would win, then I would take a giant step to the front of the pack.

Only one man, a mechanic with large circular ears named Englebert, calls me out.

"You're cheating," he says.

"I know, but it's better than the humiliation," I say.

"Still, you're gonna take a beating."

"We'll see," I say with such false bravado that Englebert turns with a scowl and walks away.

The day of the fight I have diarrhea. My shoulder hurts, my shin is fractured from a bull-riding episode and I don't want to fight. Too late now, face your beating. Move left, keep moving left, keep your hands up.

The club is as it should be as I pull up on San Pablo Avenue in the darkness. It is ethereal, smoky, spooklike. The smell of burnt tires and leather. Dozens of bikes lining the street, the dark characters and the rat and crossbones insignia. They are hopped up on juice as I pull up on my ratty Sportster, which leaks at the crankcase and has no taillight. They smile, pat me on the back, the lamb at the slaughter.

"It's not too late to back down," J.T. says to me as I get off the bike, and he hands me a beer, which I accept. Of course he is incorrect. It *is* too late. To back down is to admit cowardice, which is defeat. To not fight is to go to the back of the line, and I of course could never go back there. I had learned that lesson years ago.

I arrive at the clubhouse in a Lord Byron shirt, a black suede vest and a silk polka-dot kerchief, wanting to make my own theater and statement. A man can dress individually, of himself, be beautiful and free, appear effeminate and still punch. The getup draws snickers and ridicule. "Oscar Wilde the faggot," I'm called. I try to relax in the corner on the weight bench, and Trevor's telling me I got to go now because the cops are here and the whole thing's going to be shut down, which is bullshit. I've talked to the cops. The cops like these guys. Trevor just wants to see an ass-whooping, and he's not sure if I'll change my mind. So I strip down to my undershirt, roll up my pants to the knees, replace my boots with tennis shoes, pull up my socks to my knees and kiss the crucifix around my neck. The place is electric. They've come to see my dismemberment and I'm obliging. Trevor and an entourage escort me to the ring. It's jam-packed. People with piercings, tattoos, biker colors and glasses of liquor. I'm scared.

Fuzzy, the bald-headed, purple-bearded vice president of the Oakland Hell's Angels, does me the honor of helping me into the slaughter pen, holding the rope with one hand and giving me a shove into the plywood ring. He has that pinned-back expression of a trapped animal. He's happy.

The ring is a small one, about ten-by-ten, making running and dancing impossible. I want to at least last a round, for the appearance of things. And when Aaron announces that in this corner is Charlie, weighing in at 165 pounds, the crowd howls, hisses, laughs. And in the other corner, Mike, weighing 310 pounds—they go bananas. "What is it you want to see?" Aaron asks.

"Barbarism!"

"Kill him!"

I hear one lonely voice, the shrill of a fan who would never do this himself, but understands. "You've got nothing to lose except your heart."

The countdown comes, 10–9–8–7–6–5–4–3–2–1—"KILL HIM!" The crowd is for Big Mike and this makes me angry. Now I want to win. I will win. Yes! Down him with a jab-hook combination, show the world that, no, you *could* be your own man, you could build your own world without the onerousness of packing up with a lot of strangers, that if you stand up for yourself you'll be left alone. And so I dance left since he is a southpaw and so am I. Avoid the cross. I jab. He jabs. . . .

A left cross to my right cheek. This is what Mike Tyson calls "the truth." Everyone's a champion until he's hit with the truth, Tyson says. It's like being hit with a wet sandbag. The stars come out, and then the tea whistle rings in my ears and the concept of the TRUTH has arrived, the realization that more is coming and I probably won't win. And within that moment lies the infinity that exists between quitting and fighting.

Fight! My ears clear, the world comes back to me and the crowd is roaring. They want *a beating*.

Pick yourself up and try, man. I won't win, his arms are too long. Maybe I can make this man limp out of this alley, see, convince him that even though he is physically superior, I cannot lose, that I am not inferior but a man to be left alone. What Freud was saying in a way is that beneath the veneer of civility, one must have physical respect to get brotherly respect.

I move forward for more, the crowd howling; Big Mike aims for my head again, but I move left and the big fist only glances off me. I counter with a cross, jab, hook and stagger him. His head snaps back, his dreads dancing like garden snakes. He falls back. The crowd goes ape. They are with me now. The little man! The primordial. This is the meaning of fight club and riding on the edge and fire and explosions. *The exhilaration of life.*

Much of the rest I cannot remember. It is all white light. I make it two rounds before he pops me with an elbow that makes my torso twist, and then he delivers a neat shot to my kidney that sends a jolt of electricity through my innards, shocking and debilitating my organs. I am on my knees looking at my mouthpiece while standing above myself looking at me—thirty-nine, lost, weak, people howling nasty things. KILL HIM, and I'm thinking I'm already dead. A little man who has taken a beating for no decent reason except wanting to be wanted, wanting to prove his mettle to a group of strangers and wanting to be accepted by them. If you can't understand it, you're walking dead. The rat has eaten his cheese and I can hear them cheering and it isn't for Big Mike; it's for me, and they know before I know that I have found something that I had very nearly lost in my typing-for-a-living world.

Will.

The bout is called as I can go on no more. Aaron hugs me, Big Mike hugs me, we have a swallow of whiskey and I crawl out of the ring. Fuzzy, the Angel who helped feed me to the lion, looks me in the eye and pats me on the back and says, "Good fight. I'm proud of you, son." And Dave, the Marine, the complete and damaged man, hugs me and kisses me on the mouth, and what can I do? What can I do? I kiss him back, that whiskered cat-face fucker, I kiss him back and I understand what the kiss means now. Life is for love and for living.

And I walk back through the crowd to the weight bench where I'd left my clothes and cell phone and I'm trying to catch my breath and a beautiful young woman approaches. She is wearing a sari of gold, tight around the breasts, her hair piled high, high cheekbones, smooth skin, quite beautiful.

"I just want to tell you," she says with real dignity, "that I think you are probably a good man and I just wanted to tell you."

And there it is, that is what some women want to see. She wants to see if a man, when pushed, will fight. She wants a man with a body, a mind, a job, some personal ethics. That's what she wants, and he hardly exists. I wish I were that guy. This is just theater, honey.

I call my brother. My brother is spellbound by violence too. I tell him about the night, about the fact that I like these men, how I will never wear their patch. I tell him to call my other brothers and remind them of our own fight clubs in the living room so many years ago with the shaggy Crystal-T freaks looking on. Tell my brothers we are our own rats, our own family, a culture unto ourselves, no matter how damaged we are. We are strong despite the weaknesses. I tell him that and I tell him I love him.

Black Rock City, Nevada

It is microwave-hot and people are stoned in the sun and in this false Mecca or Buddhist temple or Palace to the Absurd—I am not sure what I'm seeing. Is it a mirage? The only thing sure is that nothing really matters here and nothing really means anything. In the end, burn it. This is the mantra of the thing they call Burning Man. The philosophy is the emptiness of this generation we used to call X. Now we don't call ourselves anything. We meander through life without purpose, charting with a broken compass. It's all made up: our family, religion, tribe. Our answer is to build nonsense in a burning alkali flat just because we can. So much ingenuity my generation has, and no place to put it. Life is a meaningless game. It is a mousetrap—a big, stupid, burning mousetrap.

And in this spirit we build ourselves a real-life Mousetrap, like the board game with the bathtub and Rube Goldberg roundabouts and the cage that snares the plastic rodent. Only this board game art piece is a quarter acre in size. It isn't a Ping-Pong ball that falls into the tub, but a burning piano into a vat of gasoline. Such is the colossal scale of our hollowness. A silly pop-culture remnant of a childhood we are still afraid to let go of. So hungry are we for shared meaning and experience that the people of my generation fawn over this ephemeral piece of "highly conceptual art" as though it equaled the Acropolis in terms of human achievement and ingenuity.

This, for what it's worth, is our Athens, this week-long Burning Man "art" festival that springs up once a year in a barren dead lake bed in Nevada's Black Rock Desert. Nothing lives here—no animal, no plant, no creeper or crawler. There is nothing, no water, no ice for your bourbon. So it is all trucked in, the bourbon, the dope, the ice, the pussy waxed naked, the maypole on which the woman swings with her privates spread wide so the public can get a good looky-loo. The flies, the outrageous art, everything—all of it shipped in. Right now, brother, a pirate ship with two crow's nests drifts by me along the endless chalky expanse, its music lighting up the moon and the mountain, and screwing going on under the mizzenmast. There is a crane reconfigured into a tulip or a Venus flytrap four stories high, its petals maw-mawing open and closed, contorting itself like a beggar of Calcutta. Maw-maw, go the pink petals. And maybe you're so hopped up on liquid acid that the flower becomes a massive vagina speaking to you and you call out to the skipper of that goddamn pirate ship because you got issues to work out.

They come to Burning Man to fuck in the temporary dirt streets, to strip down to their underwear and freak out, writhing on the desert floor. It is obvious by watching the drug-retching, the anguish, the screams, the howls, the good-looking girl slashing at her face with her own dirty fingernails, that self-expression is dangerous when too much expression is mixed with too little sense of self.

"HEY, NOTICE ME! I AM NOBODYYYYYIEEEEEE . . . ,"

forty thousand freaks scream without moving their mouths. Forty thousand stray dogs pissing all over the place.

There are the doers and the do-nothings here at Burning Man. Perhaps ten percent of the crowd holds vast, unfocused power. Knowledge of the arc welder, computer, wrench, sun. The imagination to make it rain fire, and to make the fire spell out what it is you told it to say through a microphone. Howling, as you are, in a desert as empty as your life. "Fuck the whole fucking thing," you say, and there it is: "Fuck the whole fucking thing," the fire repeats. It is the only thing here that listens to you—or cares what you say. Destruction as an artistic movement; let us call it Nouveau Nihilism.

Let me on that giant boogie bus that shines like a shark and pour me another Cosmopolitan, baby, you missed a spot on the pinky toe.

The other ninety percent of the crowd can be described as the hangers-on. There are always, of course, the hangers-on—the club kids who aren't kids, like the twenty-nine-year-old woman who's never had an orgasm and so comes here and wraps herself in colored cellophane and cuts a hole in the pelvic region and lies there in the sand, waiting for any guy with a hard-on, or a chick with a hard tongue or a fresh cucumber, to stuff it in her hole; the pseudo-hippies and greenies and freaks and that kind of shit, though nobody's talking consciousness, man, because consciousness is a bowl of leftovers from that punk-ass generation who ended up running out on us and leaving us nothing but a mountain of debt and dope and self-loathing and a filthy desert floor and a confused mind craving all the filthy things.

In a week they erect this "Las Vegas North," this seven square miles of a semicircle of neon and electronica music, flame-spitting cannons, even an airport and a hospital. If you want it, then build it, set it up, erect it, then burn it. Bring your band and plug into a generation and scream Doors songs into the night, if that's what floats your boat. In its way, *this* Vegas is better, more hedonistic, without purpose or cops. The sex is open and free. Take your dope when and where you choose. Your money is no good here; there is no money. Share and share alike. If you've got nothing to share, then just be cool. No, money is not accepted here—except, of course, in the Center Tent, the public square, where they sell gourmet coffee. Lattes in the morning, dude. Of course! Lattes in the morning and the newspaper to wipe your ass. How hard is it to boil your own coffee?

The system is alive, fungible, capable. But the soul feels dead. Pop culture, nothing more, nothing deep. No statement about a war, a dying planet, gasoline prices, religion, sexuality, none of the things we are consumed with in everyday life. We hate where we come from. The suburbs suck, so you suck, white man, your mother sucks. Tell her I said hello. They say things like, "My culture's been stolen from me," when what it really is, perhaps, is that you've thrown your culture away.

You're not a Christian anymore—you're a pagan, a Burner! A slave to that eighty-foot wooden man in the epicenter of this pop-art town, the one detailed in neon that we will burn to the ground before taking off our clothes and raping each other with our fingers. And we will go counterclockwise (against the direction of nature, no less!) and we will never touch the fire, never grab it, lick it, swallow it, fondle it. We will not commune with the life source because we know nothing of it. We are dead. And we will sing like a bunch of trained monkeys, "Happy Burnday to Us!"

Yes, it is one big monolithic Mousetrap game where things are "supposed to happen to you, man." Burning Man will "change you forever, man." Burning Man will "reconfigure your entire being, man." This is what they say at Burning Man, man.

Burning Man is an attempt to create a free, artistic society, I'm told by Larry Harvey, the founder of this whole seething mind-freak.

We are sitting beneath a canopy near Center Tent, in Harvey's compound. He's got pretty women to attend to his needs. People meander by with doe-eyed reverence as though he were the Colonel Kurtz of the desert, the Pied Piper of the Playa. Harvey is wearing a

Stetson and chain-smoking hard cigarettes, his eyes darting behind his tinted aviator shades. When he speaks, it's in a Hunter Thompson—esque rapid staccato.

"A lot of artists have been involved in the early formation of this," he tells me. "This is an elaboration of bohemia, but unlike bohemia we've done one historically novel thing: we took a scene, which is essentially communal and formal, like avant-gardes or bohemias anywhere, and turned it into a *city* and invited everyone in and said it's public.

"And you'll notice that we've taken commerce out of the equation, not because we're against commerce—we sell a ticket—but we've created an environment where people immediately interact with one another. . . . We've created a vessel, we've created a context, we've created a society in which people must interact with one another, and the medium of that interaction is a heartfelt one."

If memory serves, Robespierre said something similar before his Reign of Terror. . . .

I take his cue. I interact. I give him a gift for his time, for the inspiration, as you are expected to do here—you know, the whole anti-money, pro–unforced magnanimity thing. "Gifting," it's called in Burner parlance. I give him the only things I have left: my trousers and suspenders.

(I had arrived here in a linen suit with a blue Brooks Brothers shirt, a red-white-and-blue tie and a straw hat and was shouted down for looking like a Republican. My jacket and tie went missing at the Burning Man post office—yep, a real-life post office, run by a man in a ball cap, scarf, yellow T-shirt, his butt crack and cock exposed to the elements. I got the message.

Larry puts on my trousers and suspenders. I sit there buck-naked and we talk.

"Burning Man is a laboratory," he continues, "an experiment, not a utopia. . . ."

Harvey makes clear that the wooden statue he first created in 1986 and burned in front of a dozen onlookers at the beach in San Francisco meant nothing. The irony of Burning Man is its lack of meaning. How perfect for the empty consumerist generation, I think. Still, people came. They just dug it, babe. Fire and destruction for the thrill of it. They found something primal and vaguely religious in the giant stick man. Harvey knew he had something here. This guy had found something. *The thing. The nothing.*

The ritual became an annual event, and each year the crowds grew . . . and grew . . . and grew—from hundreds to thousands to tens of thousands. People began making their own art, conducting their own experiments in pyromania and dope-fueled delirium. It was anarchy. And somehow it worked. By the early nineties, Harvey and his merry painters moved the whole shindig out to the Nevada desert, where there was plenty of open space for their monkeyshines, their party cars, guns, fires, jet engines, giant surreal art installations—Penis flytrap, baby! Best of all, they were free from the hassles of the Man, the *other* Man, the one who runs things . . . out there.

And still, the numbers continued to rise, by simple word of mouth, by the Internet. By the time I arrived at the dance, there were forty thousand souls camped out on the desert floor, making Burning Man— or Black Rock City, as the pop-up settlement is now called—the fourth-largest municipality in the state of Nevada, at least temporarily.

The "city" moniker isn't inaccurate. It more closely resembles a giant refugee camp, although Black Rock City has its own roads, a broad esplanade, propane-fueled streetlights, bars, radio stations, bike shops, salons, what have you, all laid out in an easy-to-navigate grid system. Costumed folks set up their own neighborhoods, or "theme villages," devoted to a particular idea, philosophy, joke or lifestyle— places with names like Twilight of the Gods, Inferno Camp, Temple-Whore and Green Penis.

It's laid out in a grid like a suburb except the streets here are named not Elm and Hibiscus, but rather Ego and Hysteria.

And as in any city with a steady stream of new immigrants, there are times when people clash. Old-timers don't like the newcomers.

The ravers on the techno side of town bitch about the frat boys on the other and a whole stew in between. This is the price of expansion. This is when the city fathers, once the prophets of unbridled liberty and free expression, begin tightening the reins.

Harvey tells me that the astronomical growth of the community has necessitated the institution of rules and structures. You can't drive your fire-breathing V-8 shark car as fast as you want anymore—they've got a speed limit. You can't fire off guns at will. You can't sneak into the festival, since they've got goons patrolling the periphery. Your car is searched at the gates, not for contraband but for stowaways, since the only way to get in without paying the $300 cover is to hide *under* the vehicle, on the axles.

In order to have a community with shared values you have to impose those values. *Principles,* they're called in Burning Man's corporate literature—yes, good-bye, anarchy; Burning Man has become a limited liability corporation, with company offices and lawyers! I take a look at this manifesto of sorts, these Ten Commandments of Burning Man by which all participants must abide, this pointy-headed mumbo-jumbo about the inner self, social networks, radical inclusion, decommodification, civic responsibility.

At the heart of Burning Man's own mythos, the principle from which all others seemingly evolved, is Number 5:

Radical Self-expression
Radical self-expression arises from the unique gifts of the individual. No one other than the individual or a collaborating group can determine its content. *It is offered as a gift to others. In this spirit, the giver should respect the rights and liberties of the recipient.* [emphasis mine]

I decide then and there to take this thing to its limits, to test these folks, to see if my self-expression will collide with the "rules" of the Burning Man community.

The Burning Man looks like a big Starbucks logo to me, a glowing stick man. I hate it, I tell Larry. It's an ultimate symbol for nothing. A commodity in itself. An empty focal point. I'm against the mindlessness of it and I'm going to throw eggs at it and see if I can get the crowd to beat me to a pulp. Now, that's interesting art. Sacrificing your body. Letting mindless hipsters tear you to shreds just to remind them what lurks beneath their cool-breeze façade. That's radical inclusion, baby. That's gifting.

Harvey, I think, kind of digs the idea of a man getting beaten to a pulp over nothing. "Go ahead," he tells me. "Just try not to fritz out the neon circuits."

Rules, man, this shit's got rules. This isn't Mad Max. This is Maxi Pad. They don't like the media here? Then I'll be the embodiment of all those fast-talking, intrusive, clueless, talking-head TV morons. I will be Media Man! People should hate that well enough.

I find myself caught in a blinding dust storm in the 110-degree heat. So I do what any self-respecting reporter would do. I get bombed on vodka and wander around the flats in shorts and flip-flops. The alkali eats straight through my skin and into my bones. I've got a sunburn on my skull because I thought it'd be cool to come with a Mohawk. But everyone's wearing a Mohawk and no matter how you slice it, if everyone's doing it, it ain't cool.

I'm walking around with the pain throbbing in my brain, sort of like the thrombosis of a nagging wife who's on the verge of becoming an ex-wife. I come across three big girls in small bikinis and two men with ugly, stubby penises. My generation. This, a practice run for the End of Days. And when IT arrives, are you a leader or a follower? Are you the driver of the funky bus with the Ferris wheel or are you a passenger? Are you a woman who runs her camp with a sweet scent of cocoa butter or are you a beggar at the edge, hoping for a smile and a foot massage?

You'll get nothing, bro. Go to the port-a-john and jerk off. And inside there, please note the message scrawled on the wall. "Linda. It was great meeting you. I hope to spend more quality time with you this week." Fucking charming, man. Real fucking charming.

These are the things one thinks. I'm going to egg that mother and get my head stomped in. That's gonna be my art.

This is my generation, at least the white part of it. The black part is drowning in New Orleans right now. And me being the Media Man, my persona is the town crier.

So I'm taking my tandem bike (a bike built with my own hands, thank you very much) and I'm tripping on these mushrooms, see, and I'm riding this bike right into the Center Tent where bikes aren't allowed, even though there aren't *supposed* to be any rules here and so I figure we're even—and I'm telling the white freaksters that our black brothers and sisters, our Southern brothers and sisters, my real-life cousins "out there," are dying and that New Orleans has disappeared. And my white cousins, who aren't really my cousins, admonish me, tell me go away, that I'm ruining the party. Mardi Gras is gone and now Burning Man becomes the second biggest party in America, after the Super Bowl. Congratulations. Party on!

I throw my bicycle in psychedelic anger and I'm standing there in the gay quarter of the giant tent and who do I see . . . a Republican political strategist I know from my *New York Times* days. He's sitting alone, wild-eyed on mushrooms, his ex-wife off with some other guy, a pink puffball taped to her pussy or something—the details were foggy, his story rambling and incoherent. He didn't recognize me at first. I wasn't sure I recognized what was in his eyes. Strung out, confused, shaking from some nerve disease, dressed in biker's leather, shirtless underneath, a blinking Day-Glo penis around his neck. Here, in the gay quarter of the Center Tent. Yeah, right, the mustache. I wondered. Hmmmmm.

New Orleans is underwater and he's sitting here all alone, the political mastermind of world events. He smiles upon recognizing me and tells me, "I'm lost. I don't know where I am."

"You're at Burning Man, brother."

"No. My life's been a waste," he says. "I've done nothing good with it. It's meaningless. I've only got a little time to make something of it."

He was dying. A deteriorating spine, I guessed from the state of his hands. Like a jiggling glass of milk, hairy and soft and pale. He'd been pushed out of the power center by those men I remember clearly from the election victory party a few years ago. Arrogant young Turks smoking contraband Cuban cigars in the hotel hallway as though rules didn't apply to them—and at that moment it was easy to see rules didn't. They were in control now. The old men would be swept away. No room for the weak. The weak are to be eaten or exiled. The weak are to be left for the wolves. Now, that, baby, is real life!

And my friend sitting here, twitching and tweaking, the sandstorm howling like a dog outside, the folds of the tent flapping like a drowning bird. My friend looking for meaning in a place that has none.

"D—," I say, "there's no *there* here."

We sit quietly for a spell. Somebody is playing a sitar. A fucking sitar. I think about my mother, the military wife. She'd laugh at this one. A sitar.

I told him about New Orleans. He became lucid for a moment, his eyes clear. "Oh, my God," he said, and then wept. New Orleans was dead and we were celebrating nothingness in a desert, which could kill us, if we didn't do it to ourselves first.

And this sick man, he is pathetic. Lost and strung out here, alone and useless and knowing he is a single old shoe in a closet of garish clothes. The evening makes me melancholy. I walk him back to his RV and put him to bed. Have a glass of wine and kiss him good night. On the way to my van, I pass out on some Persian carpets. Someone gives me a blanket. I wake up thinking about my friend, the flawed puppet master. His desire to live, to win, to conquer. Such men die alone. I will end up like him, I'm afraid.

And then there are the others here, suit guys, operators, sales clerks, accountants. American subordinates, the most productive, high-strung insomniacs in the world. The whole thing spinning too fast. And existence beyond their control and no one asking for their opinions. Says one man to me about his life *out there:* "All the time, it's 'Do this, that and the other, buy this because you don't have a chance, watch TV, sit on your ass, eat drive-thru, these pills make your breath taste sweet, shut up, sit in your cubicle and do what you're told!' Out here you can blow shit up, go around naked if you want to, and nobody's telling you no. No advertising and no money here. You can trade, but no bringing in the green from out there."

"You high?" I ask him. His eyes are dazzling black saucers.

"Maybe," he says, suspicious.

"What'd you use to buy the drugs?"

"Money," he says without irony.

So for a week they put on plastic devil horns, drink cocktails with genitalia-like swizzle sticks, ingest an alphabet soup of drugs, lie to themselves, jack off in the desert, build art and then burn the whole motherfucker to the ground.

Indeed.

The Media Man bit goes okay. I get interviewed on one of the pirate radio stations, I forget which, there are a half dozen of them. I have an extreme hangover because on every corner of the city someone sets up a tiki bar and you can have whatever you want: mai-tais, mojitos, Bloody Marys, margaritas, martinis, Manhattans. MMMM. I, of course, have them all. So I'm on the radio, see, and I begin with, "Wake up, white people! It's okay if you come from the suburbs. There's nothing wrong with that. It's where you learned to read. It's where you learned to write. It's where you learned to love. It's where you stole your first kiss. So what's so wrong with that?"

Really, what's wrong with that, whitey? And then I go on some ramble about the stupidity of finding meaning in a party designed around a total lack of meaning. And then I ask that everyone put down their hookah stems and turn off the music and give a moment of silence to our dead family in New Orleans. And to the DJ's credit—his name is Max—Max shuts down his airwaves for a minute. Max, in my opinion, is a ten percenter. I am not.

At the Center Tent, a protest has started. People are angry with me, annoyed that I have pierced their private party with my mainstream camera. What if their boss sees pictures of them copulating near the toilets? One man posts a notice on the Web saying he's doing a performance art piece and that he invites me, Charlie LeDuff, to come wipe his ass. I never found that guy. All mouth and ass. No balls. There's a lot of chicken shits like that on the Internet. Fascists. Cowards. Whiners. I would have gladly wiped his ass, and then I would have jammed the sharp end of my pencil up his rectum.

They accuse me of having an agenda, of having preconceived the story before I came. I suppose it's true. I thought Burning Man would be a tribe of the new values. Peaceful barbarian poets at the fire's edge. Save the planet. Stop the war. It is here, I suppose, somewhere in the orgy of consumption and self-distraction.

There is a man in a robe and miter carrying around a bullhorn, bumming out the revelers with his shouts and protestations, his sophomoric rants against God. No, check that—he is making fun of people who believe in God in any structured way. And since nearly everybody here is white, you can say he is ridiculing the Catholics. It doesn't go over well on the Esplanade, which reminds me of the Sunset Strip with its neon and hipsters and red velveteen ropes. Not because they're into Jesus, but more like they're into themselves and the party. Philosophy is at a minimum here.

As it happens, this anti-Pope's grandfather was a missionary.

Why do you make fun of your grandfather, my grandfather, my mother, me? Why do you ridicule yourself, your own roots? I ask him.

Because it's false, and all the evil committed in the world was created in this false god's name.

Surely you believe in a greater power.

I do, but not the one they're selling me, he says.

Perhaps, I say. But you don't have to believe the entire story. You

don't have to reject it completely. It's your culture; it's where you belong, maybe the only place you truly belong. People are tribal, man,
and if you don't believe me, then put down your bullhorn and look
around. Look at the fake temple, the fake shamans, the crystals, and tell
me these people aren't searching for a tribe.

Better a false tribe of your own making than one forced upon you,
he shouts.

The one forced upon you has a reason and a root and was given to
you out of love, to help you survive. And if God is false and silly, then
why aren't you standing here dressed as a caliph? Why don't you make
fun of the Muslims, man? That would be something. But you won't
do it because you're a coward. You're afraid to offend something you
don't understand. Because you hate yourself.

And it goes this way for a while until nobody is listening to us anymore and we're both thirsty and in need of a cocktail.

Larry Harvey and his people oversee everything, down to the last detail. Everything proceeds according to schedule, according to plan.
People need some order to their freak-out or they'll freak out, know
what I'm saying? Harvey himself has found some inspiration in this
new order; he now wants to explode the Burning Man ethos, make
the thing more political, more world-conscious, less a Roman bath-
house. It seems like he's tiring of these weeks out in the desert. Maybe
the whole thing will come to an end and people will take the ideas
back to their corners of the country and rekindle the movement there.

A movement? An experience? Meaning? What does that mean? If
a tree falls and no one ever heard of it, did it have meaning? Anything?
The work of man will disappear when the sun explodes in a super-
nova. It will turn our great books and tall buildings to ash. The planet
itself will be a spent match head. Deep down, everyone knows there is
no meaning and so meaning is invented in America through new sink
faucets and car waxes and aluminum siding in pastel colors. The host

throws a party to give meaning to himself, not his guests. It's the audience that gives the artist meaning, not the art, not the fondue, not the
tongs, not the fire.

In this way, Burning Man is no different from the "outside" world
we've left behind for the week. The emptiness is still there. The fear is
still there. So we still light up the desert like the Vegas Strip. And when
you see this here, you realize the "outside" world could have developed no other way. It is the perfect culmination of human endeavor
and spirit. That is, it's rotten.

Eventually the host realizes this and grows tired of his parties and
again the nagging meaninglessness returns. He is disillusioned when he
wakes up in the morning and inspects his home—the shattered glass,
the cigarette butts, the cat on the counter licking the softened butter,
the footprints across the tiles, the piss stains at the head of the toilet.
It's an illusion. Life has no meaning, baby. You're dead the minute
you're born.

More wine?

There's nothing wrong with a vacation, but Burning Man promised something more. A new way.

Harvey's party has reached its natural endpoint. Decadence. De-
cline. He's grown old and wise and tired. "I'm sort of over it," he says
about Burning Man. He's said it more than once and the acolytes are
aghast. They've bought into the meaninglessness and found meaning
here, made a virtue of a lack of strength, acquired self-quality in deny-
ing the self nothing. And now, the Great One has the temerity to say
he is over it?

Down with the Great One!

But enough with the politics. Enough with the negativity.

There is a wedding today! A nice young couple from Washington
State. Blond, tattooed and handsome, this couple is. They are to be
married at the Buddhist Temple, a building done in red, a beautiful
piece of art built by non-Buddhists. The couple will be married in
fake animal skins by a fake shaman, a biochemist from the Northwest

who is done up in peacock feathers and blackface, the priest of the blue-eyed devil clan. It is important to say that the kids are happy and in love and this much is real. The woman in the bear head giggles. The one with the coconut tits cries. And the shaman, shameful shaman in his minstrel face and peacock feathers and bones through the septum, he mangles some Sioux tradition that he half learned somewhere. "Let us invoke the North, the great buffalo woman. Aho," he says. "Now the West, the direction of the cougar—no, wait, the coyote. . . ."

Afterward, he asks, "Did you get all that? I'd love to see that on TV."

Around the Burning Man at night, the freaks congeal. "I'm from Manhattan," some Burner squeals.

"Oh, I used to live in Manhattan. I live in San Francisco now."

"Yeah, cool, very cool. . . ."

And they start screaming at the eighty-foot stick man. "Daddy, Daddy, why won't you listen to me?" They're all stoned, playing for each other, running around in German storm trooper outfits and pumps and lingerie. Daddy! Why won't you fucking listen to me?

There is an old man, camped not so far from the Man. He sleeps in his car, which is parked near an outdoor shower where handsome young women lather themselves all over. He's seventy-five, but he's not dead and he's not stupid. Across the way from his car is an outdoor dance hall, complete with a roofed bar and liquor.

"I like young people," the old man tells me. "They keep me young."

He walks over to watch, bask in the fountain of youth, have a drink. He watches and asks for a second. But they deny the old man a drink, because he's not dancing. He's not cool. He's not youthful. His wrinkles are ugly and he offends. The old man goes away rejected.

"That hurts," he says. Yes, to hurt people is against the Concept. The Concept of Totality and Nothingness, it's driving me crazy, and my toe is swollen.

A fire spinner—one of many who practice the faddish art of spinning flaming balls attached to chains and handles—spun himself into a heart attack. Another person overdosed. They don't tell you that stuff, here in the center of the free world. It's strictly word of mouth. Rape, they don't tell you about the rapes in the toilets, except to post fliers that remind men that no means no.

See? Society cannot be escaped. It has developed perfectly according to human want and composition. It could be nothing else except the empty ratbag of self-conceit and self-denial. Rape does not disappear because you wish it so. Garbage does not vaporize in the desert. You simply haul it back to the real world. Some duck will choke on your swizzle sticks anyhow. The Wal-Mart in Reno does spectacular business the week of Burning Man. So much for anticonsumerism and radical self-reliance.

And in this spirit I take my half dozen Wal-Mart-bought eggs and on the afternoon before burning, I heave them at the man. As I do, some workers are on the platform.

They look around, then down. "Who's throwing the fucking eggs?" one shouts. I raise my hands. I'm gonna get my ass stomped now, I think hopefully.

"Motherfucker," one yells. Soon I'm surrounded by cops—not deputized officers of the law, but Black Rock Rangers, trained in conflict resolution by the Burning Man organization . . . sort of cool, spiritual keepers of the peace, but not really. They're still cops. There is a cop in every soul but they're not bad people, these rangers, seeing as women get raped in the toilets, and fire spinners drop dead.

"You'll have to leave the perimeter," says one copper whose nickname is Mongolia or something like that.

"Hey, *bro,*" I say. "Larry said I could do it."

"I don't care what Larry said, you'll have to leave the perimeter. There's important work being done here."

"But bro, I thought there were no rules to this thing."

"Everything's got rules," he says. "Don't you know they're up there loading explosives?"

My heart sank. Pyrotechnics for the show tonight. What a dick. I'm a fucking dick. Those kind of people up there, those who know how to build and then blow shit up, are working people, talented people. Party hosts. I respect them. Putting on a show for forty thousand people just because they want to. I am ashamed of myself. It was like I walked into a house party, rifled through the medicine chest, shouted obscenities in the backyard, woke the neighbors, ran into the living room, broke a lamp and then on my way out the door told them how they were raising their kids all wrong. Above all, they were trying to put a philosophy into practice; all I had were empty words.

"I didn't know," I tell Mongolia. "Please tell them I apologize. I didn't mean to hurt anybody. Truly. I respect them, and tell them for me I am sorry."

And I do leave the perimeter, but not before one of the artists runs up and smashes an egg on my head. I get my answer. I deserve it. This place has rules.

The evening has come for the burning of the Man. I have fallen in with a group of kite-fliers. Among them are two women in go-go boots, one with her breasts painted blue. The go-go girls help me paint my head gold. I wear a blue kung-fu suit one of the men has given me. He speaks elliptically about inner turmoil and unanswered angst and not measuring up to his father. His head is shaved closely except for two tufts of hair that he twists into horns and paints red. I've said nothing to him but "Be yourself." He acts as though I were the oracle and he has received the enlightenment. Still, he is a kind, gracious man.

I think it was not the wisdom that was burrowing into his psyche but rather the liquid acid and the ecstasy. The people here remind me of the international freaksters I fell in with in my younger years. A society of misanthropes who traveled from Ko Phangan to Goya to Bali, partying their balls off, swallowing bundles of heroin, shitting them out and peddling them in Zurich and Berlin to keep their own habits going. Some of them, like Rita, a sweet little Kewpie-doll face, went on to meet the Maker in a filthy guest room in Bangkok. Others disappeared. Whatever happened to you, Bones? I feel real nice as the sun sets. I have a couple beers, strap a few more to my belt and stagger along with twenty thousand others toward the Man. The electric Christmas lights around the city are dripping like candle wax. Lasers and neon and glosticks. Tits, legs, lips, eyes, eyes, eyes. Admiral, stilt clown, caveman . . . thump thump thump . . . ragtime . . . is that a motorized piano car???! . . . that's a motorized piano car . . . drummers . . . twirlers . . . fire breathers . . . thump thump thump . . . Venus fly vagina . . . oh, Mommy . . . oh, Mommy . . . Daddy, why won't you listen to me?

And like that, with the mania and the drugs coursing, there are no individuals, just a collective . . . everybody on the wave . . . IT burst into flames. THE MAN IS ON FIRE. . . .

The roar from the citizens is dull, the way people cheer at a folk concert. They whoooo, you know? WHOOOO! And then the lighters are ignited . . . WHOOOO! . . . Where's the freaking animal in people? There's a huge fire out here. . . .

And the Man tumbles off his pedestal to the ground, THE MAN, burning like a house in a wheat field and the citizens of the new world singing "Happy Burnday to us . . . ," and I'm feeling lost, man. There's nothing I feel like belonging to. Something is the matter with me. The Church doesn't do it for me. The Company does it only for itself. The Cousin continually disappoints. And now the City. Black Rock City. It feels empty and so do I. Stoned out of my gourd and I'm lonely, sister, but I'm not going into that crowd swirling around the fire now. They're all going down the drain. They're drowning, stay away from them, they'll pull you down with them.

But eventually, they do pull me in, closer and closer until I fly straight to the center, to the flame, to the beginning. Pushing through the swirl, fifty deep, freaks finger-fucking each other. And on the way, pulling in those teenage boys who are drunk and directionless and looking like they're going to bash someone's head, stomp them into mush. It'd be so easy. Who would notice? Hey, come on, boys! Let's snatch the fire. Touch it. Run through it. Let your beast bubble up from your loins and into your chest and out of your hands. Grab that

flaming stick and run away . . . and then, as they balance on the edge
of violence, I say, Okay, the fire is yours. Try not to hurt anyone. Be
men. Look out for people. Good luck in Iraq.

And they stand big and full-chested and confused. What a night.

I awake on the Esplanade along with the sun. There I lay. Mohawk.
Head painted gold. Wearing a bunny suit. The kite crew is still awake
and drinking. Across the road is a booth with a rotary phone. Talk to
God, it says.

The phone line is buried underground and leads to the Bedouin-
style tent where the crew is drinking and smoking. The morning is
hot already. Inside the Bedouin tent is a bone-handle phone, from
which God speaks. All around the playa, people wander, strung out
from the night's revelry, praying to come down, tripping out on their
inner voices, trying to grab hold of the slipperiness of sanity.

A young woman steps into the booth. The bone-handle phone
rings.

"Answer it," one of the kite crew says to me.

"Hello, Jesus Christ Incorporated," I say.

"God?" she asks hopefully. Her voice is quivering. She is on the
ledge, I can tell.

"One moment, please." I put her on hold for a while, light myself a
cigarette. "How you doin'?" I ask in a Brooklyn accent.

"God?"

"Yeah, yeah, hurry up, I don't got all day. Satan's going nuts over
here."

"God, are you a New Yorker?"

"Of course I'm a New Yorker. New York's the center a the freakin'
universe, ain't it?"

"Well, God, is it good enough just to try and be a good person?"

"Of course it is, sweetheart. That's all you can do. That's all I ask
you to do. What else are you gonna do?"

"I don't know. Really?"

"Really."

A pause here, and a sniffle, she is crying.

"What's the meaning to life, God?"

"Honey, there ain't no meaning to life. Life is what you make of it. Be good, not bad. Love your mother. That kinda thing. I gave you free will, so use it. Now, lemme ask you something, Suzie. . . ."

"Katie."

"I know it's freakin' Katie. I made you, darlin', remember?"

"Yes."

"Katie. How come you never call no more?"

". . . I don't know. . . . I'm sorry."

"You don't gotta be sorry. Just call sometimes. Get outta bed and call for me. I'll answer you. I'll be there. I promise."

"Okay."

"And Katie. Remember. You're all right. God don't make no junk."

"Thank you, God."

"You're welcome, Katie. . . . And Katie?"

"Yes, God."

"I love you."

"I love you too, God."

"Okay. Now gimme three Our Fathers, four Hail Marys. Then wash your face and go home."

"Okay, God."

"And don't forget to pick up your garbage."

"Okay, God."

"Okay, kid. Now get outta here."

Coos Bay, Oregon

Guennadi Tregroub, the sad-hearted clown, the vodka drinker, chain-smoker, the Russian fatalist, the orphan who makes children laugh, did not perform in the Oregon city of Portland. He had suffered a stroke. While at the hospital, he refused visitors because he wanted no one's pity. He is a man who makes people happy, of course. He is a clown. His job is not to make them cry. Occasionally, while at the hospital, he disconnected himself from the monitoring machines and shambled out to the foyer to have a smoke.

When Guennadi was released, he did not call for a ride back to the circus. He walked the few miles in blazing hundred-degree heat, his mind weighing heavily on the $20,000 medical bill tucked in his pocket and the imminent death he had until this point never considered.

I watch him from a distance as he

walks. He is forty-three, short, weathered in the way of all Russians who have lived a difficult life. His legs are slightly bowed, his torso built solidly but slumped at the shoulders now, his chest sunken in defeat. His eyes are focused on some unknown point, his teeth stained from cigarettes, his hair thinning. Something new, something hard and brittle, is discernible in his gait. In the country, someone seeing a man in this condition would stop. Not so in the city. Traffic roars by him, honking, reminding the clown that he is unimportant, fleeting, a speck.

"You are born into the circus and you will die in the circus," he says, walking into the teeming grounds of Circus Chimera now, past the truck that holds the snake exhibit. The deaf-mute who works the ticket stand waves—a wild, silly gesture, as though he were pretending to drown in a kiddie pool. The clown does not see him, his chin buried in his chest, a cigarette burning in his hand. The big top is staked in the parking lot of a strip mall, and the freeway connecting Portland with Seattle and San Francisco can be heard nearby.

From that freeway, the canvas of the one-ring tent can be seen, crowned with four flags, one for each of the home countries of the principal performers: USA, Russia, Mexico and Venezuela. They are framed by two neon signs on either end that read "CIRCUS HERE TODAY," when the lights are not burned out. But of course the lights are burned out. Now the signs, when illuminated, seem pitiful, vaguely pornographic. "CI C HER TO Y," one reads.

Guennadi walks past the deaf-mute, through the crowd of obese Americans, their plaintive children whining for candy, past the well-wishers among his circus family, who call out as they recognize him. The strong man first, the contortionist next, the ringmaster finally. He waves without taking his eyes from his shoes. Guennadi is not only a world-class clown, a graduate of the Moscow Circus University, but also the artistic director of the show—in short, the boss. He walks by Agostino Maltese, the youthful, powerfully built daredevil of the trapeze whose job also requires that he stand in front of the midway selling programs in his costume, a Lycra and sequin number, with eye makeup and hair goop. There is an outrageous bulge in his pants. One suspects it is a codpiece, but the daredevil will neither confirm nor deny. "Women do not pay to see small bundles," he says.

Agostino does not look unlike Harpo Marx, the greatest film clown of them all, but the trapeze artist also strikes the appearance of a smallish rooster, his head cocked bantam style, a small, sure grin, perpetually clucking at the women, his eyebrows wriggling up and down like a pair of mating birds.

"How are you feeling, old man?" the kid asks with such sincerity that the unhappy clown looks up for a startled moment as though the sun had just broken through his blinds. He recognizes the daredevil in his ridiculous outfit and smiles for the first and perhaps only time that afternoon.

The circus is a family of foreigners forged through twenty thousand miles of travel a year, up and down the highways, through small towns, cities, dumps, hollows, reservations, desert hideaways, anywhere a few bucks can be made. It is a family of wife-swappers, misfits, deaf-mutes, hard livers. Circus people tend to die young, either by misadventure or from the heartbreak of growing too old and not having the ability to go on anymore, death from the depression of being replaced by a more youthful version of one's self. The second is the more painful death, they say.

Guennadi, the master clown, walks past the snake trailer, the deaf-mute calling out with both hands now, past the concession stand and the ticket booth where the ticket girls are hiding behind large sunglasses that mask their makeup so as to not destroy the illusion that the female aerialists are anything but superhuman. He shuffles into the one-ring big top to make sure the bleachers have been cleaned and the canvas floor mopped. He smokes like burning popcorn. The clown exits through the performers' entrance, passes the row of trailers belonging to the Chimal family of acrobats and the row belonging to the Venezuelan trapeze family known as the Maltese Falcons (a name given them by the circus's American owner, though the Malteses had never heard of Humphrey Bogart or Dashiell Hammett, much less their namesake figurine). He strolls past the Russian trailers, where Katya, sweet, beautiful Katya, the contortionist, stands unawares in the doorframe of her panel truck, applying makeup in a large mirror taped with photographs of her travels across the world. There she is, standing forever in fur in St. Petersburg. There she is, smiling in Paris. Such a beautiful girl. And like the Chimals and the Malteses and Guennadi himself, she was born into the circus. The only thing she ever knew and would probably ever know. When do a contortionist's bones grow old? When do the supple muscles and tendons begin to atrophy, turn to leather, creak and complain and refuse to do as they are told? Where then would she go? Someplace lonely, perhaps. Someday, most surely.

The Russian maestro ignores them all. But I cannot, this amazing little scene, the children juggling between the trailers, playing with fire, balancing on blocks, a culture brought to this country and preserved for this country by these immigrants. They breathe life into our sedentary existence, one trapped by the television and the snack cakes. People of the high wire. The art of the daring and absurd. The trapeze artist. The clown. *El Circo,* they call it. *Tsirc.* The Circus. Russia's loss is America's gain. Venezuela's loss is America's gain. Mexico too, keep sending your finest. This great wave of immigration. We have their violinists. Their scientists. Their clowns and acrobats and daredevils. Are there no white or black folks in America who are willing to tame a lion or skip rope on a pendulum forty feet in the air?

Here in Portland, no one comes to the ringmaster's door looking to run away with the circus. No one comes looking for a job of labor and adventure. It is a lumber town filled with misanthropes and lumberjacks and aimless youth, but no lion tamers.

Guennadi climbs into his trailer, sits on his couch and lights himself another cigarette. He promises to show me the intricacies of being a clown. I am, of course, already a clown. A stupid man who hides behind his outrageousness. A scared, stupid little man who would rather people laugh at what he does than at who he is. I know that about my-self. Guennadi knows that about himself. We smoke because we are nervous and sad. The clown is my dream, an outward expression of inner stupidity and fear.

Guennadi is an orphan raised in a cheerless Moscow government block known as Number 16. He grew up a beggar and a thief, going to the town square or the train station to pick up half-smoked ciga-rettes, which he would line under his mattress on the steel bed frame, sneaking puffs during the night. And then a man from the sports com-plex came one afternoon to find young talent. What he saw in the pudgy nine-year-old one cannot say, but thankfully he saw something. Guennadi was educated in gymnastics and when he turned eighteen he was put on the street. Where to go? The army. Two years later, and then where to go? There was no family, no employment. He applied for the circus university and was accepted, the only one chosen from among fifty candidates. Mercy to the strange man who picked the boy from the crowd.

So in this way you could say Guennadi was born into the life. A life with dignity, a respectable life. The circus? you ask. Dignity, re-spectability? An American can be forgiven for missing the beauty of the thing. After all, in the States the circus is seen as little more than a sideshow oddity, a half step above the traveling carnival, a motley as-semblage of flea-bitten animals, broken-down rides, bearded ladies and methamphetamine freaks. Not so! In Europe, the circus is high art, a calling of such nobility that societies will pay to train and educate its purveyors. They do so in Russia, in France, and in Latin America as well. There, the clown studies juggling, acrobatics, philosophy, lan-guage and history. Circus performers are complete human beings. There are no freak shows, no drugs. Drugs in a circus bring death much more quickly than it should come. Imagine cocaine on the high wire. No, death comes soon enough.

The circus as the world knows it today—the traveling jugglers and acrobats, elephants, tigers, the movable tent, the calliope and above all the flying trapeze artists—is, oddly enough, an American innovation of the nineteenth century, something born from the train and long distances between towns. And while the first trapeze man was the Frenchman Jules Léotard, the first famous trapeze act was American, the Clarkonians. Their patriarch, Charles, is credited with designing the rig that allowed a flier to return to the platform without falling into the net and having to climb back up, unique at the time. The Clarkonians developed some of the trapeze's most difficult tricks, still used today, including the double-somersault with a pirouette. But if the circus was perhaps the first American gift of entertainment to the world, it was done in by future American ingenuities: first the radio, then the motion picture, then television and now the computer. Sadly, in America the circus languishes, a lonely amusement backwater. There are less than a dozen left.

Guennadi, after the orphanage, made his home in a series of trailers and tents. He tells me he toured the world with the circus; he has the photos on his wall to prove it. In 1988, his circus came to Peru: 120 performers along with elephants, tigers and bears. A manager stole the money and disappeared, he said. Hungry, the circus flew home, leaving the animals behind. During a stopover in Canada, Guennadi Tregroub stepped off the plane. Russia's loss. But there was no family back in the USSR. Just misery and a bleak apartment. Hello, North America! Hello, open road.

"Outside the ring, I am a normal person," he says with such earnestness you are likely to believe him. "Inside the ring, my heart changes. The smiling faces. I'm different inside. I'm happy. Outside, life is difficult, it is so hard to live."

He will not let me put on the big shoes . . . until I understand all of it, first and foremost the philosophy of the thing. "The purpose of the clown is not just to make the people laugh," he tells me. "I want to show through expression that I understand the difficulties of life, the work, the children, the desperation. I am the pilot on the rocket ship of illusion. My job is to take you away.

"You get older, though, like me today. When you are older you can't do it anymore and you have to quit. When you quit, you die. I know several people who quit and then died. When I quit, I'm going to die. I'm going to die. This is what I am. Nothing more. I hope my memory will be as a good clown. *If they remember me.* I lived my life perfectly, the way it was given to me. I've never been proud of myself. Never to me. It's just my job. I hope, however, that when I wave to say good-bye they will say, 'You're the best.' "

He goes on: "When I was young I never think about growing older. I never reflect on that until now. Today I know that day will come that I must quit. I don't have the energy. I realize I don't want to die. Who does? At least I did things with my life. Important things. I touched people. My heart, however, is not a robot. It is telling me, 'Guennadi, I'm going to quit.'

"The clown is a doctor for the people to cure them of their problems, for only a short time, only for a short time. Unfortunately, I don't think there is a doctor for the clown. Of course, you could say I am sad."

There is another important role the clown performs: distraction from cataclysm. Should an acrobat slip and break his neck, the trapezist fall and shatter his back, the contortionist freeze with a muscle spasm, still the show must go on, *la función debe continuar.* The broken performer is simply carted off behind the curtain, and the clown emerges with his toilet paper and his spooky calliope music or his trained dog in an elephant suit. His job is to stop the little boy from crying, to pry the mother's hands from the eyes of the little one, to keep the people from leaving altogether, dare one say, to encourage them to purchase more cotton candy. No, dear ladies and gentlemen, that broken man was an illusion. Never mind him. No such thing has happened! Sit right there and laugh, enjoy yourself! The show shall go on. How true this is, I would see.

Of course, the broken man does exist behind the curtain. His career is over, most likely. His circus family who depend on him wonder how they will eat. They have no insurance, no savings, no other prospects but to throw their bodies around two shows a day, plus a third, a matinee, on weekends. The ringmaster is most certainly making calls trying to find a replacement act when a performer crumbles, shatters, breaks, tears. He will call Budapest, São Paulo, Beijing if he must. That is how he manages to put such a peculiar family together. One falters, another is mined somewhere in the crevices of the world. The family must leave the damaged one behind, move on or be replaced themselves. The show stops for no one. Circus life is brutal, hostile. In that way, once you strip the profession of its lights and sparkling costumes, it's just everyday America. You are just a cog.

The job of the clown is to never reveal this one simple truth: life is horrible.

I always wanted to try . . . to be a clown, a trapeze artist, the ringmaster in the tall top hat and glittering tails. Boyhood dreams of the Moulin Rouge, wine and women and derring-do. Trains through the Italian countryside. If you've never dreamed this . . . then never mind you . . . you were never alive. The people of the Circus Chimera allowed me and my camera to do so.

But first I would have to start from the bottom. Physical labor.

The week's billing complete, the circus tears down the moment the last customer leaves the big top. They attack it, like ants on a dead cat. This being the United States, it is Mexican laborers for the most part who erect the big top, tear down the big top, drive the big top across the countryside and re-erect the big top. They go from Texas to Arizona, California, Oregon and back. It is spine-warping work. Chairs, risers, walls, canvas, spikes, poles, support towers, flags—all into the trucks, fourteen semis, and gone, no trace, a band of gypsies. It is boring work, but it is steady work, and to do it with these men is an instruction in humanity.

"It's boring, man," says a guy name Teodoro. "I don't like the work.

Who likes the work?" It just goes to show how far the stereotype of the Mexican has shifted in the American mind. Remember he used to be a bum sleeping under the cactus? *Mañana*. Always *mañana*. And now they are burros, animals bred to work. What they are, in truth, is men. Human beings. They hurt. They don't like to bend and they will only do so if the wage is good and lunch is paid for. Need proof? Mexico pays cheap and Mexico is fucked up. It's not worth working there. That's what the Mexicans say, if you ask them, if you labor with them, after some time, when they've touched your shoulder and you've touched theirs.

A simple laborer? Who cares for him? He is not sexy. His skills and accomplishments do not draw admirers or girls or children. And for this reason he is allocated a small cot above the snakes. Next to the big fat man who amuses himself not with books but with videotapes of women and dogs in abominable positions. Either there, or he lives in a trailer subdivided into three-by-seven rooms with walls less than a half-inch thick. I am given such a room and, while trying to catch a few winks between towns, I am kept awake by a growling bear to my left and a wild boar to my right. Hairy creatures named Arturo and Guillermo. Above me, a previous tenant has affixed a mirror to the ceiling. For what purpose a man needs to see himself in bed, one can only imagine. Such is the life of the untalented!

The talented, he is born into the circus, it is in his DNA, in his earliest childhood memories. It is what he knows, the only thing he knows, something passed down through the generations. Take the Chimal family, four generations of circus people from the Yucatán Peninsula of Mexico and now American citizens. It began with a grandfather, a man who actually ran away from his father, changed his name and joined a circus. There are eleven of them now, acrobats and trick riders who make up half the show.

There is an old saying in America among the dissatisfied class that goes something like this: I'm running away and joining the circus. Don't kid yourself, this is only a saying left over from the old American days. If you knocked on the ringmaster's trailer door today, chances are he'd send you away. They don't want you. They don't trust you. The circus life is insular and suspicious, and behind the midway and away from the lights, you're not welcome, unless, of course, you are a handsome young woman. Then the acrobats will most certainly welcome you and pass you among themselves, since, after all, they are cousins and brothers and there are no secrets in a circus family, no shame, no modesties.

Being gentlemen of the Old World, they will pour such a woman rum and Coca-Cola until she is limber enough for sexual tricks on the flying silks. Imagine! Oral copulation suspended upside down, twenty feet above the ground. And there you have it, dear ladies; you too will become circus performers in the dimly lit center ring for an audience of five dashing young men—not including the fifty laborers peeking through the folds of the canvas big top.

So jealous are the manual laborers of the supposed sexual exploits of the Chimal brothers that dirty, petty little things are carved into the outhouse walls: "*Hermanos Chimal son putas, maricones, mugrosos*"—that is, the Chimal brothers are whores, faggots, filthy.

These are jealousies most surely of the lonely heart, the work of the man who trains the spotlight on the center ring, suspects Walter Chimal, the twenty-eight-year-old strong man of the company who spends his mornings in a thick robe. He was born in the circus, literally, out back behind the big top, in a trailer. He is well built, with hair purposely styled like that of Superman. He keeps a liquor-and-panties collection above his trailer stove. He has the peculiar habit of stroking his biceps as though they were his firstborn children—healthy, handsome boys.

"Little man, I don't care," Chimal has told the lighting man. There are too many women to worry about a no-name Mexican who swings a spotlight for a living and sleeps alone in a trailer next to the popcorn cooker. What does this little no-name know about women? What does this filthy Mexican know about the married woman who will chase you around North America until you make her perform the most debased of sexual tricks and she storms home in a huff, only to reappear months later asking for more? He cannot possibly know, because women like strong men, exceptional men, not dirty, ordinary little men. If you are such a man and you are married, Chimal says, throw your wife away, she is most certainly lying in another man's bed. If she is not in another man's bed . . . she's not worth keeping.

No, friend, it is better to remain in your own little circus, your bitter home somewhere, your stinking trailer, the choking apartment where you play the role of the sad little clown.

But we are ahead of ourselves.

The circus arrives in the country town of Coos Bay, Oregon, along the Pacific Coast. I ride with the Maltese family, the flying trapeze artists. There is Gamal, the head of the clan, driving one truck filled with the trapeze apparatus. His brother Dali drives the other, the truck's transmission dripping like a broken hourglass. Also among us are their wives, Celina and Isabella, their children, their elderly mother and their sister, Habiba, and her son, Agostino. Agostino, the grandest of them all. Daredevil of the Pendulum of Destiny.

Such a life, that of the traveling performer! You should feel ashamed at your sedentary days. I do.

Eating blackberries on the side of the road. Tugboats and sand dunes and drawbridges. Bungalows and lighthouses and fishermen. ¿Viva la vida antigua! ¿Qué bonita!

The circus life is a romantic and rambling one. The education of children comes not from books but from the moment. The future never comes, it is a life of youth. And these people drive the countryside to get a look at the American. What they see is obesity, people on a cane, pulling an oxygen tank. Fat and running down from excess. That is the most striking thing about America, Celina says.

Gamal, thirty-six, is the leader of this family, the one who suffers the bills and broken machinery, the one who realizes that if you are not careful, the future will arrive and you will be left standing there with your pockets hanging out. The family earns $4,000 a month, and Agostino earns most of that, what with his trapeze antics and his Pendulum of Destiny. Gamal is aging now, at that fulcrum in life, a balancing point of fear and wisdom. "What am I going to leave my girls?" he asks. "A man can only do this until he is fifty at the most. What else can I do? The circus is all I know." He knows he leans on Agostino more than a man should.

The American circus is the most difficult of all, Gamal tells me. When I don't understand his Spanish, his wife translates for me. Always running to the next town, he says. Two days here, six performances, tear down the tent and move to the next town. It's not like the circus in Europe or Latin America, where you tend to stay for a month at a time, soak in the culture, see the sights, eat the food, visit the schoolchildren in the mountains. No, the American circus is the most difficult of all. Always chasing the dollar. The American circus is not fulfilling, he says.

The strain wears on him, it is easy to see. The hair is gray in strands, he has crow's-feet around his eyes and he is perpetually distracted. Money. Money. Money. It consumes him, putting him at odds with Guennadi, the director of the circus, and the owner, who refuses to pay him more even though the family is the main draw.

My favorite is Agostino. I call him Chapulín, grasshopper, the young daredevil who provides the two most mesmerizing acts in the show. First, the Pendulum of Destiny, a giant forty-foot pinwheel with a circular cage on one end resembling a hamster wheel and a counterweight on the other. As it spins, Chapulín scrambles in and out of the hamster wheel, performing toe touches, skipping rope and feigning falling as the pendulum swings faster and faster and out of control. After this comes the clown with his dancing dog dressed in an elephant costume and, beneath that, a dress. Then comes intermission.

Afterward it is the flying Maltese troupe featuring Chapulín, his bulge and his outrageous hair.

Chapulín is an excellent showman, shouting as he spins around and around on the pendulum, "You want more?" And as he leaps from bar to bar on the trapeze, he takes a moment in suspended animation to slap his rump, which elicits squeals from the women who had, until now, ignored the impish man. When finished, he always ends with an ostentatious and courtly bow, like a show horse. He is absolutely magnetic.

Outside the ring, he is another man altogether: self-conscious, shy, self-effacing. I ask him about the women and he says, yes, before the show none ever pay him any mind, but after the show he has so many offers that he is full before he ever gets to the dinner table. Funny, but I never see him with any women.

I am told his demeanor is very different from that of his grandfather, Rosario Maltese, known from Arabia to Paris to Caracas as the Great Tunissiani. The Great Tunissiani was a circus acrobat before and after World War II. He made money, good money, as a performer with Le Cirque de Paris. He was known to spend this money on women and well-wishers at the Parisian hotels, just as Hemingway did. But there was a phony thrill to being Hemingway. Lion hunting, war reporting, deep-sea fishing. Invented adventures, temporary and purchased adventures, the adventures of others. In the end, remember, Hemingway did not like being Hemingway. Hemingway blew his brains out.

The Great Tunissiani, on the other hand, lived an adventurous life and died of old age. He was an Italian soldier taken prisoner in Africa, an immigrant to Venezuela, a traveling member of the Ringling Bros. Circus, a stuntman in Tony Curtis's *Ali Baba and the 40 Thieves,* a lover of fine wine and women, an insatiable man who fathered Gamal at the age of sixty-five. The Great Tunissiani liked being the Great Tunissiani. When he died, he left his children two things: a small, struggling circus and the knowledge to save it. The family indeed resurrected the circus, brought in hippos and such things, and in the end, the eldest brother took it for himself.

Chapulín is the product of Tunissiani's daughter, Habiba, and a man she met as she traveled the Venezuelan countryside with the circus. Predictably, the union of a rancher and a contortionist did not last, the contortionist and her son returning to the road, the rancher returning to the land. The sedentary life. "Hah!" Chapulín tells me in his good-natured way.

That night, after the first performance in Coos Bay, the Maltese family takes me up to the platform. The plan is for Guennadi to teach me the basics of clowning and the Malteses to teach me the basics of the trapeze. By the coming Saturday, the last day of the show, I would perform aerial clownery—that is, I would make a spectacle, climb the ladder, jump with the bar in my hand and scream as I swung toward the catcher. The catcher would yank my trousers off, seemingly unbeknownst to me. I would only realize this after I fell into the net, breathed a sigh of relief and then looked down. Humiliated in my striped underpants, I would once again scream as I ran offstage, my hands over my privates. My heart! Man, that sounds fantastic—and easy enough.

Before I take to the ladder in my stocking feet, Gamal says to me something like, "Remember, courage must be stronger than fear. And also—don't look down." He says it in Spanish. I do not know what he is saying, exactly. It was translated to me later.

Fear. When your bluff is called and the trapeze artist says go on ahead, take that bar and your life in your own hands and do what you will. Will . . . the battle within. There is the thinnest of lines between thrill, survival, fantasy and will. I climb. Thirty rungs. Forty feet onto a wooden plank no wider than the length of my foot. The net below is an antique, thin, made to fit between an old trapeze apparatus. It is perhaps nine feet wide. It looks like a G-string. Thin. Thin. Thin. My arms are dull, my triceps throbbing. My heart is racing. It's not the height that enervates you, but the optical illusion of the tent. It is cone-shaped, and so no focal point helps. Looking forward draws your eyes upward to the top of the big top. This turns your knees to water, since everything appears to be sloping. Looking down. Look down. No, never look down. I'm dizzy, frozen, my hand biting into the bar, which is wrapped in clean white powdered cloth. I try focusing on it. The bar is reassuring somehow in its cleanliness, the order of it, the attention paid to it, the white softness of it.

They are all down there looking expectantly. Walter Chimal, the big lover. The deaf-mute. The ringmaster. Katya, sweet Katya, smiling widely for me. Guennadi, with his stern face, his arms folded across his chest. The fifty laborers peeking in through the folds, I can sense them, I can feel them breathing. Chapulín and Celina on the platform with me. Gamal shouting instructions that I don't understand. Dali swinging upside down from his catcher's perch. "Point your toes," Chapulín tells me. I take the bar and leap. . . .

Over the next few days Chapulín becomes a dear companion to me, a little brother of sorts. Wherever I go, he goes. What's wrong with that? We laugh together. He asks about women, too shy to talk with them directly. To bed down a sexy contortionist behind billowy curtains, we agree, must be the finest thing the circus has to offer. Imagine that! A contortionist. Neither of us, we agree, possesses the skill.

He doesn't smoke or drink, but does so with me at the Indian casino, which is hosting the circus in its parking lot. It seems to me there will be few happy people coming to the show. A gambler never leaves the table if he's winning. The loser goes home; he does not want to see dancing dogs.

I get Chapulín a cigarette and a big glass of Chivas on the rocks. He takes two swallows and I have to walk him back to his trailer. The Great Tunissiani would be proud. The casino parking lot is filled with RVs belonging to a different sort of drifter and thrill-seeker. Old people, these ones, people who look like their dogs. Gamblers, widowers, riders of the circuit of faux adventures. They stand with windbreakers on, cupping a cigarette in their hands, watching as Bowzer urinates. They look lonely. Their skin looks like wax paper. They look as if they're going to die.

"Death," croaks Chapulín, the youthful daredevil looking onto this unique scene of Americana.

Chapulín began his trapeze training at the age of thirteen and it ended badly. He was attempting the Cross of Death, whereby one trapeze artist attempts to return to the bar from the catcher's grasp while a second attempts to leap from the bar below him into the catcher's hands; they cross in the air, thus giving the trick its name. Young and callow, Chapulín did not listen to his instructor, Gamal. He let go of the bar too late. The timing was thrown out of synchronization and they collided in midair. Chapulín broke his ribs and clavicle and punctured a lung. He lay unconscious for two days. That would have been it for me, I tell him. For him, it's the only life he knows.

"I am afraid every time I go up," he confides. "Every time." This is shocking, considering that his athleticism seems so reckless and effortless. Then he repeats what his uncle told me, probably the liturgy of all daredevils. "Remember, courage has to be stronger than fear."

The Pendulum frightens him most—the forty-foot whirling steel contraption held in place by two thin wires. There is no net to this one. "My mother, she was born into the circus, and she won't watch when I do the Pendulum," he says. His mother knows when his calliope music begins to play it is time to return to the trailer, sit in a lawn chair, have a cup of tea.

Over the next few days, I do the trapeze a little more, attempting to jump without fear, though this never happens. I can turn around now, return with my feet on the platform and even hang by my knees.

Guennadi, for his part, is a stern instructor, demanding a serious attention that I did not think, until now, applied to clownery. It is in the eyes. Clowning for a small group of children, for instance, is easy. Clowning in the center ring is quite another matter. There are no eyes to lock on to. It is only white light and a few silhouettes. You cannot see or hear the audience's reaction, and so you must guide them, using your eyes and your body language, toward the illusion you wish to take them toward. It is acting, and as in acting, you must believe, and it must show in your body language that you are . . . funny. But it is the eyes that are important, the eyes must emote a certain confidence. "Crowds are much like dogs. If they sense fear or hesitation, they will turn on you," the maestro says.

"Remember the philosophy. Make them happy; take away their problems. A clown gives people energy to go back to their work. To be funny, you must be serious."

Country crowds are better than city ones. Urban sophistication breeds out a certain sweet naïveté, engenders an unwillingness to be charmed, an aversion to whimsy. There is a numb self-satisfaction in the city dweller, the burden of having seen it all, and so nothing seems to impress him; not space flight, not even a daring young man on the flying trapeze. Country people, on the other hand, are kindly, appreciative, and decent in their circumstances. Farm children, when they are taken to a circus, will squeal with delight, not whine out a never-ending list of demands as city children do. Maybe this has something to do with spending one's childhood wringing amusement from stones and twigs and fishing poles. Who knows?

Country women, when they attend the big top, clutch at their breasts, their mouths ovular with fright, their faces contorted in amazement as the daring young man attempts his triple-somersault. City women tend to inspect their nails. I am happy to be performing for a country crowd. The appointed time is drawing near. Tomorrow, the one-thirty matinee.

The morning is crisp, the tide is low and the smell of the sea hangs over the circus grounds. It is one of those dreary slow-motion days, where the sun's essence casts the sky with shadows and you walk about with a feeling of nausea. Today is trapeze day and I am still afraid, afraid of the eyes I cannot see, afraid of failure, laughter of the wrong kind. I go to Katya's trailer because she will paint my clown face for me. Her place is clean and pleasant and I remove my shoes before entering. She too is pleasant, chirping away in the peculiar language of this circus—a patois of English, Russian, Spanish.

"Good morning. *Cómo está? Harasho?*" she asks.

"*Dobre utre,*" I answer in Russian. "Good morning."

Her face is fantastic, square with clean white teeth and blue eyes. She is nineteen and I feel alone for her. What does the circus promise? What will she become in this vast, hard country, where the promise of opportunity can murder you, the myth can crush your spirit? As it is, her mother kneels to a man in Las Vegas because this man has a house in St. Petersburg.

She paints my face in the classic manner, large white half circles over the eyes, red cheeks, a small upturned smile, a white dot on the end of the nose. She steps back with my chin in her fingers. "*Klass!*" she says happily. "Excellent."

Chapulín adds a few dots and curlicues, and powders my face so the makeup won't smear and loans me outrageous size-nineteen shoes. Guennadi offers me one of his old clown outfits, ill-fitting trousers with suspenders, a floral shirt, a cap and a tie.

"How are you today, my friend?" I ask.

"Not too well. My heart aches today. I'm feeling a little depressed and out of sorts," he says. "No matter. Good luck today, and remember what I told you. Serious to be funny. Okay?"

"Okay."

I sit in his dressing trailer, nervously going over my routine: waddle out to the trapeze apparatus. Shout that I want to go up. Climb up to the net, tug on it, hop around, run with a scream as Chapulín leaps out onto the bar and swats his ass. Wave my fist and climb up to the platform. Okay. Got it. Now knock my knees, feign nausea, take the suspenders off my shoulders and hold them in my teeth. Take the bar. Leap. Swing with my legs out. Dali snatches my pants. I don't notice because I'm scared and hysterical. Swing. Turn. Swing some more. Fall into the net and take a big breath. Look down. Notice the pants are gone. Look out at the crowd. Scream once again with embarrassment. Run around the net. Roll off. Cover my privates and run offstage. Good.

I practice my facial gestures in the glass of a framed photograph of Guennadi's clown college days, one in which two totems of men stand three-high on one another's shoulders holding a net. Another man has just been launched into the air and three below wait to catch him in their arms. Guennadi is somewhere among them, I'm sure. An audience, its members dressed in neckties and winter coats, encircles them. My reflection in the glass, I see it and think we are similar men, Guennadi and I. Happy outside. The joker. Prankster. But inside there is an endless well of sadness. The only escape from fixating on your reflection in that dark pool is to play the ass, to feign happiness. To drink yourself silly. Vanity, thy name is Clown.

The show has already begun! I can hear the laughter from the dressing trailer. I venture outside and my adopted circus family smiles. The laborers give me the thumbs-up. The deaf-mute laughs without a sound. I play with the Maltese children, and I am very good at this clown thing. I make them laugh, pull my finger, hold my leg. Such a beautiful life, the circus.

Chapulín's music is playing, that spooky calliope. He is inside, performing on the Pendulum of Destiny. The crowd ooohs, then aaahs, one final gasp and then it breaks into applause. He must be doing the jump-rope bit. Habiba, his mother, is sitting in a lawn chair near her trailer, drinking iced tea.

It is all so normal, as normal as a circus scene can be. The contortionist is stretching against a pole. The children are juggling again. I'm walking around in gigantic shoes. That spooky, ubiquitous calliope music. That goddamn music.

There is a gunshot, then a thud, then the calliope stops. That doesn't sound right, I think. I look over at Habiba, who has fallen out of her chair and is quivering in a flaccid, sobbing mess. There are screams around the circus grounds. The female acrobats go ashen, then begin to sob, their big gooey eyes of mascara leaking like motor oil. The men stand blank-faced. I run into the big top. There on the ground lies Chapulín, unconscious, groaning, swollen, pallid. The Pendulum is cockeyed. One of the cables gave way, snapped, that was the gunshot sound. People are filing out the door. Mothers have hands over their children's eyes.

Good God, Chapulín! Death. It swirls around the circus.

The performers—clowns and acrobats, that is—put Chapulín on a board and shuffle him backstage. They do not wait for the ambulance. The show must go on. *La función debe continuar.* Guennadi shambles out with his little dog dressed in an elephant costume and the crowd begins to laugh. The captain of the rocket ship of illusion, I think. Such a good clown.

The paramedics arrive and put Chapulín in a neck brace. He has come to. He can wiggle his toes. Still, the paramedic says he has probably shattered his back. It's over for Chapulín. No more circus. I lean in to him and tell him I love him. We'll have a beer next week, I say. He smiles and croaks, "Thank you, baby," just like Elvis, just like I taught him. Lupe, the matriarch of the Chimal clan, is rubbing liniment into Habiba's neck. The Russian magician is smoking. Gamal looks dead, holding the broken cable clamp in his hand. Guennadi is clowning and the people are laughing and Chapulín is off to the surgeon's table.

There we all stand, somewhere between melancholy for the past and fear of the future. No one says it, but the people of the circus know it—there are nothing but hard times and dark clouds for the Maltese family. Dali says to me, "I saw him fall and I turned old."

After a prolonged silence he says, "I want to get out of the circus life. But what else do I know how to do? Nothing. Is there any work in Los Angeles?"

Crow Agency, Montana

Before he was butchered on the slopes of the Little Big Horn, General George Armstrong Custer was reported to have dined on a luncheon consisting of a bacon, lettuce and tomato sandwich, a gherkin pickle and french fries. It is said that he ate at the trading post off Interstate 90, a cheap tourist trap with garish teepees in front, not a mile from where he died.

As he prepared to die—and he surely knew he was going to die—the general stood in the shade of a cottonwood tree near the river with his horse and a number of subordinates, drinking Pepsi-Cola from a plastic bottle.

Today was a reenactment, the 129th anniversary of the so-called massacre of the Little Big Horn, where, according to legend, every man of the Seventh Calvary was slaughtered, some decapitated, others cut to pieces so that their spirits would be too consumed with finding their feet and fingers to bother seeking revenge against their killers in the next world.

It is said that Custer was the last man to die, that he fought gallantly at the top of the hill like some flaming Hollywood swashbuckler until he was felled by a savage in paint and feathers. Which is not to say that this General Custer, this Little Big Horn reenactor sipping his soda pop, was not in fact the original Indian fighter who met his death on June 25, 1876, at the hands of a mounted Sioux warrior.

Consider that this Custer too had the blond curly locks, the buckskin jacket, the same agitated demeanor that must have plagued the first and original Custer when he realized he had wandered into a hornet's nest, an Indian camp perhaps ten thousand strong.

This latter-day Custer told me that the Indians believed he may be the reincarnated Custer. How odd, I thought, how providential. Not only had this man discovered who he was in his past life, but that he was actually noteworthy in that life and people today happily paid to watch him go through the old college moves.

And how sad it is, I thought, that in this life you pine for those old glory days of a past life much like an elderly soldier retelling his boring went-to-town war stories.

"They call me Son of the Morning Star," he told me this sweltering afternoon as I stood there in the shade and soft ground. "As for me, I don't know where Steve ends and the general begins." This was undoubtedly true, as this Custer, sometimes known as Steve Alexander, a surveyor from Monroe, Michigan, lived in one of Custer's former homes and had a cell phone greeting that said, "You've reached the general . . ."

Beneath the cottonwood were various adjutants to the general, among them a staff sergeant, a meaty man with a thick handlebar mustache, and a private, a thin man in spectacles. They spoke to him as if he really were the general, referring to him as General, asking about his wife, Libby, when in fact his wife's name was Alice. One wondered whether Libby too had been reincarnated and by a twist of the stars had happened to reunite with her former husband, both in these, their new mortal coils.

To think!

The white men, it was clear, took their reenacting very seriously. Each year, they traveled thousands of miles from far-flung points across the continent, their gear jammed into trucks and rental vans, to play war at the Little Big Horn. They camped in Civil War–period tents on the banks of the historic river, which runs through the Crow reservation in rural southeastern Montana. Or they slept in town and strutted around like overweight peacocks in the Army blues. The battlefield itself was owned by the Real Bird brothers, Crow men who made a healthy chunk of change off these perennial playactors, these white men willing to fork over the contents of their billfolds for a role in the Wild West show.

To the east, the reservation bordered the tiny town of Hardin, an exit like any other exit on the American interstate: a couple of gas stations, a couple of casinos, a McDonald's. It too used to be part of Crow territory until the turn of the twentieth century when the whites decided they needed it. The reenactors made it their headquarters, biding their time in raggedy hotel rooms and snacking on Big Macs as they awaited their date with destiny. I split time between a teepee and a little dump on the Hardin strip. It had a waterslide. Across the street was a sandwich shop, which, for whatever reason, seemed to be the hangout for the young people in these parts—white, red, black, brown. There you could buy moccasins out of a trunk, or a blowjob for twenty bucks, or a dime bag of meth.

Back under the shade of the trees, the bluecoat sergeant was going on about the time Fort Lincoln burned and what a job it had been to rebuild that one.

Strange characters, these reenactors. I'd been with them for some time and I'd broken them down into five solid categories:

First, there was the type teetering on the mental precipice, those who believed they were either reincarnated or had somehow been here before, an itching feeling like the ghost of a foot that is no longer there. The reenactment for them was a spiritual awakening, not unlike a pilgrim's journey to the desert.

Then there were the former military men with a hankering for the camaraderie and discipline of the old Army days. This type tended to be the man with the outlandishly waxed mustache who appeared in small-town newspaper photos on the Fifth of July, standing beside a flagpole in front of the red-board schoolhouse.

There were the broken men, without military service, lost souls looking for a place to belong and a solid sense of purpose, although they tended to flutter on the outer edges of the campfire, seeing as they had no real war stories to tell and so felt bad about that.

There were the guys who would never grow up, the telephone repairmen and such who worked in the black ghettos and were unhappy in their circumstances. After a few swigs of whiskey they'd tell you that it was fun to play cowboys and Indians with real guns and horses and real Indians.

And finally, there were the "stitch Nazis," little autocrats and junior high school instructors of American history, know-it-all pedants who would bicker until the sun went down about how, exactly, the brass buttons of the cavalry dress uniforms were affixed to the woolen coats with yellow piping.

The sergeant in the blue coat was not an ignoramus but rather a thoughtful and intelligent man who spoke eloquently of philosophers, the Federalist Papers and the final moments of Custer's life.

"Why does a grown man spend thousands of dollars on memorabilia and horse transportation to come out here and glorify war?" I asked him, just moments before the show began.

"So history is not forgotten," he said with the surety of a Realtor who is convinced you will be satisfied with the overpriced house you have just paid for. "Think about that," he said. "There are people out there now who claim that the Holocaust never happened."

I said, "Yeah, but did you ever consider that the blue coat you're wearing today represents to some the holocaust of three million indigenous people in North America who stood in the way of Manifest Destiny?"

He stood slack-jawed for a few moments. Such a thing should not be asked at this moment, Custer wringing the neck of his cola bottle in anticipation. Indians in the background making a grand entrance in front of the grandstands. Death and gunpowder in the air, and I should ask such a loathsome thing! "The legacy, right or wrong and forever shifting, should be preserved," he said tersely.

"Besides, every hero needs a villain." He said it with a smile.

It was a good point but bullshit just the same. I wondered how it would go over if, say, once a year a group of German-Americans put on SS uniforms and reenacted the goings-on of Bergen-Belsen in the streets of Milwaukee.

I looked at Custer, a man who in his regular life surveyed the lines where the trees would be torn down and strip malls and tar and cheap chromium tanning salons put in their place. Just up the way near the battlefield, near the teepees where the general had his lunch this morning, there was a Kentucky Fried Chicken, its logo, of course, a big white mustachioed man in a string tie. Colonel Sanders.

"General," I said earlier to him, appealing to his nineteenth-century personage. "What have you done? All you've brought us is a KFC."

"Sometimes," he said without a pause, "the general takes the Colonel with him."

The Battle of the Little Big Horn, in real history, was won by the Cheyenne and the Sioux, the most obdurate of Indian peoples, who refused to submit to reservation life and so were hunted down by the U.S. military to make them do so. Little Big Horn was the high-water mark of their history, their Fourth of July, so to speak, the day on which Indian people actually won one against the overwhelming numbers and technology of the whites.

The Crow, for their part, didn't share in the moral triumph. They had chosen to collaborate with Custer and the cavalry, not only as a matter of survival against the expansion of the United States—Washington had promised that in return for their service the Crow's territory would remain unmolested by settlers—but also as a way of once and for all ending their domination by the Sioux, who had pushed the Crow off the best hunting grounds and into the mountains. In the end, the Crow got the land.

The Crow land is good land. The grass is tall and rain falls here. There are plenty of horses and the water is clean at the base of the mountains. The sky is large and fingers of lightning touch the ground on many afternoons when the sun begins to cool and weather fills the space. No such thing happened today, however. The sky was debilitating and the soldiers melted in their woolen uniforms. Very tough men indeed, standing on the far ridge of the actual battlefield, ready to play dead on the ground where men actually died, their blood spilled, mixed in the mud, made into seed and worm, eaten by birds, only to fly again. Most definitely there must be bits of bone and teeth still lodged in the earth here, and I felt funny about the whole enterprise.

Even so, it was a boyhood dream to lead a cavalry charge down the Little Big Horn, so many times had I fantasized about it as a youth, pored through the pictures, always to play the Indian, the winner. It ranked up there with riding a bull and playing professional football. As it happened, I would die eight times that day on the muddy river, more of a shallow, babbling brook lined with sharp, flat stones. I would die for the sins of Yellow Eyes standing over there in his buckskin coat, a wide brim beaver-hide Stetson, the man who, I was told by an informant, just lunched on a BLT.

At the time of the real Little Big Horn, the country spasmed with hysteria about the Stone Age red menace. How could this be, just as the national centennial was to be celebrated nine days later in Philadelphia featuring the new telephone of Alexander Graham Bell and the mimeograph machine of Thomas A. Edison? The Sioux and their Cheyenne cousins would eventually come to suffer a complete beating and near extinction, culminating in the Ghost Dance vision and the massacre at Wounded Knee fourteen years later. Ironically, one of the greatest Indian warriors and spiritual leaders who led the Hunkpapa Sioux at the Little Big Horn and to whom the Ghost Dance vision was bestowed, Sitting Bull, would spend the year of 1885 as a player in Buffalo Bill's Wild West Show, making him perhaps the ultimate American war reenactor.

But the Sioux live far away from the Crow now and they had no representatives participating today. The Cheyenne, whose reservation borders the Crow's, whose reservation in turn borders the battlefield, also boycotted the Crow-sponsored reenactment. The tribes are bitter enemies, their enmity stretching far back, far before the first white man ever set foot on the continent. Consider that Crazy Horse, the greatest fighter among all red men, who led the Oglala Sioux at the Little Big Horn, is said to have taken only four scalps in his life. The last two were Crow.

Before the Little Big Horn, the great Crow war chief Plenty Coups had a vision, it is said. He saw a hole, and a wind swept everything into it—everything except a chickadee in a tree that watched as a spotted buffalo pulled covered wagons across the earth. This was interpreted to mean that the white man was coming and everything else was going to die. Plenty Coups decided it meant that the Crow should capitulate to the white man and help him in his campaign of Manifest Destiny. For this Plenty Coups has gone down in white history as a great peacemaker.

To some the Crow are the Uncle Toms of the Indian world. And interestingly, the Crow do not represent themselves in their own reenactment, considered by most to be more "authentic" than the Little Big Horn pageant in nearby Hardin, which features fat white women playing Indian warriors. No, the Crow portray their bitter enemies and victorious rivals, the Sioux and Cheyenne, brave warriors who fought and died that day. For the truth is that after leading Custer to the sprawling encampment of the Sioux and Cheyenne—where the Army's plan was to attack the village from three directions—the Crow scouts either slunk away or were dismissed by Custer. Either way, no Crow died on the battlefield that day and none would die today. The Real Bird brothers and the Crow men played in the show for two reasons: dollars and cents.

So who was left to play the Crow? Who would do such an obtuse and rotten thing? Who would dredge up bad memories and a shameful history? Who would have the temerity to kick sleeping dogs?

I decided to be a Crow scout modeled after White Man Runs Him, one of the craftiest scouts and a favorite of Custer's. He wore war paint of white clay stripes down his face. Of course, the handsome, wiry scout did not die in real life, but this reenactment wasn't as authentic as they would have you believe. Custer, in all actuality, probably died within twenty minutes; he was not the last man, as the Errol Flynn movie, or the reenactment, would have you believe. At least a hundred men of the Seventh survived that day, as did a horse named Comanche and a bulldog that was taken along for some reason.

Details, unimportant scraps and gristle. Details get in the way of a good story.

Many of the cavalry today would not die either, preferring to trot over beneath the shade of a stand of cottonwoods. They would rather do that than fall off their horses and sully their old bodies and expensive reproduction uniforms. If the soldiers would not die today, then certainly a Crow scout could, maybe should, if we were to atone for Custer's sins.

But first I slipped into the character of Half Yellow Face, the sacred pipe carrier of the Crow scouts, who accompanied Custer to the edge of the valley and, upon hearing of the foolish plan to attack, spread the tobacco to the four winds in preparation for the certain death that would befall the cavalry.

"You and I are going home today," I said fatefully to the general with the Pepsi bottle. What an advertisement that would make, I thought. I'd have to call someone on Madison Avenue.

"Listen," I continued. "Can I get a little lock of your hair as medicine in today's battle? I mean, think of it! A piece of Custer's scalp."

He looked at me as though I were about to ride into battle naked, with my ass painted red and a feather duster shoved up it.

"I don't have a knife with me," he said hopefully.

On cue, an obsequious aide-de-camp, a corporal, I think, who looked as though he worked the graveyard shift in a french fry factory, scurried onto the scene. He clicked his heels together and said, while holding a blade point up, "General!"

The blade was dull, but the general did not wince, thus relieving me of a little antipathy of following him into death.

"I've got to be in Gettysburg next week" was the last thing he said to me before he was butchered with a plastic hunting knife.

Atop the hill, the white men, mostly Vietnam and Korea veterans who saw nothing good in war and yet spent their retirement glorifying it in the name of education, waited for the bugler in the bushes to sound the charge. Horses whinnied and dust hung in the air like dry stiff laundry. Someone shouted out to me—and not for the first time that week—to keep a lookout for savages and hostile redskins. It is important to tell you here that I am a piece Indian. Anishinabe, we call ourselves, the first people, the most powerful tribe who did and still do inhabit the area of the Great Lakes, the people who in fact ran the Sioux off the fertile woodlands and onto the inhospitable plains where life was difficult, until the European brought his horses and guns. The French say Ojibwe; the English Chippewa. It is also important to say that I have an overwhelming dose of French blood coursing in my veins. This means I am routinely mistaken for an Italian.

When I came out of a bar in Hardin called the 4 Aces with an Assiniboin friend of mine, she was recognized under the dull street lamps by an acquaintance of hers from their home reservation. The guy was a typical shabby drunk with clothes that looked like he'd picked them out of a trash can and nails so badly discolored with dirt it looked like he'd slammed them in a door. He looked me up and down with disgust and said to her, "What'chu doing hanging out with honkies?"

Honky. My grandmother was a mixed-blood who grew up on Mackinac Island, Michigan, on the eastern side of the island, behind St. Anne's Catholic Church where she was baptized. She scrubbed the toilets and cooked the suppers of the swell white people who vacationed there. Late in the Great Depression, she ran away with a sixteen-year-old white kid. She saw her chance out and took it.

They had six children and when they divorced, some of the children were dumped in a Catholic orphanage high in the northern lake country. By the time she remarried, most of the children were young adults, confused and self-destructive. This confusion, naturally, was passed on to her grandchildren.

You *do* carry your people's sins, and those sins manifest themselves in curious ways. If my grandmother was ashamed to be red, saw no percentage in it, then I am excessively proud. It is compensatory. In America, most of us have lost our narratives, and so in need, we tend to stylize one and cling to our precious drops. I did not grow up on a reservation, but I have a tribe, a clan, and a pipe. I'm a Catholic, but I know the lodge. Identity is a witch's brew. Consider that some of the strongest black nationalists are some of the lightest-skinned. Malcolm X had tawny skin and red hair. August Wilson could have passed for white—in fact his father *was* white. I have never claimed to be Johnny Tall Bear, but I am his cousin. When I heard the sergeant on the hill calling Indians savages, I got pissed. No one likes being called a savage or an octoroon or a honky.

The guy who yelled redskin on the top of the hill, I had met a few weeks earlier at a school cavalry buffs like to attend to learn the nuances of field operations and buffalo guns. I told the man then, as we stood in a group smoking bad weed in a paddock that stank to the hilltops of horseshit, to please knock it off. He gave me an "aw-shucks, I'm just staying in the character of the period and you really shouldn't take offense" sort of line.

But when I heard him say the words again on the top of the hill today, ramrod-straight, tall, his face marbled to the consistency of boiled meat, I resolved right there that I would shoot that motherfucker in the face if the opportunity presented itself. Never mind history. The bullets weren't real and so you didn't have to acknowledge your death anyhow. That's the thing about Americans, we have a great capacity to reinvent, embroider.

So, if I fragged Sergeant Peckerwood in the face with a dummy bullet packed with cotton wadding, who'd care? The overweight tourists in their sun hats and safari shorts sitting in the grandstands on the far side of the river wouldn't care. Authentic? My ass. You're dead, white man.

No one really knows what happened that day at the Little Big Horn anyhow.

Some things are agreed upon, however. Custer died. Ironically, the general who beat the beehive would eventually have it swarm down on him. In 1868, the United States government signed a deal with the Sioux, the Fort Laramie Treaty, which set aside, ostensibly forever, a tremendous parcel of land for the tribe—about the size of the western half of South Dakota. The territory, officially closed to white settlement, encompassed the Black Hills, sacred ground to the Indians and plentiful with game. But westward-moving whites thought this territory proved too good for the indigenous. They wanted a crack at it. And so Custer volunteered in 1874 to take a mounted survey. He reported abundant and beautiful fauna, fish, hoofed animals. He also reported the presence of gold, sounding the death knell not only for the Cheyenne and Sioux and every other tribe in the West—but also for himself.

The rush was on, and try as it might, the U.S. military could not keep the peace between the avaricious whites and the increasingly belligerent reds. Eventually, the federal Indian Department ordered all wandering Indians to relocate to their assigned reservations by January 1876 or face the consequences.

Many of the Indian bands were in their winter camps and so never got word of the decree, and it is doubtful that had they gotten word they would have obeyed. One might as well ask the sun to rise in the West than to ask a free man to live in a trailer park and eat welfare cheese.

Instead of hit-and-run, which had been their preferred fighting tactic, the Indians would for the first and last time make one concerted stand: they included the Blackfoot, the Cheyenne and the bands of the Sioux Nation. The Oglala were led by Crazy Horse; Sitting Bull commanded the Hunkpapa. They were accompanied by their cousins, including the Miniconjou, the Brulé and the Sans Arcs.

Three columns of soldiers were dispatched to fight them. Colonel John Gibbon would ride from the west. General Alfred Terry would come from the east, with Custer in charge of the Seventh Cavalry under him. General George Crook would come north from Wyoming. They were accompanied by Crow, Arikara and Shoshone scouts.

A week before the Little Big Horn, in a neighboring valley known as Rosebud, Crook came upon a thousand warriors. In the ensuing skirmish, the general lost nine soldiers and a Shoshone scout. The Indians lost perhaps thirty, but it could not be considered a victory by either side.

Crook reasoned that because rations were low and the Sioux might order a counterattack, it was better to retreat. His column camped about fifty miles to the south, near Goose Creek, where he and his soldiers enjoyed a fine three-week vacation of big-game hunting and fish-ing. They caught more than fifteen thousand trout during their holiday.

Meanwhile, neither Gibbon nor Terry nor Custer was informed of Crook's whereabouts or his run-in with the Indians. By then, the Indi-ans had moved west into the area around the Little Big Horn River.

George Custer may not have been bright—he finished last in his class at West Point, or thirty-fourth, as he liked to say—but he was courageous. During the Civil War he led the charges of his Union troops at a time when it was customary for commanders to watch from the rear. At least fourteen of his horses were killed beneath him. His repulsing of a Confederate flank while leading a mounted Michigan brigade is generally considered one of the turning points of the Get-tysburg battle. He was brave, no doubt about it. And lucky.

It may have been this luck, a lust for glory and presidential ambi-tions that caused him to divide the Seventh and go it alone before Crook or Terry or Gibbon arrived. His intelligence on the field condi-tions and of his enemy's comings and goings was incomplete. He did not know that many of the Indian warriors that day were armed with repeating rifles. It wouldn't have mattered, most likely.

Custer led about 650 to 700 men, plus Crow scouts, some civilians, the bulldog and even a war correspondent, Mark Kellogg, whom the Associated Press continues to this day to claim as their first correspon-dent to die in war. Kellogg worked for the *Bismarck Tribune* and the As-sociated Press may have picked up his reports, but he was not their employee, says author Sandy Barnard, who has written extensively about Kellogg and the Little Big Horn. But facts should not get in the way of a good history.

Custer divided his command, sending Major Marcus Reno and Captain Frederick Benteen with three companies each. The general went with five. One was left behind to guard the pack train. The sub-ordinates went south as a blocking tactic, as Custer attacked the mas-sive encampment from the north. The Crow then took their leave.

To make a long, convoluted and sketchy story short, Custer led every man who followed him to his death. He most likely tried to cross the Little Big Horn River at the point where we were reenacting today and he was repelled. He was probably chased up the slope of the hill and killed within a few hundred yards. Benteen and Reno retreated to the top of a hill and held on for three days until the Indians left. They survived.

Custer lay dead with a bullet in his left temple and a bullet in his heart. He was found naked except for his socks, but his corpse was whole, sitting upright and propped up between two other naked bodies. His hand was supporting his head, like he was thinking or napping. It is at this spot that the national monument sits with a sign reminding tourists to curb their dogs.

Though much lore surrounds the identity of his killer and the circumstances of his death, much is unknown. Suffice it to say, no Crow names are part of that story.

As for Custer, his death in a relatively unimportant military campaign shocked a nation and created an industry. Thanks to Hollywood, the prematurely balding, impish little Indian fighter is forever the handsome and swashbuckling Errol Flynn. His legend is preserved through knickknacks and coffee mugs and refrigerator magnets.

In the end, after hanging around town for a few weeks, I'm not sure who won. The Sioux won that historical day, and paid dearly for it. Today, the Lakota territories are the poorest corners of America, bar none, more impoverished than Detroit or Gary, Indiana, Appalachia, or the Bronx. The Crow, for their collaboration, got a nice reservation, but it is really just a crumb from a stolen loaf. Unemployment there is eighty percent, kids get pregnant before they graduate from high school, many live on government handouts and the language dies a little more each day. It's the kids who are unfairly blamed by their elders for the loss of the Crow traditions. Somehow, the adults reason, a spiritual fungus has infected their children and this has led to a turning away from native ways. The parents or grandparents don't blame themselves for turning away.

A language, after all, is most certainly not lost in a single generation. It is lost through time, through domination, brute force, embarrassment, assimilation, laziness, self-defeatism, television. It is as if the Indian kids were handed the antique family mirror in a million shards and blamed by their parents for not keeping it polished.

The whites in nearby Hardin do slightly better. Still, the kids are on methamphetamine. There are few jobs.

The only winner of the Indian Wars, it seems, are the shareholders of the train that cuts through the reservation, hauling a never-ending stream of coal, gas and lumber.

The tourists came early today to the national monument just up the hill from the Real Bird property where the reenactors slept in their tents. They came in their Winnebagos and Starliners, the rewards of a lifetime's work. Toil at some middling job for forty years and you get a washing machine and a mobile camper. You cart your shriveled puckered ass around the country without ever having to get out. You drive for days, hundreds of miles, a thousand miles, more. You arrive at a point of interest, you roll down your window, take a picture of the placard marking some historic spot and you continue on. The whole goddamn American existence has become drive-thru. When they bother to get out of their trucks at all, these people, white people really, gather under the awning of the National Park Service, where a ranger in a Smokey the Bear hat lectures them on the comings and goings of Custer that day. The whole thing looks like a *Leave It to Beaver* episode, except all the little kids are twice as large as they used to be. Corpulent little piggies; fatties out for a week with the grandparents; the old lady a dried-up wet nurse; the old man a saggy-bottomed crank who seems disappointed in this little piglet.

"Grandpa, why did the Indians move away?" the little boy asks.

"Because we made them," says the salt of the earth. "Because we killed them," he corrects himself. "So we could live here."

So much for the white man's perspective.

The Indians, for their part, told me they were banished from the Little Big Horn grave site because a couple of years ago on the anniversary they had ridden up the embankment and "counted coup" on the graves of the dead soldiers. Counting coup, depending how you look at it, is either an homage to the fallen opponent, or a mockery of his death. *Coup* is the French word for "blow," and an Indian counts coup in a couple of ways, I've been told. The first opponent to go down or die becomes a trophy of sorts. Any warrior who touches this body in the heat of battle collects a token of bravery. Count one. Touching an injured enemy is considered an act of magnanimity. The fallen now carries the burden that his life is indebted to his adversary. Count two.

Anyhow, the Indians weren't allowed to ride up and count coup anymore because the local white people complained that the Indians were desecrating graves. The Park Service banned the practice. This only added to the Indian perception that the whites were racist.

And so today the Sioux, having ridden for many days from the Dakotas, galloped up the northern embankment of the national monument, far away from the memorial obelisk, mounted on calicoes, carrying eagle staffs and coup sticks, ululating. Some Indians were blondish, some had blue eyes, but that's the way it is in Indian country now; you can't sleep with your cousin. Nearly every Indian is infected with Caucasian blood. They wore heavy metal T-shirts, Nike tennis shoes and blue jeans and possessed large, doughy bodies. On an adjacent hill, the Cheyenne prayed to the four directions, their drums competing with the Sioux drums. The white people sat under the awning, with the canned announcement and the Smokey the Bear lecture. The Crow were nowhere to be found.

Under a tree, I talked to Don Many Bad Horses, a Cheyenne spiritual man, tall, with white equine teeth, a prominent nose, dressed in black despite the scalding sun. He looked like a cross between the guy on the Buffalo nickel and Johnny Cash.

He told me that not only would the Crow men who mimicked the relatives of people who were not theirs be cursed, but so would their families. Besides, he said indignantly, the Cheyenne weren't being paid a nickel of the money the Real Bird brothers were charging for their pageant.

"I don't like that at all," he said. "When you imitate somebody who is a medicine man, it's totally wrong. If they keep doing this, gradually their family is going to die."

"So replaying war is a bad thing?" I asked him. "War's bad. You shouldn't do it for fun or money, is that right?"

"That's true. In my belief, they're going to pay for it. Someone should tell them. I will tell them myself. I am not scared. I am still a true warrior."

"You wanna come?" I offered him.

He hesitated. "Right now I'm kind of too busy to do something. My work is not finished yet . . . got to do some work."

I said, "I'll give them your message, shall I?"

"Yeah, you do that."

I had met Many Bad Horses about a week earlier when the Cheyenne were reenacting their victory at the Rosebud battlefield. There was no charge.

At the Rosebud, I was hanging out, trying to bond with my Indian cousins, make the scene, telling animal jokes, when three white guys in bluecoat uniforms walked up and asked me if I wanted to be their captain in the reenactment. It seemed their captain had been detained in his hometown by an insurance adjuster.

I felt funny being a white killer. I was trying to get in touch with the Indians and now I was going to be pointing a gun at them. I'm no Cortez. They were going to hate me. Think I'm Italian. Christopher Columbus or something. A honky.

I wouldn't have done it, but I had a TV show to do and we needed pictures. So I put on the white elkskin jacket with the brass buttons and gold brocade, I took a single-shot carbine and headed out into the field of grasshoppers and flies and started unloading on some kid riding down the hill in an eagle-feather bonnet; we were supposed to be re-creating the legend of how Half Buffalo Woman saved her brother. Little bastard. I kept shooting. I was enjoying it.

One of the white men, Rod Beattie, an aging former paratrooper and powerhouse mechanic, said something interesting to me through the cloud of gunpowder: The war in Iraq and the war of the Plains have similarities. One culture has the technology, the other lives in the Stone Age. And resist as they might, the Arabs are going to be dragged into the modern world, just as the Indian was dragged in. The Muslims can't win because, like the Indians, they are divided by clan and custom. Sunni, Shiite, Kurd. Shoshone, Sioux, Crow. It's all the same in that respect.

"There is no way to stop the march of progress," he told me after we'd unloaded our blanks and were awaiting our invitation to come into camp and have a doughnut and a Coke. "I don't know if what's going on in this country you could call progress, but no matter how you look at it, the Muslim is going to be part of it, whether he likes it or not."

"Well, I don't like the place we're headed, you know? Fat, stupid, scared and jerking off to porno," I said to him.

"Neither do I," the sergeant said, holding his guidon of a split U.S. flag. "That's the way it is, though."

"You think the Indian got fucked?"

"I think he's still getting fucked."

I had a memory at that moment. It was when *The New York Times* had dispatched me to eastern Turkey during the American invasion of Iraq in 2002. Diyarbakir was the capital of the Kurdish nation that spread over a number of countries, including Iraq, Syria and Iran. Fearful that the Kurds would try to carve out their own independent nation, other Muslims had slaughtered them.

I had arranged a clandestine meeting with a man who could put me in touch with the PKK, a rebel Kurdish militia at war with the Turks. When I walked into the man's gray office in a gray building in a gray and muddy sector of the city, I was shocked to see posters of Sitting Bull, Chief Joseph and other Indian leaders. The Kurds did not know who they were, but they did know the general history of the red man and felt a brotherhood with him. The Indians got fucked and so did they.

But getting kicked around can go a long way. Survivors fetishize themselves as much as others do. They become a romanticized improvement of what they really are. Many Bad Horses tells me he's been to Europe quite often. The French and Germans can't get enough of the Indian thing, as if Indians possess some deeper understanding, some special insight into the phantasmagoria of the next world. In fact, a BBC crew was running around town during Custer week, doing some movie or other about the Seventh Cavalry and the Indian wars. I don't know why Europeans should even care. No one in America cares to know anything about the Battle of Hastings.

What the BBC crew failed to notice, and what the average American does not seem to know, is that there really is no Indian brotherhood. The Custer week brings that out. And for that reason, at the reenactment, the Crow do not announce the name of the Crow actor who is portraying Sitting Bull or Crazy Horse. "It is not the Indian way," the announcer tells the tourists.

More truthfully, the Crow know the Cheyenne and the Sioux read the newspapers. They might see the name of the man portraying Sitting Bull in the caption underneath the photograph. The Cheyenne, you see, have phone books and telephones and shotguns too. Better to let ghosts rest.

But I had a message to deliver to the Crow producers of the show, the Real Bird brothers. Sitting under a tree drinking coffee, I asked one brother, Kennard, how the show could be as authentic as he claimed when the Crow portray the Sioux and not themselves.

"We've offered this to anybody. Anybody can come in and put this together because the cavalry will be here and the Indians will be here and you write your own version and do it," he said. "This land here where Custer tried to cross the river, that's the same thing as Plymouth Rock, or the place where Columbus sailed off from, or Billy the Kid rode. This is historical land. I mean, it has a lot of spirit. So then our deal here is the land is the star. As long as the river flows and the grass grows, we have to continue living. It never ends. We all have to be together."

"I got one more thing. It's a message," I said. "And I can carry it back because he didn't want to come. His name is Don Many Bad Horses."

Real Bird's face lit up with friendly recognition.

"Oh, Don Many Bad Horses. Yeah, that's my partner. Yeah, I know him."

"You know what he said? He said if you do this and you play war with the memory of his ancestors and people that carry that medicine, if you do that and you make a profit, then your family will be cursed. And you should know that."

Real Bird did not flinch. He went stone. "He can say all of those things, and that's who we are. We have people coming after us all the time, and so if he wants to do that we'll just continue living too, yeah."

I returned to the teepee pitched on the banks of the Little Big Horn where I had stored my gear, only to find Don Super, the other Custer scout, smoking weed out of my sacred pipe. I had mined the stone some years back out of a quarry owned by Dennis Banks, a Chippewa and leader of the American Indian Movement. The stem was a birch branch from Michigan and the whole thing had been made by my hand. The pipe is meant for ceremonial and spiritual purposes, and so I was pissed to see Don smoking dope from it.

"Hey, what are you doing, man?"

"Oh, you're not supposed to smoke grass in it?"

"No, it's a religious pipe," I said. "For fuck's sake."

Don looked sad and I felt bad about that. He was a melancholy person, a fifty-eight-year-old veteran and former interrogator and interpreter during the Vietnam conflict. The experience had profoundly affected him to the point where I suppose he was ashamed of his work. So many died for no apparent point, he told me. All it led to was a proliferation of heroin in the United States, he believed—the government shipped it in and used the money to support a covert war that he readily participated in. He was tall, rugged, hair the color of nicotine, hollow blue eyes and soft-spoken. He had a perpetual mellow, hangdog way about him. You could smell the morning breakfast wafting up from the mess tent, flapjacks and Canadian bacon and the sound of a drum rolling over the valley, and Don was standing there, staring off into the distance, smelling of reefer.

"Don, why are we doing this?" I said as a sort of apology.

"I don't really know," he said. "My wife doesn't understand, she says it's glorifying war. Nothing good ever really came out of war, but I do it, I suppose, to keep the history alive."

As much as I liked Don, it was something I'd heard over and over and never fully appreciated or believed. Men who hated war, had participated in it, continued to suffer from it, playacting war? The best reason I had heard came from Colonel William Reeder, Jr., a chopper pilot who was shot down in Vietnam and taken as a prisoner of war. He was forced on a long march north during which every prisoner died except him and a South Vietnamese soldier. He was locked away in a cell at the Hanoi Hilton for more than a year.

"I got to thinking about American history, my own history, that's what kept me alive, just thinking about that," he told me. "I realized how little I really knew about my country. And I vowed once I got out, I would learn all I could. That's what kept me alive, thinking about that."

After he was released in a prisoner exchange, the colonel, who now walks with a cane, taught history at the U.S. Army War College and was director of artifacts for the U.S. Cavalry Association.

He was proud, not ashamed, of his service, and recently returned to visit Vietnam. It turned out the Hanoi Hilton was near the hotel where he and his son were staying. Reeder's son convinced him against his own feelings to go for a look at the old prison. The colonel's cell had been demolished, but another just like it stood and the feelings came rushing back and his hair stood on end.

Go on, Dad, go in, his son encouraged. It was time to bury the past, he said. And so the colonel stepped tentatively into the cell, sat down and clasped his hands between his legs.

His son slammed the cell door shut with a laugh.

How easy is it for a man to forget his ancestors' horrors? When will the memory of Vietnam grow so old that we begin to think it would be fun to reenact it? Do they reenact war in Europe? I wondered. I'd have to ask the BBC crew.

On the hill, the bugler sounded the charge. Don Super, playing Mitch Boyer, the half-breed scout, and I, the amalgam Crow, led the charge. I was dressed in a painted striped face, bear headdress, sweetgrass choker, striped britches and suspenders, deer moccasins, a Remington .44 on my hip. We flew down the hill, craggy rock and wild rose and sage and the river before us. Winnebagos stuffed with shriveled old people behind us taking photos from their seats. To our right, seventy-five mounted cavalrymen, including a guy on fifteen-day leave from Iraq who chose to play war during his time away from war. His wife cried in my teepee thinking about it. And the marble-faced sergeant who kept saying kill the redskins. That guy was going to get a close-up look at my .44.

Don and I made it to the river, the calvary a few yards behind. At the banks, we saw a horde of Sioux and Cheyenne (really Crow men in body paint) making a rush for us. Don and I peeled around and made a break out of the river. Now I was feeling it, like a real horseman, a Hollywood stunt guy, and I played like I'd been shot in the back and took a blind dive into the river. Shot off my horse, spaghetti-western-style. I died the first time that day. The only problem was I fell off the wrong side of the horse, to the right instead of the left, with the river current running right to left. So as the Indian horde stampeded across the river, I drifted straight into them, nearly causing a ten-horse pileup. But the Crow are expert riders and I was stepped on by a horse only once, on the toes. The nails turned black and fell off a month later.

I got bored lying on the bank of the river. The mud stank like a rotting opossum. I decided I wasn't dead.

The battlefield was helter-skelter with a hundred Indians running around. The warriors were cheap-looking in their synthetic hair, store-bought buffalo and black-bear headdresses, barefoot, barebacked and breechclothed. I stood there admiring the spectacle when a warrior rode up behind me and shot me with a plastic arrow in the back. Goddammit, dead again. A third Indian walked up behind me and tomahawked me with a rubber mallet. Dead thrice. I lay dead for a while for the spectacle of things before getting up. This was stupid, I thought—I was unloading my pistol at the Crow and none of them would acknowledge their death by falling off their horses. In this re-creation, not one Indian was going to die, it was obvious.

The fourth death came by bullet.

The fifth time I died was in hand-to-hand combat with a couple of warriors, and we all laughed at this. The sixth time, I was struck with a spear made from a broom handle, then shot with a gun. All the while, I was making my way toward the white motherfucker who called us all savages and did not apologize. I could not find him in the curtain of smoke and horses.

I was hit with an arrow for my seventh death and lay there for a while, catching my breath and enjoying the beauty of the sky and field. Warm, perspiring, out of breath, staring at the clouds. I poked my head up.

"Yoo-hooo, boys, I'm not dead."

A warrior stopped his horse then. He wore a savage expression.

Something wasn't right with him. He raised a hatchet and it was real! I grabbed his wrist and wrestled him to the ground and there was the stink of booze on him. This freak thought this thing was real, and as we tussled, I rolled over on the blade of the hatchet and it cut up my ribs on my right side. I gouged him in the eye, and he relinquished the weapon, scrambled to his feet and went looking for Custer.

Henry Real Bird, one of the Crow brothers who hosted the reenactment, had told me of the guy who played Sitting Bull a couple of years ago when it was still cool to play Sitting Bull. Sitting Bull, it seems, fell off his horse in front of the grandstand, causing the crowd to gasp and cover their eyes. He lay lifeless. The paramedics took him away. But Sitting Bull was not dead, he was just inebriated.

Now, I lay not twenty feet from Custer, who was bitching that he was being roughed up too much by a couple of warriors who decided Custer should die many times today.

"Hey, now!" I could hear Custer squeal.

"Take it easy," one Indian guy said.

"Fuck him," said the other, with whom I had just wrestled. He was sawing on Custer's scalp with a plastic serrated knife, clutching a handful of flaxen locks in the other. They were beating him up pretty good. I had to smile. I didn't know if this guy deserved it, but the original Custer got what he deserved. And since he was reincarnated, I went over there and popped a cap in him.

I peeked around for the other white man I was going to frag. I saw him off in the distance under a stand of cottonwood, still mounted, preferring not to play it real, where every white man dies. He preferred to keep his uniform dry, his bones in their proper place. He was probably talking about his golf game. Whatever. The white man had cheated again.

Reenacting war seems like a stupid thing to do, outrageous, in fact, when you play it on the ground where the blood was actually spilled. American men, I think, won't we ever grow up? That's what I thought, anyway, until I looked into the water of the Little Big Horn, where the Indians were washing off their war paint and the whites were watering their horses.

They were smiling and shaking hands and laughing—talking about horsemanship and all the ways they died and being photographed together. Funny, fake war promotes racial brotherhood, in a place that desperately needs it. Today was a good day to die. The dark shroud of death had claimed Custer and I went for a buffalo burger.

A few days later, I limped into the Billings airport. Broken toe, bruised ribs, and saddle sores. The BBC crew was sitting there at the café eating bad food. Well, what did you think? I asked one of the men, a tall angular fellow with the haughty demeanor of some middle-level officer in the Queen's Brigade.

"Interesting," he said down his nose. "Some real problems here with race and integration," he said.

I told him that's not new, that he certainly must have seen that, for all the problems we have here, Americans do a better job of integrating strangers than any other people. "I mean, there's not a white man left in London," I told him. "The horde moved in and you all ran away."

He gave me some lame argument that while white English do indeed live in the outer ring of London, the rabble within tend to integrate more fully with *each other*.

Because there is no Chinatown, no Little Baghdad, no Little Khartoum, somehow England's immigrants are happier and more satisfied than America's, he seemed to reason. The Americans should learn from the Brits, he lectured.

I didn't think anything more about it until ten days later, when four British-born men, three of Pakistani extraction and one Jamaican, took a train to London and blew up themselves and fifty-two commuters. So much for the Brit's theory of his happy immigrants.

A simple rule can be learned at the Little Big Horn: the triumph of the conquerors makes them the carrier of their subjects' disease.

Detroit, Michigan

Remorse for what? You people have done everything in the world to me. Doesn't that give me equal right?

—CHARLES MANSON

Two homicide detectives sat in a Chinese joint on the north side of Eight Mile Road on the east side of town. It was bright outside, cold light poured through the plate-glass window. The view outside was cheap architecture, depressing and nondescript. As homicide cops most always do, they talked murder. Their conversation went something like this:

"There was this time over in the Sixth when an Arab made his wife get down on her knees in the front yard," the white detective said. He pronounced it *Ay-rab*. "She was cheating on him. He made her beg for her life before he cut her head off with a machete. He tossed her naked body in a Dumpster.

"She had a great set of tits," he said matter-of-factly, almost as an afterthought. The waitress came by and poured him more tea. He paused, wiped his lips and smiled. She walked away. He continued, "Those tits were so fantastic that every guy in the precinct stopped by to look at 'em. You hardly even noticed the brain stem poking out. Her head was stuffed in a sack."

"Those Ay-rabs don't take no shit like that, man," the black detective added. "A cheating wife, I mean. They're old-school those Ay-rabs."

"Very true. Anyhow, she had a great set of tits. You couldn't help but look at 'em. Nice big balloons. I'll never forget those."

Tits. You can't help but stare at them, whether they're attached to a headless corpse or they appear in your run-of-the-mill crime scene photograph. Tits cause more murder than money. Tits cause passion. Passion leads to sex and sex is death. Nobody knows that more than a good homicide dick.

The men finished their lunch and drove back to headquarters to fill out paperwork. A lead on a caper they were investigating had run its string. Dead end. Even dead ends needed to be documented or you didn't get paid in the Dead Squad. At precisely four P.M., the black detective put on his trench coat and went to see a man about a dog.

"Night, Mike," he said.

"Night, Tony."

The white detective, Mike Carlisle, took a dirty ashtray from a metal drawer, lit himself a cigarette and opened a window. It was late October and Detroit was getting cold. Carlisle smoked like a damp log. He was tall, around the six-foot range, well built, somewhere between forty-five and fifty-five years old with a square ruddy face, blue eyes. He preferred his suits like his coffee—black. He was a hardboiled character with a humor and vocabulary that matched his suits—dark. He carried a pistol under his arm and a badge on his belt, Number 4339. He put on a fresh pot of coffee.

The Detroit homicide bureau was a terrible place to work. The motto: Aspire to retire. The office was filthy from neglect. The shades, there were none, save for a piece of brown paper covering one of the windows. The floors hadn't been mopped since Prohibition; electric cords hung from the drop ceiling and led to nowhere. The mug-shot computer did not work and was collecting dust in the corner. In another corner, crime scene evidence sat in a shopping cart near the entrance in brown envelopes marked "Biohazard." Sometimes the packages sat for days and leaked while waiting to be taken to the crime lab. Murders were still logged into an accountant's ledger by hand and many times there was no toilet paper in the bathrooms. How did you expect a cop to get off his ass when there was no toilet paper to wipe it?

And when Carlisle spread out a photo collage of the most grisly murders he'd had the good fortune to work, you started to understand that murder had leached into the most personal recesses of his life.

Take, for instance, the snapshots of the hookers, all black, who had been beaten with a blunt object, had their clothes torn off and then their corpses raped. The scene was always the same: some filthy back lot or abandoned house, which are everywhere in Detroit. This one lay on a soiled mattress, a smear of blood showing she had been dragged to her final resting place, a used condom at her side. She had been bludgeoned on the left side of her head, revealing that the killer was right-handed. What was disturbing was that she was displayed spread-eagled, like a Da Vinci drawing, her chin and toes pointing upward. More disturbing still was the angle at which the crime scene photographer had taken the photos. That is, straight up her crotch, as if the photographer couldn't help himself, as if the killer or killers knew what lurked in the heart of every man. Crotch. Crotch and tits. The murderer mocked:

See them maggots and the blood. You like that, pig? No difference between you and me. Shine your light tight up in there, pig. . . .

Carlisle excused himself, as there were some family photos mixed in with the pictures of insanity. A fishing trip; his son in his naval uniform; Carlisle as a kid playing in a rock 'n' roll band; Carlisle hugging his wife.

"Don't know how those got in there," he said with a shrug.

There were other photos of other women with their heads smashed in, spread-eagled in some forgotten corner of this dying city. The DNA matched on all of them. A serial murderer from '02, who hadn't killed since '03 as far as anyone knew. The killer just disappeared. Vanished. Took a poof pill.

This case in particular distracted Carlisle. He was considered to be among the best homicide detectives in a city known as the Murder Capital of America. He used to work the Cold Case Squad, but that was disbanded earlier in the year because of budgetary problems. Not that the squad didn't have enough work to do. There are, detectives say, ten thousand unsolved murders dating back to 1960 in the Motor City. So far, since he returned to the homicide desk earlier in the year, Carlisle was a perfect 11 and 0 in closing out murder cases. He prided himself on a good job, that he earned his money, like he was contributing something to society even though nobody gave a shit about dead whores.

Detroit was once a beautiful city, known as the Paris of the Midwest with its wide boulevards and elm trees and Tudor-style mansions and working-class bungalows. Money was everywhere, even for an uneducated man, thanks to the factory jobs at Ford and Chrysler and General Motors. Detroit was the end point of the great migration of poor blacks and whites from the South and European immigrants flooding in from the East. Then the bottom fell out. It was a perfect storm. There were devastating riots in 1967. The whites left in droves and they took their money with them. Then came the oil shocks of the early seventies and then better-made cars from overseas and Detroit began to collapse. Factories closed or moved to the suburbs or to the South and finally to Mexico. The city was buried in a blizzard of crack cocaine. Then blacks began to leave. What was left in Detroit was a dark, desperate center.

Today, Detroit is the most violent of America's biggest cities when adding up rapes, burglaries, assaults and killings. Detroit officially recorded 385 murders in 2004, though detectives say murder cases came closer to 500. They suspect someone upstairs of cooking the books, re-classifying some murders as justified, for "publicity reasons," detectives other than Carlisle told me. Justifiable murders, they said, don't count.

The car jobs dried up and as a consequence the city was broke. To balance the budget the current mayor, Kwame Kilpatrick, ordered the layoffs of 150 cops even though Detroit is one of the few cities in America where murder is on the rise. There is about one cop for every 300 residents of the city. These are hard times for Detroit. Hard times mean murder, Carlisle said. Unemployment leads to poverty, poverty leads to drugs, drugs lead to misplaced passion and passion leads to murder.

At the time of this writing, Detroit had a fifteen percent unemployment rate. It was the poorest city in America, where one-third of the people—and half the children—lived in poverty. It is the blackest big city in America, where nearly nine in ten citizens are of African descent and nine in ten shootings are of blacks. Detroit is broken. If you get in a car wreck in Detroit, detectives said with all seriousness, citizens will call for an ambulance, but not before they lift your wallet and belt and shoes. It has been said that Detroit was the first Third World city in a First World country.

Some people die because they're stupid. Consider the killing of Quick, an east side drug dealer and hustler. He was shot in the face by his woman, Unique, because Quick cut off her dope.

"You shot me in the eye, bitch, go get my glasses," he told her before getting a ride to the hospital.

They didn't rush. On the way, Quick wanted Burger King because hospital food, he knew, was terrible. He took a piss in the bushes, then walked himself into the emergency room. He was pronounced dead a half hour later. Moral of the story: fast food is bad for your health.

In Detroit, they don't get even. They get odd. Take for instance the case of a desperate man so angry at his life's circumstances that he incessantly bickered with the landlord's wife, who lived below him, just for something to do. One day he snapped and hung himself by the neck out his window, stark-raving naked. He had done it perfectly. That is, when the landlord's wife went to open the morning blinds, she got an eyeball view of his swollen and quite dead scrotum.

"Fuck you bitch," his suicide note read.

The narratives are endless:

"I had a guy stab his woman to death with a fork," Carlisle told me. "His reason was that she served him chicken instead of pork chops. 'Hey, man,' he says, 'I don't play that shit. I'm the man of the house.'

"'Dumb fuck, only thing getting to Jackson State Penitentiary before you,' I tell him, 'is the headlights on the bus taking you there.'"

He laid out more photos. A quintuple homicide from '85—a shooting, a stabbing, and strangulation, the trifecta all in one. Five people. Mommy, Daddy, Uncle and the two children. The uncle was bound and killed on the toilet. Daddy in bed. Mommy in bed with her legs spread open. One child in his bunk bed. The girl on the floor, looking very peaceful, as if asleep almost, except for the blood. Carlisle had a suspect wandering around in Ohio, but he'd been waiting six months for the samples to come back from the crime lab.

It's easy to grow cynical. Cops are people, after all. They know other cops are assholes, that prosecutors are assholes, the mayor's an asshole. Judges are assholes too. They don't want their children making a career in the department. They don't want the kid divorcing his wife or collecting morbid photographs or spending long evenings in the bars staring at the bottom of whiskey glasses or having to sneer through broken cheekbones. Carlisle didn't drink as a habit.

"More people are murdered around Christmastime in Detroit," Carlisle said of one photograph, the tree shining in the window, someone dead underneath. "I think it's to avoid buying Christmas gifts." Carlisle had gone hard.

He emptied the ashtray, turned off the coffeepot, closed the window. He drove home to the east side, past the corner in his own neighborhood where a kid was gunned down two weeks before. The teddy bears and candles were still there. Carlisle was the last white man in the neighborhood. He opened the door to his little house and there you saw the whole thing, all nine hundred square feet of it. The sort of box that if you tripped coming in the front door, you found yourself falling out the back. He took off his gun and placed it on top of the refrigerator. Changed out of his work clothes, washed his hands and removed the foil from a plate that his wife had set on the stove. The phone rang. It was the mother of a guy who shot himself in the head. She had some information, she told him. He told her to come downtown in the morning.

The lady came in full of piss, a fat white woman with missing teeth. There's no way her son could have shot himself in the head, no way, not her boy. By the way, he was right-handed. Why would he shoot himself with his left hand?

Carlisle explained it again: The men were drinking until the daylight. They were no-good men. The shot was consistent with a suicide, no odd angles, no scuffle and he had been talking about doing it all night. The detective was being as nice as he could. The woman had feelings, after all, even if her son was puke. But this case wasn't worth it. There was no extra money in it, no overtime, which is what really got a detective going, overtime money. The woman left the shabby interrogation room unhappy and on her way out, she tripped over a moldy Tupperware container that looked as though it had been lying there the better part of a decade.

The first case of the morning came. It was Carlisle's turn on the rotation board. Dead white male discovered rotting in his living room in the southwest side. Detectives respond to all calls of found bodies, becoming involved only if they suspect foul play. As he arrived at the house, a neighbor asked, "The smell is something powerful; would you like a mask, Officer?"

"No, ma'am," he answered with amusement. "This ain't my first day on the job."

. The house was typical for the southwest side, prewar two-story, a mix of siding and shingles, a sagging porch, peeling paint. Neighbors stood on their porches, drinking malt liquor in the early afternoon. Inside, it was so dirty it was hard to find the body. But there it lay, black and bloated, only the long straight whiskers revealing that he was once a white man. His pants had slithered off his waist and his genitals had gone purple.

His pants were down, Carlisle explained, because after he died, he bloated, then shrank, and during this accordion process his pants managed to work their way down his thighs. "I always wondered why their pants are always pulled down," said the cop who had slithered through the window.

The burner in the kitchen was still going. Carlisle turned it off. The guy had been dead a week and nobody noticed until the stink got loose. The two cops stood in the doorway, sucking for fresh air. Carlisle stood over the body among the flies in his dark suit and polished shoes, unperturbed, cracking wise.

"The cause of death appears to be drowning."

"Drowning?" the cop asked.

"Yes. This man drowned in his own filth. Look, he even messed his pants."

There was not a bare spot on the floor. The dead man's beard was neatly trimmed, which suggested he was functional. A purple man died as he lived—alone. The shades were drawn. The man was a shut-in. He never came out and so no one noticed his absence. Drowning in filth and no one cared. Death in a dying city. His end would probably come at the bottom of a pauper's grave. The final rites administered by a man he never knew, a religion he did not practice. A prison crew leaning on their shovels over a grave he'd share with two dozen others. The tombstone would read simply, "2005."

The morgue men came to the door with a body bag. A comedy team, it seemed, one thin, the other stout. "Oooh-weee, he's gonna be soup when we pick him up. Likely be leaking all over the place," the stout one said.

"We got shovels," the thin one mumbled as he pulled on rubber gloves. "And we got plen'y a room in the truck."

About this time, a neighborhood kid came running up the street. "A guy just pushed into Jesse's house with an AK-47."

"What?" one of the cops asked, belligerent-like.

"A white guy in a mask, with red hair, he just walked up to the house down there with an AK-47 and asked where Jesse's at and just pushed the door in. There was gunshots!"

"How you know it was an AK?" the cop asked. It was a stupid and unnecessary question.

"Man, I know what an AK looks like. It's down there, the house with the plant on the porch."

The cops did not move. They did not radio in to headquarters. There would be nothing gained chasing a guy with an AK-47. There was no overtime in it. It wouldn't help your bowling score. Wouldn't do much of anything except get you killed.

Carlisle came out having heard the kid's commotion. As the detective, he was in charge of this scene. The orders were his to give. "Okay, boys, you head down there, where the shots came. I'll call it in and take this kid's statement."

The cops moved hesitantly, like housecats at an open door. They must have taken five minutes to get down one block. I got there before them on foot. A silver car was going the wrong way down the very street where the gunshots were heard. The cops warned him to slow down.

Jesse, the thin light-skinned man who'd had the gun put to his face, said he would not sign a complaint. No one would be arrested for the shooting or the break-in. This was fine with the cops. The cops could go home at four.

The thing was, Carlisle knew that most likely he'd be back in this neighborhood a couple of weeks working on a homicide case. "Jesse'll handle it himself," Carlisle surmised.

A fresh call came in over the radio. A nude woman in an east side alley, a condom stuffed in her mouth, gunshot wounds to the head. "Probably not a suicide," he calculated.

The detective drove the Ford Freeway across town and pulled into a vacant lot along Chalmers. A crowd and a news truck were already there. Carlisle rolled up his windows and locked the doors. He put on his suit jacket, dark with pinstripes, and got the rundown from the plainclothes gathered around the entrance of the fallen-down garage.

"Just a pros', Mike," one of them said. Just a prostitute.

Carlisle borrowed a flashlight from him. The body lay to the left of the entrance, just out of sight from the crowd on the street. She was black, corpulent, late thirties, homely and worn-looking. Her head was caved in on her left side. She was stripped nude. Her bra was torn, like it had been ripped off. A pink prophylactic and its wrapper lay next to her. She had on clean white socks. Most disturbing, she was laid out like a starfish, posed with her arms out, her legs spread, her chin up. The photographer took crotch shots.

Carlisle shone the flashlight on her vagina. "You recognize her, Johnny?" he said to a young uniformed cop who had turned his head away. "I mean, you dated her, right?"

"Naw," Johnny croaked, still looking away. A half smile broke across his face. He looked like he was going to be sick.

I wasn't going to be sick. I was going to cry. My sister lived a street life too. A tough life. A black-and-blue life. She died young, at age thirty-five, on the west side of the city, in a notorious section known as Brightmore. She'd gone partying with some shady people she'd met at a dirty bar. They decided to go someplace. God knows where someplace. The driver of the van was wasted and decided he had to get there in a hurry, going eighty down a residential street. Before the van crashed through the fence and then through the garage, my sister leaped out, wild enough to try and save herself. She lived life hard and she squeezed the juice from it. She jumped out of the van and straight into a tree. The three in the van survived.

The case of my sister—her name was Nicole Marie—went ignored. Her file grew yellow in a pile of other yellow files—the sons and daughters of some other women out there. It would have stayed that way for my sister and our mother if not for a cop who cared, a cop like Carlisle. At least the driver did some time. My sister was not trash. Neither was this woman. No one deserved this.

Carlisle poked her with a pencil. She didn't move. She died from a good bludgeoning, not a gunshot. He mined for clues among the garbage and discarded auto parts. A good detective thinks nothing, assumes nothing. He lets the details come flooding to him: crack pipe, condom, torn and bloody clothing, bashed head—left side. She appeared to be an experienced hooker, judging by the Narcotics Anonymous key rings hanging from her purse, which lay in the weeds. There was a fresh package of unopened luncheon meat about ten feet from the corpse.

"What do you make of this, Mike?" I asked, pointing out the cold cuts.

"Don't believe all the baloney you see," he said deadpan, before returning to his work.

There was blood spatter on the wall, none on the ceiling. No murder weapon could be found. He probably took it with him, probably a hammer, maybe a construction guy.

"Looks to me like he makes an arrangement with this girl. She being experienced, she's not going to go to an abandoned building with a stranger and lay out naked on the ground for the guy. She's a whore, but she's got dignity. So she's probably gonna suck his cock, smoke a rock, a scenario like that. She goes down to suck him off, and boom! He's beating her to death with something. Then when he's done killing her, see, then he rapes her. You can tell that by the bra, it's been ripped off her, it's torn at the edges. You can't strip a big hooker like this naked, manhandle her, put on a rubber, rape her and then kill her, you see what I'm saying?

"He probably killed her first. I'm saying this sick fuck gets off on the killing, and then rapes the corpse just to finish the job. We got a real nut out there somewhere."

The meat wagon arrived. The two pick-up men from the morgue got out. "You boys again?" Carlisle asked.

"Yup," the thin one answered. "We got plen'y a room in this here truck, yes, sah."

Carlisle drove back to headquarters, located at 1300 Beaubien, a neo-classical and once-beautiful building designed by Albert Kahn. Now the steps were crumbling, the lead paint was peeling, pipes corroding. The seventh floor had been condemned a few years ago because of pigeon droppings and mold. The third floor was nice, polished metal and marble. The third floor was where the chief had her office.

That corpse looked familiar. The torn clothing, the condom, spread-eagled like that. Carlisle reached into his drawer for those photos and walked them over to the lieutenant's desk.

"That dead prostitute on Chalmers, she was laid out just like this." He showed the lieutenant a Polaroid of today's crime scene. "Same MO. Bashed on the right side of the head. The place is abandoned and dirty. I think the guy's back."

"Maybe it's not him," the lieutenant said. His eyes said something else. The lieutenant had a thin face, intelligent-looking, not hard. His last name was a jumble of consonants. They just called him Vinny.

"There was a condom," Carlisle pointed out.

"It doesn't appear used."

"It might have shriveled up if it was used. It might not," Carlisle said.

"The lab will determine that." The lieutenant stroked his stubbled chin. "At this point take it as it comes. ID her. Find the next of kin. Find the boyfriend. See if she was fighting with anyone. Take it that way. Don't raise no red flags with the brass about a serial killer. Then they'll be breathing down our ass. There will be a task force, paperwork and triplicate. Keep it quiet and see if you can dig up those old files. If it's the same guy, then he's been laying low for a couple of years. Maybe he was in prison or something. When we get the DNA from this, we'll see if it matches the others. But for now, keep it quiet. I assume you want this case."

"Something tells me I don't, but yeah, I do," Carlisle said.

"Jesus, this is an ugly city," said the lieutenant.

Beyond the garden-variety girlfriend who shoots her boyfriend in the face, it's difficult to solve homicides in Detroit. For detectives, it's one disappointment after another. The computers are broken, some of the evidence handlers are incompetent, the lab has a half-year backlog. While other departments across the country have a database of gang members and nicknames, Detroit does not. The department is politicized; cops have been laid off. The Cold Case Squad has been shuttered. Radios don't work in basements, the headquarters are filthy, bums sleep on the steps, no toilet paper.

Then there is the consent decree. Federal investigators condemned the department as the most troubled force they had seen in ten years of scrutinizing police nationwide. Detroit led the nation's large cities in the number of per-capita shootings of citizens by police. A Justice Department investigation in 2003 found that police detained homicide witnesses without required court warrants and that fourteen people died in police lockups from 1998 to 2001—making it worse than Abu Ghraib in Baghdad. One woman—a material witness—was held for five days in a cell on the notorious eighth floor of police headquarters, fed baloney sandwiches and left to sleep on the cold slabs with the roaches and rats. Eventually she told what she knew. This is how murders got solved and this is why people don't like the cops in Detroit.

Black people never have. White cops harassing black men at a blind pig ignited the '67 riots, the deadliest urban unrest of the century until the Rodney King riots in Los Angeles in 1992. It was the watershed moment for the city. Detroit was the fourth-largest city in America in 1960 with 1.7 million people, the population 29 percent blacks. With the riots began the white exodus. In 1970, the city shrank to 1.5 million, the black population at 45 percent; in 1980, population 1.2 million and 64 percent black; now there are less than 900,000 citizens in Detroit, nearly 83 percent black. The city is surrounded by overwhelming white suburbs, more than 3 million strong. But try as they might, they can't keep it that way. Detroit is witnessing a new phenomenon. Black flight.

The population is falling in the city and murder is still on the rise. Because of the federal consent decree, police layoffs and closed precinct houses, less than half of Detroit's murders in 2004 had been solved.

When Carlisle got back to his desk there was a message. Someone in the neighborhood recognized a photo of the dead prostitute. Her mother lived a few blocks from the crime scene. Carlisle wrote down the address, put his jacket on and headed back to the neighborhood. It was getting dark.

As he stood on the warped porch of the white Cape Cod, a gunshot sang out a block over. The dead woman's mother answered the door. She was drunk and fat and nervous. She asked the detective if she could smoke.

"It's your house," he said. "Mind if I smoke too?"

Carlisle smoked. He lit her cigarette. She smoked. A man crept out from the kitchen, sheepishly asked Carlisle for a cigarette, and then an aunt crept out of the kitchen, sheepishly asked Carlisle for a cigarette, and then a cousin and then someone else. Everybody smoked but nobody knew anything. The dead woman hadn't been home in days.

Carlisle closed his notebook and excused himself. Before he could reach the door, the uncle bummed another cigarette. Carlisle was glad to go home. It was dark on the east side. No place for a stranger to be. Not even a cop. Especially a cop.

The morgue is busiest on Mondays. On Mondays it's standing room only. After a bad weekend, the metallic tables are occupied by victims of misadventure and done-me-bad. All in various positions of repose and color and odor. Some have their chests spread open, some have their skull tops sawed off like a coconut. Others are covered in a flesh blanket pulled up to their chins so the guts can be pulled out and weighed. Monday is the busiest, but today was Wednesday and Wednesday was busy. Detroit. It's always busy. To date, there had been 9,762 deaths in Wayne County. More than 400 of those had been investigated by the Detroit homicide bureau. There were still two months until the new year.

As the technicians plucked guts and brains from the cadavers, they chirped about their sex lives. Rhythm and blues played from a radio. The place stank like spaghetti sauce.

Carlisle had come to collect the fingernail clippings and the rape kit. In Detroit, it's the detective's job to handle the evidence, from crime scene until trial.

"This your case, Mike?" a photo technician asked.

"Yup."

"Serial killer?"

Carlisle paused, looked him dead in the eye. "How'd you know?"

"I remember his work. I went back a couple of years and pulled the pictures. Got another one just like it last month, a few blocks from this one."

"Really?"

"Yep. Yours looks to me like she got beaten with a brick. There's gravel ingrained in her skull, but it hasn't been punctured. Got defensive wounds all over her wrists. The other woman they found dead up the block last month was spread out like this one, the cause still un-known."

"Not a beating?"

"Don't know, no marks on her."

"Okay, you see any more like this you let me know, okay, Joey?"

"You got it."

At headquarters, he stuffed the nails and the rape kit in the cooler, then carted out a cardboard box of the old cold cases of dead prosti-tutes. The bottom was falling out of the box. Word had gotten down to the third floor; it was now classified as a "case of interest."

Carlisle laid out the photos and the other detectives got curious. The one with watery eyes, chewing on a PayDay, said, "Hey, I had a girl killed in an ice-cream truck and the guy laid her out like that."

Carlisle read his crime encyclopedia last night. This guy was what you call a disorganized serial killer. That is, he didn't torture sadisti-cally, do things like cut nipples. He worked on impulse. He made no attempt to hide evidence. The condom was left right there next to her. There were no patterns to his crime, just did his thing, so to speak, be-cause the urge came upon him. Serial killers ninety-nine percent of the time prey on their own race. They graduate up from killing pup-pies and such. They tend to kill prostitutes, victims of lust. Society doesn't raise an eyebrow. The man probably hated himself, was penni-less, was angry this was the way he had to get sex and so she had to pay for it.

"There is a fine line between the cop and the killer," Carlisle con-fided to me. "I mean, I've got to know why—why does this fucker do this? I also wonder what it's like to realize that you're being killed. The victim, the killer and the cop. Now it becomes a competition. For me, this fucker has to be stopped. When I'm gone, maybe they'll say I did something for society."

A plainclothes sergeant I'd never seen before walked up to Carlisle's desk and stuck his nose in. He was a greasy, dark-skinned white ethnic in a suit that hung loosely on him like it was ashamed to be on the big dope. The guy gave off a bad-cop feeling and he came over to play the long underwear bit. Carlisle frowned. The guy was too dumb to notice the gesture.

"What? It looks like a pattern?" Sergeant Grease Ball asked.

"That's what it looks like."

"Your case?

"You're sharp today."

"That's a good case, a lot of overtime." Sergeant Grease Ball smoothed his fanny. "They wouldn't be calling the Feds in it, would they? I don't like them Feds poking their nose around."

"Look," Carlisle said, staring straight into Grease Ball's black eyes. "The brass, they don't want this getting out, stirring up panic and the newshounds. We're gonna take it slow and easy and see how it progresses. Not a word. Understand?"

"Sure, Mike, sure, of course. You need any help, you let me know."

"Yeah, I'll do that."

Sergeant Grease Ball and his suit bumbled through the row of desks, three on each side with room to walk in between. Carlisle's coffeepot sat at one end. The exit was at the other. Sergeant Grease Ball used it. No one watched him go out.

Carlisle called to his partner, Tony Wright. "You wanna head back to the crime scene? I want to take another look for that murder weapon."

"Sure thing, Mike, let me get my coat."

Carlisle was more disgusted than yesterday, when the corpse was lying there. The crime scene technician had mailed the job in, leaving behind the bra and most of the victim's clothes. "Fucking unbelievable," he growled, and then called for someone to come collect it. The clothes were covered in maggots. Underneath was a piece of broken cinderblock. On the bottom, it was stained with blood and hair and scalp.

"Bingo, there's your murder weapon," he said to Wright.

A new evidence technician had come by at this point, was fumbling around in her van when a smallish shabby black man, maybe forty, with wild yellow eyes started talking to her.

"What's all the fuss, she's just a old fuckin' street girl walking up and down the street," he said without prompting.

"She was still entitled to a life," the technician said.

"She jus' a raggedy thing, no one is gonna miss her."

"Maybe, maybe not."

"I bet it's only one or two people doing all the killing of these girls. That's what I think."

The technician began to get suspicious.

"Why don't you tell it to the detective?" she said, and waved Carlisle over. Wright remained near the garage.

Carlisle came over, the technician went about her job.

"Hey, Officer," the black guy said. "I'm a good person. Anything I can do to help you? I don't like to see anyone hurt for no good reason. It ain't right."

I lit myself a cigarette. He bummed one and admired my jacket. I offered my flame. He took it and inhaled, complaining the smoke wasn't menthol. He was twitchy and morbid in nature.

"No, it ain't right," Carlisle said like he was barely listening.

"My old girl, see, was on heroin. I'm not into that. She was going to get help, she told me. And she was supposed to be at rehab. Then she showed up dead outside the dope house over there near Fenlon."

"I'm sorry for your loss," Carlisle said. "What was her name?"

He gave her alias "Nina Simone." Wright was handling that case. This guy seemed to know a lot. Carlisle didn't let on.

Most murders get solved through a snitch. Sometimes the snitch is the killer himself. There is no such thing as coincidence in murder.

"It ain't but two or three people doing this."

"Doing what?"

"Killing these girls. This one here, I known her as Kiki. She just got back from rehab. I seen her Friday. Known her the past fifteen years or so. Big girl."

The dead woman had been in North Carolina for eight of those years.

"Were you here yesterday, when the investigators were here and the crowd and the news truck?" Carlisle asked calmly, smoking his tough cigarettes, looking off in the distance. He knew sometimes killers did that—returned to the scene. Sometimes it was the satisfaction. Sometimes the guy was snooping around to see how much you knew.

"Yeah, I was on the corner over there by the gas station. I didn't want to interfere with your investigation, so I stayed over there. Real sad what happened to Kiki, though."

"Yeah, it sure is," Carlisle said. "Listen, you got a name and a phone number where I can reach you? In case we find something, you might want to know about your friend."

The man gave his name. Andrew S——, his phone number and his address. He lived a block away.

"Anything I can do, sir. It just ain't right to kill a person for no good reason, anyhow."

"I'll call if I find anything," Carlisle promised.

The detectives drove back to 1300 Beaubien, where a wino was sleeping on the limestone steps of the station house. The rap sheet on Andrew S—— was waiting on Carlisle's desk when he got there. It was long enough to hang the man: assault with intent to do great bodily harm (twice), stalking (twice), drug possession (numerous times). He kept company with prostitutes. It showed that he had lived at addresses near the other murders on the east side around the time they occurred. He'd been sentenced to jail around the time when the murders stopped.

He was in violation of probation for an assault charge and there was an outstanding warrant for his arrest.

The men decided to go back and pick him up. After a cup of coffee, they put on their coats.

"Aren't you going to wear a vest?" I asked Wright.

"Vest. There ain't no vests." He laughed.

Wright, black, round-faced, fortyish. He dressed in dark suits and white ties, was good-natured and aspired to retire, get through the day, go to the bar, meet some women. He grew up on the city's east side, around the Buffalo Homes. He learned to hate the cops because in his time the white cops came down to the neighborhood and beat the hell out of black boys like him. Wright joined the Detroit faction of the Black Panthers as a teenager. He was with them up to the time they started shooting up police stations. He decided he could do better for black people if he became a cop. He became one of *them*. That was twenty years ago. And twenty years of policing a city of despair and degradation has an effect on a man's mind.

"See right there, Charlie?" He pointed to a building we passed on the way to the suspect's apartment. "Right there, we was making a dope bust and we broke down the door and the guy was in the back room and his kid, who was maybe two, was in the front room. The kid yells, 'Daddy, it's the po-lice.' And then the kid made his fingers like a gun and started making like he was shooting. Pow! Pow! Pow! Two years old. These people teach them at an early age to hate the po-lice. Unbelievable, and you ain't going to fix it."

These people, he said. How quickly your people become *these* people.

One of those people called. The mother of the puke who killed himself. Isn't it possible, she asked Carlisle as he drove, that these men convinced her baby to kill himself? That they encouraged him and that he never would have done something like this on his own?

It's possible, he said.

Well, doesn't that make them responsible? she asked.

"To God, probably," Carlisle said, "but not to the law."

Having someone to blame meant the world to her. And Carlisle let her have it.

She thanked him and hung up.

Carlisle, not a religious man, muttered, "Jesus Christ."

They pulled up to the curb in front of Andrew S——'s apartment. It was the kind of neighborhood with boarded-up houses and paper plates blowing through the streets, a small area so boundless with desperation, a man could spend his whole life wandering around here and never find a way out. A group of young black men were drinking beer and carrying on, up on the second-floor walkway. You could see their silhouettes through the screen door. They made the unmarked car, the suits, and me in a buckskin coat.

"Shit, this don't look good at all, nigger," one man in a bandanna said to another. "Uh-uh, this don't look good at all."

I put my finger to my lips. They shut up. Carlisle rapped on the door. Wright stood behind him. No answer. Carlisle rapped again. No answer. He looked in the window. The light was on.

I went around the corner to see if he had hightailed it out the back. I was bored. I watch television. Sure enough, he was halfway in a car.

"Andrew," I said. "Where you going?"

He recognized the buckskin jacket from earlier in the day. He was breathing hard with fear, like I'd just jumped out of a closet.

"Nowhere, sah," he said, flummoxed.

"Why don't you step out of that car, then, and wait for the detectives?"

"Yes, sah. Lemme just get my tools out of the trunk."

I was getting nervous here, hoping the detectives heard me from the porch. I was swimming in waters where I didn't belong. I said, "No, Andrew, why don't you just stand there with your hands to your side?"

"Yes, sah."

The detectives came around the corner. Wright looked at Andrew, then he looked at me, and shook his head.

We went in Andrew's apartment. It was clean. There was a TV, an overstuffed couch and a kitchenette. In the corner was an altar with a painting of a black Moses hanging over it. On the table was a stuffed owl looking up at black Moses, which was balanced on a Bible and an incense urn. There were candles, an hourglass and a porcelain elephant, animal horns and a walking staff. There was also a photo of one of the dead prostitutes.

"What you gonna do, arrest me?" He giggled nervously, like a guilty man. "I didn't kill nobody. I just came to help y'all, is all. You ain't gonna arrest me, are you?"

"Yes, yes, we are," Carlisle said. He said it sweetly, like warm milk. "You got a warrant and you're going to have to take care of it. Now, if you sign this paper allowing us to search the place, we'll put in a good word with the judge. Assuming you don't have no weapons or drugs in here, okay? You don't got no drugs in here, do you, Andrew?"

"No, sah, just some seeds on a tray in there. A little bitty of seeds is all."

"I ain't worried about that, Andrew."

"Yes, sah." He sat at the kitchenette and signed the paper. He mumbled about God. Wright soothed him.

Andrew said, "It's meant to be. I gotta get my life worked out."

"Yes, sir, you do. That's all. See the judge. Get it worked out, is all," Wright said. "Go in front of the judge with your head down and say you're sorry. Get there early. Do the right thing."

They put him in the car without cuffs and took him downtown. The consent decree forbids detectives from taking suspects downtown in cuffs. On the way, Andrew started talking about his former career at the Water Department. Wright too had worked at the Water Department. They had similar acquaintances. Ray. Ray was a common friend. Such a coincidence. Detroit, the smallest big city in the world.

That's how the art of the confession is run. If the suspect is vinegar, you are sugar. He is sugar, you are vinegar. If he's a Christian, you're a

Christian. He talks of his kids, you talk of your kids. Andrew blabbered about getting right. What exactly he needed to get right, he did not say. They sat him at the desk next to the evidence refrigerator. Wright just nodded his head. Mmm-hmmm. Got to get it right, Andrew. Got to get it right.

Andrew said, "I'm sort of happy. I'm glad, actually. I'm going to sort it out. Get it all right. There ain't no way. I can't do it anymore. There's no way. I can't do it. I got to get right with God.

"But it's so hard living out there in the ghetto, you understand? I got to defend my manhood. I get the challenge, that's when I lose it, that's when I get mad."

I noticed he was wearing elevator soles.

Carlisle motioned me into the next room. The Department of Corrections had sent his incarceration record. Turns out Andrew S—— had been in jail for the better part of '02 when the first batch of prostitutes were murdered. Carlisle shrugged his shoulders. "Not our guy," he said. "Too good to be true."

The detectives took the excited little man into an interrogation room anyway. Could be he killed our woman in the garage. They came out a half hour later, and Andrew S—— was taken across the street to county jail.

"Dead end?" the lieutenant asked.

"Yeah, but we got a DNA just in case," Carlisle said. "I asked him and he gave it up. Says 'you can take my blood, you can wipe my ass, I didn't do nothing.' Probably a job for you, Vinny. Taking that ass sample."

"Not without a clothespin and a rubber glove," Lieutenant Vinny said. "Go home, guys, you did a good job this week."

I was more disappointed than they. I wanted an end to this story. Something good to say about the city and the cops. The story needed an ending. On the way to the elevator, Wright noticed the floors had gotten mopped. It felt like a victory.

"Wow," Carlisle said.

"Like you could eat off them," Wright marveled.

Fridays, detectives try to catch up on paperwork, and maybe cut out early. Carlisle got a call near the end of the day. At least the guy had the decency to die near the bureau.

He was an old man, dead in a long stairwell in midtown at Garfield and Woodward. He'd been living in the stairwell for twenty years. He lived in the apartments upstairs until the city condemned them. With no place to go, he moved downstairs.

The stairwell was made up nicely. It was carpeted, swept and the bedspread had frilly lace. The guy died in bed with his shoes off, his arms folded over his chest. He looked comfortable. He died across the street from a hospital.

"He drank hisself to death," said Mary, who lived in the next stairwell over. Mary didn't look like she got to the salon very often. In fact, Mary sounded a little like a Mark. "He wanted pussy fo' he died, but I wasn't giving it to ol' nasty in there. He'd drank anything. Drāno if he had to."

Carlisle shone a flashlight on the man. Eugene, age fifty-two. There didn't appear to be foul play. He went to his car to write up some notes.

"Isn't that something," he said. "The guy's younger than me. You die in this town and someone like me shows up and gives you five minutes of attention. That's all she wrote. The president dies and he gets a parade, a cannon salute and a riderless horse. The whole shebang. But this guy fucked up less shit than the president ever did, if you think about it. It's sad when it ends up like this."

The coroner's wagon came a while later.

The meat men got out. The same two guys.

"We got plen'y a room in this here van. We got plen'y a room."

Three months later, the DNA results were in from the lab. The serial killer was indeed back.

A few months later, the killer struck again. Except this time, his victim lived. Working from her murky description, Carlisle and other detectives found the man working at a local Burger King. DNA match. Case closed.

Tulsa, Oklahoma

Oklahoma City, Oklahoma

New York City, New York

Fashion is a form of ugliness so intolerable that we have to alter it every six months.

—OSCAR WILDE

Amarillo, Texas

Oakland, California

Black Rock City, Nevada

Coos Bay, Oregon

Crow Agency, Montana

Detroit, Michigan

Cleveland, Tennessee

Miami, Florida

I'm sitting in a 757 on a tarmac at LAX on an airline that rhymes with Dong and whose logo is a white spermatozoa-looking thing and I'm on my way to New York—capital of glam and soft-work-for-a-living—to try my hand at the cutthroat world of male modeling, to explore the vanity of the stronger sex, the weakening of his will and his slow, inexorable subjugation by the manufacturers of face creams and moisturizers.

The best way to see the transmogrification is to live it. Be the IT BOY. Face on a Times Square billboard, on the back of a magazine, on the downside of an uptown bus. Get paid because you're pretty. Get laid because you're happening. Get fake muscles at a gymnasium rather than real ones at hard labor. That's the dream back in my hometown, because there aren't too many other dreams there. That's why I'm coming here, like the kid with dreams from Allen Park, Michigan, or Mobile, Alabama. And you can only hope a kid like this will break through or break out before he gets his drink doped up and he's carted out in the back of a meat wagon. I've at least got a shot, since I'm traveling around with a movie camera and a soundman with a big fuzzy microphone on a stick, and who doesn't want to be on television? I'm counting on the subtle game of quid pro quo.

So I'm on my way. I left my wife in a puddle of tears at the counter of Dong Airlines. The clerk told her she would not be flying to New York due to some reservation snafu and to fix it was going to cost several hundred dollars. This made my wife cry, that and the fact that I told her we should take a break from each other because she wasn't really appreciating what I was giving her. You know—giving her. My good looks and a plane ticket. I was halfway to IT, in my mind anyhow. She wasn't giving the proper respect and I let her know it and she was melting into those tears and I got it going 'round in my head and could really use a drink right now, what with this Chinese guy behind me yanking on the headrest. But I'm thinking perhaps I shouldn't have that drink, it could puff up the eyes or mottle my complexion. It's bad enough as it is. I shave with soap and wash my hair once a week. My teeth are a little yellow. Hair? My forehead is becoming a six-head. Maybe I'll have a tomato juice and two cucumbers to put over the eyelids. New York, if you've never been there, will kick you to the curb. Especially when you're bloodshot and puffy.

"The martini bar is open," the stewardess says.

"Ohhhh!" squeal the two male passengers in front of me, one with hair blow-dried into the shape of a vagina: two plumes piled high and swept back and parted down the back of his head.

The other guy is nothing: a cheesy ball cap, weak chin, typical white guy, pear-shaped.

"Oh, Jesus," I'm mumbling.

I order a vodka tonic, a premium vodka that will receive no advertising in this space. Suffice it to say they don't have my premium vodka, so I order premium whiskey. I'm agitated. Departing Los Angeles, the capital of isolation, for New York, the capital of alienation, my wife in tears. How ugly. Miss, another drink, please?

New York is the city where a nebulous factory is pumping out a new reality, where lines between traditional masculine and feminine roles are being blurred; a smokestack pumping out gender obfuscation. A new masculine beauty myth is emerging in an ultra-competitive city with an ultra-competitive job market and men are being told that brains and charisma are no longer enough; they must now look the part as well if they're going to get the *edge,* whether it be in the boardroom or the bedroom.

They're telling you men what it is to be beautiful and you're buying it. They are creating a whole subgenus. The alpha-pansy. The last untapped market for sure is male ego and body-type insecurity. Body waxes and cucumber masks, you'll buy it.

Girdles and eyebrow tweezers that run on batteries and saucepans and a shopping magazine to help men understand what pans they need in this new world. The only problem is it reeks of GAY. You're not convincing a brother in Alabama or Allen Park that it's cool to purchase a one-button velvet Armani jacket and a pink tie if he's thinking it's GAY. That is the trick here, Dickey.

Manhattan. Jet lag. Whiskers. Greasy hair. I am hung over in a cab. Too much primo whiskey. Horns are bleating; the sun is stabbing into my eyeballs like toothpicks. The streets are crowded with people and rotting garbage. Vendors on the streets are selling knockoffs on Fifth Avenue. Fake Prada in front of the Prada store! The balls on that guy! It's noisy. A rat in the sewer grate. The city is in full swing. Everyplace in the Times Square canyon is papered in neon and cunt and cock; images of fashion and beauty, from the billboards to the stores to the people walking down the street. New York is the kind of place where beauty is so commonplace, so taken for granted, that people don't look anymore like they're enjoying it. They look sick in their nice clothes. Pasty, ill-fed, drunk on bad coffee, seething.

I've got an appointment at the Condé Nast building at 4 Times Square. It's high glass and chrome and the talent working there is young, Swedish and African girls carrying someone's latte. The place is subdued cool New York, like, you don't know anything going on out there, Mr. Whiskers, and you're not going to get anything going on in here either. The elevator doors are polished steel and you can't smoke in front of the place.

I'm wearing a black suede vest, silk spotted tie in a Winchester knot, powder-blue Brooks Brothers shirt, pinstriped pants from the Gap, silk socks, wooden-heeled shoes and cocoa butter in my hair to keep it down.

I go to the offices of *Cargo* magazine on the fifteenth floor to see Ariel Foxman, an ambitious thirty-one-year-old who is the son of Abe Foxman, president of the Anti-Defamation League. Anyway, young Foxman is not selling God or civil rights; he's selling this magazine, one designed to tell you what crap you're going to need to make it in the world of the urbane man. He's selling consumerism, the last true religion in the United States. The office is spare with a large desk and framed covers of his magazine that hang crookedly on the wall, and he complains to his PR person about this. "I've got to get those redone." And he turns to the female aide and says, "Let's get those redone." A man who makes things happen! I'm in the right place. . . . The view from his office is a spectacular one of Times Square, and it is not lost on me that here, he is the puppet master of male: pale, thin, narrow-shouldered and safely locked away in a high glass tower.

"There has been a discovery in the last ten years that guys are vain," he tells me, looking me up and down like I'm some kind of homeless guy who's taken a seat next to him at an outdoor café.

"Men's vanity, that's the new gold rush."

The trick, he says, is to tap into fashion and grooming, the super-competitive itch in men to get a leg up on the competition, so to speak, to bore into the modern man's anxiety of not knowing exactly what a modern male should be, even though we are the ones who export the image of the ideal man across the world. Brad Pitt is the guy, but Brad Pitt pays another man to dress him. There is a mint derivative in shaving creams that suppresses razor bumps.

Style versus stylish. Style, unlike the stylish, is unique, innate, personal and cannot be copied. Stylish is purchased off the rack.

Well, what's wrong with me? I ask him. Nothing, he says, casting an eye up and down, then back up again. And so I'm wondering whether he—as the disseminator of style—is watching me for clues about what a straight guy with dough will buy or whether I somehow follow the lead of his magazine in my grooming and dressing tastes without ever having heard of the publication. Would I buy what he's selling? And as I'm thinking this, he proclaims me perfect! He's noticed the belt, the silver earrings, the off-white teeth, the slim build. I'm suspicious of guys like this. It goes back to high school when I wasn't getting past the velveteen ropes and into the pants of the chicks with big blond hair and Gloria Vanderbilt jeans. I was never cool and so I loathe mass-produced cool.

"You see, you too are vain," Foxman fusses, drawing closer, inspecting the vest and spotted ties. He's close, but not quite getting it.

"Yeah, but I don't need *you*," I say. "I was vain before you ever started selling it."

"Perhaps," he says, but informs me that vests will be the rage this fall. Fat men, gay men, suburban men will all be wearing vests. Silk vests, leather vests, wool vests. Who determines this, I do not know. There is a plexus, it seems, between Madison Avenue, Fifth Avenue and the fashion houses. Thousands of vests of all stripes and sizes are being mass-produced for the fall collection at this very moment because it has been decided it's vests.

Perhaps they are stealing from me. I've been wearing vests for years and been ridiculed for it. Now I'll be in for a hot minute before I get ridiculed eighteen months from now for being out of date.

Be that as it may, we quickly get to the topic of men's makeup. That is, men's *products*. Men and makeup sounds too GAY. I ask him if he knows the ultimate hair cream that triples as a hand moisturizer and razor-burn emollient. He says he does not know.

I lean over the editor in chief's desk and offer him the crown of my head. "Smell. Go on, smell my head."

He's taken aback.

"Go on, then, smell it!"

He does, flinching, dabbing, bobbing like a woodpecker at a tree. Then, realizing it doesn't bite, he takes a few whiffs of my scalp, arches his eyebrows in a small appreciative way and tells me it reminds him of the candle Jews light after Sabbath.

"Nope. Cocoa butter," I proclaim.

He nods like it's going in his next issue.

I tell him I shave with soap. He gasps. Soap contains wax, he informs me, which clogs the pores and dries the face. Foam contains alcohol, which will age the skin prematurely. No, gel is what you want, gel with glycerin: $14.95 a tube at Saks.

I ask him if I look fat in my clothes. Absolutely not, he says with a leer. "How about my calves, you like my calves?" I ask from atop his air-conditioning vent, my pant legs rolled up, spread-eagled against the window like a perp at a housing project.

"Excellent," he assures me.

There is a three-story banner outside the window on the old Times building across the street, where the ball drops on New Year's. On the banner is a model selling something.

"I want to be there, like her," I tell him.

"What do you mean?" he asks.

"IT. I want to be IT. By the end of this week I want to be up there."

"Good luck," he snorts.

"Okay, can I be in your magazine, at least?"

"We could try," he says rather unconvincingly.

A tall, nice-looking woman takes some Polaroids of my mug. I look like a bloated sailor on shore leave who has been found in an alley and can't remember his name.

Not looking good for me. Thinking quickly, I make a date with Foxman for a drink. Sometimes, to make it in a man's world, you have to sell your dignity.

Men's fashion is now a $10 billion industry in the United States. Men's skin products (makeup and creams) add perhaps another $60 million to the economy. Even venerable Avon now carries a men's line. Men's plastic surgeries multiplied threefold from 1997 to 2003, to more than eight hundred thousand procedures, according to the American Society for Aesthetic Plastic Surgery.

One uptown plastic surgeon on Fifth Avenue told me that the number of men coming in for elective surgery doubled in the last five years.

Why? I asked him.

The media is telling him he doesn't measure up, the doctor says. "It's not just the rich Park Avenue guy. It's cops and everyone else. I had a bus driver come in here and request liposuction. He says he feels self-conscious, that he thinks the women on the bus are staring at his love handles."

It seems that guys are getting in touch with the girlish alter ego that lurks underneath the mustache of every man. The term for this new breed is *metrosexual,* coined in the mid-nineties by a writer named Mark Simpson, who read the writing on the wall. The way he saw it, if a man didn't go shopping, stand at a makeup counter, rub gels into his wrists and daub wrinkle remover on his crow's-feet, then the consumer machine was going to convince him he should—that he *should* go shopping, that he *should* be more sensitive about his grooming, his nails, his genitalia. The machine would make magazines for him, tell him to be more sensitive and worry about his appearance. In short, it told him Budweiser bad, Pinot Grigio good. History may not remember his name, but give Simpson credit, he was the first guy to see it.

And to see it is to believe it. This is where the modeling comes in.

I go with my camera and fuzzy microphone to Click Models. The agency is on the penthouse floor of a building in the garment district. It is a large, busy, open-air office. There are a couple other guys waiting around looking ridiculously fit and thin and waifish, but with muscles and Adam's apples and nice hair.

People walk by without so much as glancing at me. I'm feeling self-conscious about the whole thing. After a while, a short, curly-haired woman walks over and asks for Charlie. I'm Charlie, I say. She says she is Stephanie Grill, head of the Men's Division and daughter of Click's founder, Francine Grill. Francine made her name in the seventies simply by finding talent with off-angular faces and dark-colored skin. Such an outrageous idea.

Stephanie sits far away from me, across a big table near the reception desk. She says I'm an attractive enough guy and have good bone structure, but it's a look more fit for the bars that the fashion pages. I'm not quite old enough to fit into the older male modeling category and not young enough to fit into the mainstream Abercrombie category. There's not a lot of work for guys like me who fall in between. I'm not quite tall enough or built enough. My hair and skin need work. My clothes are atrocious. I like her, she says it nicely and with a smile. She makes it seem a virtue to look like crap.

She tells me she'll give me a shot, though. You know, the movie camera and fuzzy microphone open doors. She tells me she's got a model apartment someplace on the west side of Manhattan, if I need a place to stay.

She scolds me gently, telling me I'll have to put an end to my carousing and spend less time reading and more time in the gym. A guy named Paolo takes me to the roof and again I stand for Polaroids, but this time I've got to take off my shirt. Looking at the Polaroids, I realize it's true what I've suspected for weeks now. I'm dying.

Here's what I learn, from Stephanie. The guy between thirty and forty is being sold a bag of shit. The industry wants me to believe I'm less. So they give me pictures of younger guys and tell me I've got to look like that. If I just wear what he wears, all my dreams will come true.

There is a second swindle concerning the male model. The thirty-five to forty-five-year-old model with the salt-and-pepper hair. He looks mature, like he's got stuff going on. So think about it: they're selling older guys a younger older guy, thereby convincing the older guys, who by now should be beyond the hang-ups of wanting to be hipper and more youthful, that they should be hipper and more youthful like this younger older guy.

It's working. The jobs are there. One-third of Click's models are men. And the more salt-and-pepper, the more bread. Still, modeling is like pornography and prostitution. They are the only industries where men earn less than women.

"The whole thing makes me sick, but that's the business," Stephanie tells me. "If you want a shot at it, then go get cleaned up."

I get a haircut, a shave, facial, manicure, shoe shine, and two beers and a scotch at a men's salon in midtown, a new phenomenon, I'm told, a chance for the man to pamper himself and get his nails clear-coated. The place has black sinks, many fine women laughing at stupid advances, a wooden bar, two private rooms and a shoe-shine stand. The funny thing here is that they do everything the old barbershops used to do except give you an actual shave. It has to do with arcane New York City barber licensure rules. It's ridiculous that I'm standing in the men's shitter with a disposable razor and a thick beard shaving myself in a male beauty salon.

The good masculine moment comes when the facialist closes the door. She's a younger woman with a nice pumpkin rump. And when the door closes, it's like a psychiatry appointment in reverse.

She's telling me men are confused. It's nice to have fine skin, but look at these suits outside the door in the salon. They're desperate: balding, overweight, their necks spilling out of their collars.

"Men finally begin to suffer," she says. "They don't know what to be. You know that old thing about putting yourself second. Family first. The clothes don't make the man. That's disappeared. They're self-absorbed now, like women, tricked like women. Women don't know what to be and they're taught that from the time they're born. Be beautiful or smart or whatever. Squeeze into these shoes. Once you get old, you're thrown away. Women don't know if they should have children or a career. It's like your youth gets wasted worrying. You don't even know if you should commit to a man, if he'll throw you away. And now it's the guys' turn to worry."

She is married, she says. "I don't know if monogamy is possible. I think it's a leftover anyway."

The point here, gentlemen, is your wives are cheating on you with smooth, nicely scented men. In the spirit of this, I get my chest waxed by a Romanian woman with good tits. She's got a shop on Fifth Avenue across from Central Park. I scream so loudly she ends the session prematurely because I'm scaring the customers. The wax leaves my torso looking like a plucked chicken. It's as itchy as wet wool on testicles.

I need a wardrobe to go on casting calls and I arrange to go shopping with Michael Flocker, who wrote the bestseller *The Metrosexual Guide to Style*, a handbook for the modern urbanite. The book is tripe, but it has sold so many copies that even the great fashion magazines like that from *The New York Times* have had to recognize it. I meet Flocker in front of Saks. He's wearing a noticeable and badly applied base. Makeup, I call it. Rouge, he calls it. His breath is terrible, something like canned sardines.

Michael, I ask, pointing out his bald spot and poorly polished shoes, how would you know anything? You probably live in a crap apartment in Manhattan, you probably have no lover or prospective lover and you wrote that ordering a Harvey Wallbanger makes you look like a dildo to women. How would you know what women want?

"I understand generally what taste is," he says. "Besides, I have female friends, and you do, of course, have to take it with a grain of salt."

Men's fashion and vanity are as old as humanity, says Flocker. And consider that Native American men put bear grease in their hair and adorned themselves with antlers and animal hides, quills and shells. The Bushman of Africa might wear a bone through his nose or rings about his neck. Louis the XIV wore ruffled linen and powdered wigs and makeup and thought himself so beautiful and interesting that he invited people to watch him pass the Royal Stool. Shakespeare wore tights and a high collar and a silly little beard.

The difference, of course, is that stuff wasn't passed down by way of mass consumerism, details designed to drive you crazy and shift the very next season. What we're experiencing is the nature of a mature and decadent society in which people don't worry about how they will eat, Flocker says. If you don't have to work with your hands, you might as well paint them.

The guy is brilliant, but it's got to be more succinct for television. With the camera rolling, I say, "Michael, here's what I want you to say: say for me that the American man is confused."

He says, in a nice, concise sound bite, that men in this country are searching for identity through manicured nails and hair product.

"That's fine," I say. "But we might have to edit this. So what I want you to say for me is that American men are *not* confused."

Understanding, he gives me another sound bite about how men in this country are not confused, how male fashion and grooming habits are no different from the time when our grandfathers went to the barbershop for nail filing and hair tonic.

"Cut," I say, as the camera keeps rolling. "That's great, but it might not work. Here's what I want you to say. Say for me that we *don't know* if the American man is confused."

He gives a nice rundown, saying it's unclear what is going on with the American man, that we aren't sure if he is wallowing in the depths of self-loathing or if he's sprouted gossamer wings and is flying off to fairyland in a suit cut to an hourglass figure.

It's a swindle. People will say anything to sell themselves.

As I leave with a black suede overshirt (Polo, $500), a black under-shirt of linen and Spandex (Michael Kors, $200), and white slacks (Polo—at $60, a real steal!), he turns and says, "Thank you so much. Please just don't cut me out of the film, okay?"

You betcha.

Behind the pretty pictures in the fashion quarterlies is a world of ratty carpets. Rob Klein is an old photographer who will take my head shots for free. His teeth are an aging wooden fence, he wears a beret covered in white cat hair and ovular John Lennon–style glasses, and when he peers over them he looks like a raccoon in a trash can. He is neither impressive nor unimpressive in nearly every way and has a vo-cabulary peppered with language from the seventies, predisposed to little gems like "Hey, babe," and "Groovy." He is an anachronism in a world where the old are discarded because they are a sickly little re-minder of where we all go, if we're lucky—to the land of irrelevance and decay in a shabby apartment covered in cat hair.

Now he takes head shots of wannabe models. For instance, when Corn Pone Carl gets off the bus from Iowa, Klein's partner, J.T., a dwarfish man with a rapid-fire pitch, is there with a card promising to help the boy reach the spires of Times Square with his beauty.

J.T. refers these marks to Rob, who takes head shots of them, for a charge.

Klein says he wears the beret to bed, never wanting to be reminded of his baldness. After we take some bad photographs of me scowling and uptight, we go to his joint uptown, with his fat cat. He is shooting pictures of a former nude model who's had eleven plastic surgeries. She likes the fact that we've got a camera and Klein's got her walking around with her top off. A former boyfriend smashed her face—this was the reason for surgery number one, Klein tells me.

His apartment is filthy, and the overflowing cat box in the bathroom could use cleaning. He sleeps on the couch. The woman pretends not to notice it.

"Getting old," Klein says. "Kids, you try to tell them, but I don't know if they hear you. They get bored real fast. Smart-aleck kids. I'm old, but you'd be lucky to be where I am, I tell them.

"The male model, he sees an image and he has no clue what it is. 'I'm a glamorous male model,' he thinks. But what he doesn't know is how many fashion designers are gonna feel him up. What kind of humiliation he's going to go through. You know how much rejection you get?

"You're a party boy until you're not a boy anymore, and then what? It hits you real hard. One day you look in the mirror and nobody else is looking at you anymore. Youth culture is very unforgiving. You're old one day and they don't want you around.

"So, I don't care. They snicker about the beret, so what? I can run faster than any of these kids. I don't like my hair because it's thinning. I tried a beard, but people told me I was too Jewish-looking and it started getting gray. So I tried different hats and this worked. It's my image. I like the look, I like the idea and I never take it off. Never.

"I don't want to admit being old. The fact of the matter is I'm like Warhol. I got a Warhol scene going here. I'm doing interesting things. I have people in and out. A mini-factory—models and actors and filmmakers. I encourage creativity around me. I could be a nut, but I feed off the energy of the younger people."

Klein sounds bitter. And he's right. The woman with the plastic face and silicone tits slips her shirt on and disappears.

I get back to Click to find the address of the model apartment. Joey Grill, Stephanie's brother, is the idea man at the agency. He bought a flophouse on the Bowery. The plan was to convert the chicken-coop bedrooms there into hovels for models—five feet by six feet. He bought the building but couldn't get the bums out of the building because of city law. In the end, it worked to his advantage. As it turns out, the city pays him fifty bucks a night to house the homeless and models only pay $200 a week.

"I'm making way more money," he crows. "I'm down to thirteen bums. But it's still more profitable. It turns out the bums take care of their places better than a bunch of lustful males who treat my property like a frat house."

I notice my Polaroids are stuffed behind a wheel of Scotch tape.

I go to the model apartment. I knock, a good-looking guy answers, we open a beer and watch TV. This place too is filthy. He tells me it's weird to come from some farm area, as nearly all the boys do, and then you're in New York and some fag is telling you to take your shirt off. And you used to play football and milk cows and beat up on faggy kids at high school beer parties and here you are worried about your hair and stomach muscles and hair on your chest. And standing in front of a fag half naked makes you start thinking maybe you're a fag, and that's what they're thinking back in the Dairy State: you're a fag. But they're also secretly wanting to be you because they're the assistant manager of some storage cage or some such.

There are posters tacked to the apartment's wall. By far the favorite among the young men is that of Paris Hilton. Girl of the year, trendsetter, liver of life, the latest media creation in a hundred years of media creations. She is old money, but the twist on her is her delicious low class. Her affinity for showing her beaver around town and her prowess at fellatio. The IT girl does nothing but be IT; being seen is her job, life as pop art. Youth. Women dress like girls because a woman can't act her age anymore. She's got to compete. Not only do women need men, they need to be needed by men. The only problem is that men want younger women. And so the woman ages and makes a spectacle of herself in her tight skirts and pumps. Oh Paris, baby.

Among the models here is B. Cherry, a blond, good-looking, solidly built Texan who preaches confidence and good diet. His hair is combed forward from the crown, which he reflexively primps in any shiny surface that catches his eye, whether it be a chromium fixture, a window or a windshield. I can't help but think he's going to make it.

Randall is from Alabama. He got his break because his mama pestered and phoned the agency until they took him. He is a lithe and soft-spoken boy with a Southern lilt in his voice and a Ringo Starr hairdo. He is modest and talks about how he voted for Bush because Bush is consistent and shares his values. I wonder if Bush would dream of making a living by taking off his shirt for a homosexual.

Tim is waking up from a drunk. He is blond, six-foot-three, independent and uncommitted. He hates taking his shirt off for homos and sleeping on a filthy mattress at two hundred bills a week along with the cockroaches. There is a bright side. He's in New York to drink free liquor and screw some rich guys' daughters. If he gets work, great. If not, his dad is rich.

I rent the movie *Zoolander* and bring it to the apartment to watch with the guys, it's a spoof on the life and times of the male model. They watch with rapt attention, there being a noticeable lack of books in the apartment.

"*Zoolander* is like the total opposite of what the guy models are like, but the way they portray the industry, like the people that run it, man, is very accurate. Very accurate," a model says. "They portray all the models like, let's go have a gasoline fight, orange mocha frappuccino, or whatever the fuck they are.

"The dudes are from all different parts of the country and we just chill, go out and party and have a good time and stuff like that, but the people that run the business are the shaky ones."

"What do you mean?" I ask.

"Well, this industry that we're in is run by gay men and a couple old ladies. A few women here and there, but it's all gay men."

"And a few old ladies?"

"Yeah, and every casting, you got to go in and strip down to your underwear and turn around and they take Polaroids of you and the whole time they're eyeing you up like, 'Mmmmmm' [makes a fey gesture, puts a finger to his lips and mimics someone looking up and down], and that was the hardest thing to get used to, man. But it takes time."

"So you got used it?"

"You either get used to it or you get the fuck out of it. Some people can do it."

"Where you from?"

"Newcastle, Pennsylvania. That's, like, more cows than people. It really is. I grew up showing steers in 4H and shit. Can you imagine going from that to New York City and bars? Total culture change. I'm dealing with it. I got to go back every couple of months to get my mind back on a normal track.

"I went to college for two years, got bored with that, decided fuck it. Came here. Now I'm here and riding it as long as I can, you know? If I'm done within a month, so be it, but if I can ride it for ten years, then I'm all about it."

We get wasted that night on vodka and orange drink. Pretty boys. They're a dime a dozen. There are no open beds in the apartment, so I sleep in the filthy bathtub. I notice condom wrappers and Q-Tips behind the toilet. Inside the hall closet there is a ledger of women's names scribbled on the door. A list of all the females they've shagged this one memorable summer. Number 34 was a woman in her mid-thirties. They called her "Grandma."

I lived a good seven years in New York when I was writing about the city. And it's odd to me that after the three years since I've lived here, the city should feel so soft and effete. When I left the city, the dust of the World Trade Center still hung in the air, on windowsills, in the cracks of stoops. The attitude then was animal. Drink heavy. Whiskers and firemen and even cops were the ideal man. There were long lines at the uniform store just down the block. It was a kiss-a-sailor sort of atmosphere. Now the place is soft with men walking around in suits with overstuffed shoulders and pink ties and painted nails. There is plenty of money around, and money makes men bold. Self-satisfied, self-centered and self-important. New York, I realize, has gone European.

"Shoot me, shoot me," says a portly man in a salmon shirt and Polo sunglasses with both hands occupied with shopping bags. He says this to the camera we have propped on a tripod on Broadway and I'm remembering a time in this city when if a guy yelled something like that, you couldn't be sure if someone wasn't going to drill him.

The boys from the apartment show up in white T's and blue jeans and cheap cool sunglasses. The job is for a relatively new line of suits designed for guys my age who want to appear as though they spend idle afternoons sipping Pernod in the palazzo around the Spanish Steps.

I don't get the job. I'm told I'm not right for them. Too old, which is laughable because I'm exactly the man they want to buy their clothes. I'm just not the kind of guy they want to *sell* their clothes. A Swedish guy from the apartment gets the job.

All the casting calls I go to are the same. I'm told I'm too old; you're not the type we're looking for; we'll call you back; handsome but . . . nothing. No IT BOY. And I've got a camera following me.

The project is bust until Rob Klein calls to say he has gotten me into a show. A pretty low-level show. On the bright side, I will be modeling a rubber suit created by the Baroness, perhaps the world's greatest designer in fetish latex wear.

It's being held at the Show on Forty-first Street, a half block from Bryant Park, which used to be a pauper's field but is now the center of Fashion Week.

Rob Klein appears hours before the show in his cat-infested beret, which slopes like a banana over one ear, giving off the look of a chocolate and coconut soufflé gone wrong. He wears a knotted cravat. He is producing this show.

Preshow warm-ups: There is a flapper girl singing in a flat voice. Klein is telling a white boy freak in dreadlocks and baubles that he's looking absolutely terrific. Klein tells a young black guy that he's gonna be a star; he says the same to a woman in a sparkling bra. She will be hosting the show, Klein tells me.

He tells me he wants me to model three different lines, but I refuse, not being enthused about the clothes. I will only wear the rubber suit and I want to come out at the end of the show. The crescendo. The IT BOY.

Klein is flipping out. "Look, babe," he says in his antique vocabulary. "You wear something else besides or it's done, dig?"

Backstage in the dressing room there is a flock of nubile young women of every stripe: straight, lesbo, white, black, yellow, cocoa. They all say they like a personality in a man, which is deceit. They like a man with a wallet. Money makes a boring man interesting, ugly men darlings, poor men rich. The dressing room is a freak zone of low-level design, all about aspiration and middling chances, marijuana and cheap warm champagne.

"If I lose ten pounds, then they say I can be in *Playboy*," says a sweet little grape who goes by the stage name April May. Lovely. Lovely. Tasty. Tasty.

She says she has an appointment in Los Angeles in two weeks, which is doubtful if she is a J.T. client. If she could just stop eating the McDonald's, she says. "I'm just a slave to McDonald's."

She has dimples on her ass and little blondish puppy hair, accentuated by a sunbed tan. A photographer friend of mine is trying to convince her to let him take shots of her stripping down in the toilet, trying to convince her that his only motivation is art. There is the cheap champagne going around and a smidgen of cocaine and the Baroness, the great diva of rubber who wears giant orange hair framed with white striping, is saying stuff to me like, "Darling, if you don't feel fabulous, you can't look fabulous," and "Beauty and fashion are as cutthroat and mean as a bike gang."

I've had to oil up to squeeze into my rubber pants and now I'm bubbling. Rubber pants, rubber top, purple rubber coat with the high collar, a codpiece stuffed in my pants constructed from two pairs of Ms. May's silk stockings, slashes of eye makeup and black polish on all twenty nails. I'm getting drunk on the smoke and warm champagne and the emcee is fucking everything up down there. She's forgetting the designers' names, bumping into the models as they careen down the runway because she forgets it's not about her. Everything is slightly off.

"Come on, everybody, it's sexeeeee," the emcee shouts with her arms in the air. "Come on, get crazeeee!!!" The place is a morgue, a meat locker, filled with Michael Flocker and strange acquaintances of the producer.

Finally, my name is called. I pull back the curtain at the top of the stairs and descend barefoot and rubber-clad, as debonair as Astaire himself in my mind's eye.

They're clapping! Roaring! Roaring. Laughter! Laughter? Yes. They're laughing at me. Like the *Carrie* movie. They're all laughing at me. Over his camera lens, I see the photographer who was trying to make April May in the toilet, he's laughing. Flocker's laughing. I've sold myself. Confidence, now, don't lose control, steady . . . focus on the focal point, chin out. I've done the sit-ups and push-ups, manicure, haircut, chest wax. I've slept in a bathtub, for God's sake. And they're LAUGHING! Teeeeeee-heeeeee.

And then as I stop on the end of the runway before I make my pirouette, I see that they are happy. The boredom of bad clothes and the emcee and the scene. Trying to look like something they're not and not quite making it. Everybody feels insecure, but get a load of this guy in the S&M suit! *No,* sir, these are laughs of happiness, a nod to theater and haughtiness. No, they love me. I'm stupid. Yes! It is laughter of love!

I stand there with a snarl, my hands on my hips, revealing my great pumpkin of a codpiece. I am fabulous. Decadent. I am the IT Boy in this bizarre little corner for a fleeting bizarre little New York minute. I have broken through. Made the scene, man, crossed over from the metrosexual into ZIGGY STARDUST! I am Jim Dandy Candy!

The Baroness is announced and she trips the light fantastic. She is mesmerized by the adulation, lapping it up like a cat at the saucer. She will not leave the lights. She takes a series of ornate bows with the attendant hand gestures, her breast becoming unmoored, I'm worried, from her pink rubber bustier.

And I'm thinking, Fucking hell, come on. I've got to shit, the rubber is tenderizing my intestines and the champagne has gone to my ass. As we exit the stage and return upstairs to the changing room, the low-level showbiz press wants my photo. J.T. wants to represent me. I tell him, "Let's do lunch." And this seems to satisfy him. A few girls want to meet me and my camera in L.A. Rubbing on me like mewing kittens now, they've figured out I'm the most convenient ticket out this evening. A designer invites me to some swell party. I don't go. I remember that Narcissus drowned while falling in love with his reflection. I make it to the toilet just in time.

The next morning I sleep late, pack and get on a plane. A large guy, some cowboy sitting next to me in Bermuda shorts with a forest fire of red hair covering his legs, asks me in a thick country accent, "Sir, how did your nails get black?"

It was too hard to explain. I told him I was a house painter.

Cleveland, Tennessee

Jesus says if he strikes you, offer up the other cheek. Now He
didn't say what to do after that.

—JUNIOR MCCORMICK

The church, I was told, was about an hour south of Chattanooga. But once I made the turn off the highway, I found myself driving through swamps and cotton fields and I was utterly lost in the sameness. It was growing dark. Eventually I came upon a shallow river and then a hairpin turn in the country road. On the other side of the road was a shack, a mechanic's garage. Against it leaned a withered, stringy fellow chewing tobacco. "Church of the Lord Jesus?" I shouted from the car.

Two eyes peered out from under his ball cap. Thaddaway, he said, without saying anything, throwing his chin toward sunset.

I went thaddaway. About two miles down the road on top of a hill stood the church. I drove past it, trying to collect myself. I was anxious, I admit that. This was Deep South and these people, from what I'd been told, didn't mind dying.

They were a sect of Christians who drank strychnine and handled poisonous serpents because they believed that's what God told them they could do. And if you believe the literal truth of the Bible, then that's what He did tell them they could do:

> *And these signs shall follow them that believe; In my name shall they cast out devils; they shall speak with new tongues; they shall take up serpents; and if they drink any deadly thing, it shall not hurt them; they shall lay hands on the sick and they shall recover.*
>
> MARK 16:17–18

But sometimes it doesn't work the way the Lord promised. A half dozen years ago, John Wayne "Punkin" Brown, Jr., died while handling a four-foot rattlesnake during a sermon at Sand Mountain, Alabama, not eighty miles from here. He preached on for fifteen minutes before he died in front of his flock, who had tried to cool him down with an electric fan. As it happened, Punkin's wife had died of a serpent bite three years earlier. They left five young orphans.

"It's the will of the Almighty," Brother Junior McCormick had told me over the phone. Brother Junior was a friend of Punkin's and a pastor of the church I was idling in front of now. Most of the serpent handlers in Appalachia are friends. A lot of them, I would come to find out, are related.

For instance, the pastor of the church where Punkin died had a cousin, Brother Glenn Summerford, who was convicted in 1992 for trying to murder his wife by shoving her hand in a box of rattlesnakes he kept in his backyard because he thought she was cheating on him. God must have been standing near, because though she was bitten twice, she didn't die. Brother Glenn went away for ninety-nine years.

These are serious people. I figured probably not the kind who take well to a Northern Catholic, even if he comes wanting to know Jesus.

That is the terror of being a reporter. You are always in someplace you are not supposed to be, asking questions that no decent person would, things that would make your mother ashamed. Imagine standing in the doorway of an apartment in a Brooklyn housing project on New Year's Day, asking a woman how she felt now that her son was the first homicide victim of the year. Or asking an inebriated hobo the last time he had enjoyed the company of a woman; or asking a black football player if he thought whites were genetically more intelligent; or a candidate for governor if he really did admire Adolf Hitler; or an Iraqi holy man how it was, exactly, that he escaped the torture chambers of Saddam Hussein when many of his colleagues vanished. The enterprise of reporting is frightening, but then again, it is this shard of terror that makes it exhilarating. This is one reason why so many correspondents chase war. That, and ambition.

As for the subject, no matter how much he feigns disinterest or disregard for the reporter, he feeds on the attention, like a dog on a chop. This is the magnetic repulsion that exists between the observer and the specimen. I was counting on it as I pulled up the gravel driveway to the top of the hill.

There, an old stiff-hipped man dressed in black was sitting in a sedan next to a severe-looking woman with a bun of hair pinned to her head. In the back sat a toothless man chewing on his gums and a boy about nine years old, obese and bald, with an alarming disinterest in his eyes. This was Brother Junior and his clan.

Junior McCormick is not a well-educated man. His percentages and philosophies are culled from a single source, the Bible. There is nothing contrary or coal-eyed about him. He smells of Old Spice cologne. Brother Junior is the type of Southern man Northerners thought they had long ago dominated, assimilated, nearly extinguished. But here he was, and I was staring at him standing on top of a hill in rural northern

Georgia as he lifted a box with gold writing on it that read "Mark 16." I could hear the rattlesnake writhing inside.

He excused himself to put his Bible and box inside the church, and while I waited for him, the young boy stared over and never once moved his eyes away. I was relieved when Brother Junior came back outside to talk.

We were outside his small stone Church of Jesus Christ, he looking past the small cemetery at the foot of the hill onto a valley of short greens and pecan trees. Looking at him, he appeared a simple man, late sixties, white hair and white goatee, dressed in Wal-Mart black and inexpensive shoes, a sort of impoverished version of Burl Ives. He had rheumy, deep-set blue eyes. His handshake was weak, and when I took his hand I noticed the middle finger was withered. I asked about it. It seems Brother Junior was bitten on that finger some time ago and it had died away. In fact, he'd been stung by poisonous serpents on more than a dozen occasions since he took up the practice three decades ago.

"Generally I didn't worry too much about it," he told me matter-of-factly. "I didn't go to no doctor. Only the first time I got bit did I go to a doctor. Most of the times I been bit by cottonmouths. Now, that's a very, very painful thing.

"A lot of time, I just wasn't anointed," he continued. "Once you get the Ghost, the ability is always there. Now, if you don't listen to Him . . . well . . . I can move too quick. Now, I might get ahead of the Spirit, and then I'm in trouble."

All this talk about movin' and anointin' and gettin' the Ghost spooks a lot of folks. And the serpent handlers aren't the only ones who talk this way. The South is packed to the barrel lip with charismatic Christians—Pentecostals, Baptists, Methodists, Nazarenes and countless other fundamentalist sects and denominations—speaking in tongues, shouting fire and brimstone, claiming miracles and singing and weeping and carrying on as if Jesus Himself were waiting just outside the church door to announce His Second Coming.

"Oh, people thinks we're crazy, but that's all right," Junior told me. "I'm not trying to impress people, just trying to impress the word of God on 'em's all. That's what He commands us to do."

And the word of these Christians is spreading—to Africa and Asia and South America, from the Grand Concourse in the Bronx to Melrose Avenue in Los Angeles. People are leaving Catholicism and mainline Protestant churches, seeking a more personal and electric relationship with God. They want more than the idea of God; they want to *feel* God. And they've found what they're seeking in this Southern-bred Christianity. Now it's being said that Brother Junior and his fellow "conservative" evangelical Christians are slowly, inexorably casting their religious shadow over the political and cultural landscape of America.

But here in this gravel parking lot, Brother Junior seemed so modest, so simple, I doubted he could take over his brother's car payments, much less the world.

Still, I knew that here I was on foreign soil.

I had been told by a local minister near Grasshopper Valley in Tennessee, where snake-handling is thought to have begun, that two hillbillies had shot up a trailer because a woman from New York had recently moved in with her children. When asked why they had shot the trailer up, the hillbillies said it was because she was Catholic.

The minister asked if they knew what a Catholic was. The hillbillies admitted they didn't know what a Catholic was except to say that they knew a Catholic weren't no good.

But Junior wasn't like that at all. He was quite welcoming, actually.

"I don't mind y'all being here," he said. "God says we got to be brothers."

Brother Junior and his people are hill stock, descendants of the Scots-Irish who have inhabited these Appalachian hills and hollows for more than two centuries. It was these people, these insular mountain dwellers, who birthed snake-handling and other variants of strict Holiness Christianity when they came down from the hills at the turn of the century and ran into an industrial culture they viewed as corrupt and hostile toward them. And so they threw up a wall. Jesus. Like every persecuted group in the world, they turned to orthodoxy, fervor, self-righteousness. To assimilate meant cultural annihilation. It meant you disappeared, you went extinct. So they prayed. And in that spirit, the Appalachian region took on a cloak of religiosity. It's been said that there are so few atheists in Appalachia because Appalachians *need* God.

Today, they watch as city slickers come in and buy up the farms and put up their fences, the representatives of a cosmopolitan Northern culture that has for years portrayed the Southerner in its films and books and television programs as ignorant, lazy. This can make a man resentful, but Brother Junior told me he was not interested in pop culture or in the things of Caesar.

"I'm jus a poor ol' country boy," he said. "Don't come from much and don't have much. I got a little biddy ole trailer out in the country and I'm satisfied with that, I s'pose. God promised me a reward in heaven and that's where I'm spending my mind to concentratin'. A man can get his mind mixed up worrying about what he don't have. He stops seeing what it is exactly that he does have."

McCormick's people are a landless class with weak jaws and hard eyes and sloped postures that make them look as though they were set out to drip-dry on a hook. They are against dancing and smoking and drinking. They frown upon proud and fancy forms of dress, earrings, makeup and short hair on women, and women in the pulpit altogether. Their ancestors brewed moonshine and butchered hogs and worked the coal mines.

Brother Junior was retired now, having gotten by on odd jobs: the chicken house, rubber plant, cotton mill. "Everything a country boy does to get by," he told me.

He excused himself as the guitars started to twang inside the church. The service was about to begin. I stayed outside to have myself a cigarette behind a car. It was a beautiful summer evening. The cicadas screaming, falling half dead from the trees, their legs twitching like pin-wheels. I squashed my cigarette underneath my boot and listened.

"I was lost but now I'm found, brothers and sisters! I know where I live. Some call it home. I call it heaven!"

Amen!

"The spirit of God is in you if you been borned again, hallelujah!"

Amen!

"Can I get a witness?"

Amen, Brother Junior.

"Hallelujah!"

Yes, hallelujah! Yes, Sweet Jesus!

"I used to get drunk in the bars. When I was out there, the devil had me all messed up. I used to get drunk at the bars and I'd wake up with my eyes shut and before I'd opened them, I'd reach over ma head and I'd feel for them jailhouse bars. Oh, Lawd, I was in a bad place, fighting and drinking and cattin' 'round. I used to drink in the bars and now I drink in Jesus' bar. Now I drink the Holy Ghost, now I get all worked up for Jesus! I got pardoned by Jesus!"

Glory!

"No, I don't care if they put me down. I go with the name of Jesus! BabaShlalalalabee!"

I sat near the front pew in case any of the others happened to get the anointing by the Holy Ghost and might feel the urge to drink from the bottle of strychnine or put a torch to their hand or take that big rattlesnake out of its box and do a jig.

Down here in the Georgia foothills they believe the Bible hard. Literally. And sitting here was like being in a storefront church a hundred years ago.

I sat near a window with blood-red curtains. Behind me, the Holy Spirit had manifested itself, come down to earth into this little chapel with the purple wainscoting and shaggy carpet, a place so humble, I felt that if I leaned against the wall the place would slide down the hill until it snagged itself on the tombstones below.

The piano was off tune, the woman playing the steely guitar croaked like a swamp frog, the tambourines and harmonica, the Appalachian voices, the tinny quality of the microphones made my hair stand on my neck, and I liked it. You *could* feel God here. The dozen or so people sang: *Some call it heaven, Whoa, I call it home.* The praising and singing and calling for blood, it sounded as though people were having needles shoved in the soles of their feet. A woman with an angular, sunken, poverty-stricken face, the kind you find in Dorothea Lange photographs, was standing in the pew behind me, consumed by the Holy Ghost, babbling in tongues. A one-word language.

Lalalalalalalalalalalalalalalalalalala!

Brother Junior took up the serpent from the wooden box, properly anointed as he was now in the Holy Ghost. He danced a jig and spoke in tongues. I turned toward the back and his fat little grandson had gone wide-eyed. His gum fell out of his mouth and stuck to his chest. After a few minutes of this, Brother Junior gingerly placed the serpent back in the box and closed the lid with his foot.

Now Brother McCormick and his two heavyset cousins, all three preachers and all three the sons and grandsons of serpent-handling preachers, anointed the congregation with oil, applying it on our foreheads the way priests do with palm dust on Ash Wednesday. It was vegetable oil. Crisco. Simple people. People so white, they looked like they were powdered. The grandson of McCormick came to the altar only because his grandmother pulled him forward. He was overweight, maybe 140 pounds, a shaved head the color of ivory. The boy looked like a cherub and an inmate with his deep eyes and black clothes and round white face. He looked scared and his gum fell out of his mouth again, but this time he did not move to retrieve it, his eyes did not waver, he stumbled toward the altar. The worshippers laid their hands on him, praying for the healing, the touch of God. The boy flinched like the devil had poked him with a prod. He returned to his pew, but not before bending over and putting the gum back in his mouth.

After the service, we drank soda pop and ate store-bought cake. We gave each other the "holy kiss" as commanded in Romans 16:16, and I wasn't frightened anymore. It was a pleasant evening. Among us was a woman with a sunken mouth. Another with hair to her knees. A man with a solitary tooth, the band members, the preachers, the children. Miss Lilly, Brother Junior's wife, asked me about Catholicism.

"Do y'all worship Mary?"

No theologian, I did the best I could. Do we worship Mary? Or do we pay homage to the mother of Christ? I couldn't be sure, I told her. It seems like some worship Mary. This is a sin, I know. Idolatry. What could I say?

"What about Purgatory? What's Purgatory?"

"It is supposed to be a temporary place of suffering below heaven for those who have not fully atoned for their sins." Beyond that, I said, I don't really know. The Church doesn't talk much about Purgatory, or Limbo, or Hell, for that matter. Cornered, I told a joke about altar boys with parts down the middle of their hair.

They laughed.

I told Sister Lilly that I don't truly understand the mysticism of my own religion, only my need to have a religion, a culture, something I can say I belong to. I want to believe the Jesus story. Lord knows I do. It just seems so far out.

"Yep, mm-hhmmm, darling. You jes' keep on trying. Jesus'll make His way into your heart. You jes' keep calling. He'll answer."

The men talked in the corner about snakes like some men talk about classic cars. Brother Junior showed me the jar of strychnine they keep in the lectern, just in case.

Then talk turned from rattlers to politics. Benny Phillips, big and jowly and gentle, said he voted Republican, for Bush, because he felt Bush could handle the war in Iraq better.

Brother Junior voted for John Kerry, a Democrat, because he was concerned about his Social Security and thought Bush was a prodigal son incapable of leading the country. Brother Junior was a vestige, a white churchgoing Southern Democrat. Most of his friends had left the Democrats long ago when the Democrats started pushing the blacks on them. The Southern white man abandoned the Democrats and now the white Evangelical is the base of the Republican Party. They view the Democratic Party as lesbians, colored people, atheists and college professors. The Democrats offer them no caucus, no clubs, no pride in their heritage.

They are told to be ashamed of their peculiarities and their history. East Coast liberals have tried to take God off the money and out of the courthouse and out of the Pledge of Allegiance. Brother Junior might be a holdout, but not for long. The Democrats better find something that speaks to him.

"Cable television tells me all you guys vote Republican because all you think about is abortion and prayer in school," I said.

"Oh, no no no, not at all. I voted for Bush, I thought he could handle the war better," said Brother Thomas Harbuck, a package carrier and a man who clearly enjoyed his cake. "So I voted for him for the safety of our country."

Brother Benny said, "In fact, the abortion issue did not enter my mind. Because that is not a presidential thing, that is between a human being and his God."

Brother Junior stroked his mustache and nodded his head.

"You guys aren't dumb rednecks like they say?" I asked.

"Oh, no, we're good people," says Brother Thomas.

"But that's what they say. I live in L.A. I know what they say."

"Yes, sir, they do, but that's all right. We got families and we love our families and we believe strongly in our faith. We love the Lord and

I try and I pray and when I try to sing a song or to preach, I try to be a blessing to God's people."

The night had gone dark. The cicadas had gone silent. And as we filed out to the parking lot, Brother Junior invited me to his home. He told me he had hardly ever been out of Georgia, except to Tennessee, because he never needed to be. I told him I'd see him Tuesday.

As I drove back to my dump motel in Cleveland, Tennessee, I was thinking about those faces. A joke about hillbillies came to my mind and I wondered if it was possible for a man to be his own uncle. It is. Think about it. I laughed until I realized for the first time in my life that I am my own cousin by marriage since my parents are step-brother and sister.

When I got back to my hotel, I called my mother to inform her of this.

"Well," she said after a strained silence, "you ought to fit right in down there."

A lot of places claim to be the buckle of the Bible Belt, but the real heart of it must be southeastern Tennessee. The Pentecostal Holiness movement blossomed here in the early part of the twentieth century. It took root in Los Angeles but began on January 1, 1901, when a Kansas Methodist minister named Charles Parham witnessed one of his acolytes speaking in tongues for three days. Six years later, one of his students, a black man by the name of William Seymour, held a multi-racial revival on Azusa Street in Los Angeles. During those meetings, his interracial congregation became anointed with the Holy Spirit and began speaking in tongues and writhing on the sawdust floor. Nobody had ever seen such things. The revival made headlines, but the movement and its adherents were repudiated by good society as kooks, drunks and spittoon vomit. Despite the bad reviews, the seed of Pentecostalism blew back to the Tennessee hills and took root.

In the eyes of many, things got even kookier around 1909, when an illiterate bootlegger named George Hensley began preaching at the Church of God near the town of Cleveland, Tennessee. Hensley was said to be preaching the Gospel of Mark when he took a large rattlesnake from a box and handled it for a spell, telling his congregation to do the same or be doomed to eternal hell. Word spread.

Hensley toured Appalachia and was run out of a string of towns. When he returned home from one particular journey, he discovered that his wife was screwing their neighbor. Hensley attacked the man with a knife and was sent to prison. Hensley did not have good luck with women. He was married and divorced four times.

By 1928, the practice of serpent-handling, never widespread among the majority of Pentecostals, was deemed blasphemous by the Church of God. Hensley was stripped of his ordination after one of his acolytes was bitten. It was conveniently decided that Hensley was a backslider. He moved to the coal region of Harlan, Kentucky, and kept up his ministry, but the tide had receded and the converts were fewer and fewer.

By the 1940s, however, serpent-handling experienced resurgence after some of Hensley's followers held a revival in Grasshopper Valley. The practice again flourished until a man died from a rattler bite and the state of Tennessee legally put an end to it in 1947. But Hensley and his believers never stopped, calling themselves the Church of the Signs Following. Hensley himself was said to have been struck over four hundred times before absorbing the fatal bite in 1955.

Today, Brother Junior estimates there are a thousand, maybe a few thousand, serpent handlers in the hills today. Though the practice is illegal, the law generally looks the other way, seeing as it is a religious practice. Should a practitioner die, well, that is either natural selection or God's will. Perhaps a hundred people have died since Hensley began the art of it.

In nearby Dayton, forty miles from where Hensley held his first serpent, the famous Scopes Monkey Trial was conducted in 1925, pitting the forces of creationism against evolution. In that trial, John T. Scopes, a Dayton schoolteacher defended by Clarence Darrow, was convicted for teaching Darwin's theories in public school.

Chattanooga, twenty miles to the southwest of Cleveland, on the Georgia border, is said by the National Abortion Rights Action League to be the largest American city without an abortion clinic.

Southeastern Tennessee, there can be no argument, is the buckle of the Bible Belt.

In terms of Christianity, Cleveland is perhaps the most important place you've never heard of; the headquarters of several large Pentecostal churches, including the Church of God of Prophecy, with its three-quarters of a million members, and the Church of God, Cleveland, which claims seven million members worldwide. Pentecostalism and its derivative—charismatic Christianity—claim more than twenty million followers in the United States and five hundred million worldwide.

I didn't know this before I came. To me Cleveland was just another American strip-mall town, with the same fast-food restaurants catering to the same overweight people.

I had come to Cleveland to meet Brother Mike Ferree, a freelance Pentecostal minister who had a small church in town. Ferree was a Christian throwback, one of a handful of preachers still holding old-fashioned tent revivals. He traveled perhaps sixty thousand miles, three hundred days a year, in his Cadillac along the sawdust trail, ministering to anyone who would have him.

Ferree was tall with a sharp Adam's apple. He wore large glasses that made his wide mouth and large teeth appear wider and larger, like he could swallow you whole. He kept his clothes in the trunk and an electric razor in the glove box.

He took my hand and looked me up and down as we stood on his wooded property near his converted trailer.

I asked him what he thought of me on first appearance. What he told me he thought he saw was an East Coast liberal who lived in Hollywood and worked for decidedly the most left-wing newspaper in the country. "So why are you here?" he demanded.

I told him, "Because the country most surely looks at you like some kind of backwater hayseed, a man trying to lay his views on the country. They think men like you are out there trying to repeal abortion rights and force pregnant women to seek out some witch doctor who worked with a clothes hanger in the back of a butcher's shop. People think you want to return Jesus to the classroom and erase Darwin from history. And you want Adam and Steve to go back in the closet.

"Not *my* thoughts." I meant to assure him of my objectivity. "Just general conversations I picked up at work and the bar."

"I see."

I also told him that I was on a spiritual quest; that I was a Christian who struggled with the Christ story. That I had everything a man could want—money, prestige, a house, a good woman—and still I felt hollow. Even Christ doubted when he was on the cross at his moment: "Father, why hast thou forsaken me?" Christ doubted and He *was* God, I said.

Ferree's face twitched like a bug on a griddle. I had made my first cultural mistake. Above all, Appalachian culture requires humility and subtlety.

"I do this for the souls of God's children," he replied. "I could have had money. Probably millions of dollars. But I'm not about that. Jesus never intended for a preacher to live better than his flock. That's a sin. . . . But let's get something straight. I don't need you and you don't need me. So don't come barging in here like some kinda big shot. I'm in no need of that."

He was right, and our relationship was poison from then on. A certain disdain and distrust had polluted our first handshake.

Nevertheless, we drove to Knoxville together, where he was to tape a commercial on Christian radio to promote a tent revival he would be holding the next week up near the Virginia border.

During the car ride, Ferree told me his was an episodic conversion, not some long intellectual path to God, but rather a light shining through his depravity. He was a former heroin abuser who had once planned to murder his future wife and once, while high on the stuff, shot himself in the leg. He had been shot twice while dealing drugs, he said. One bullet was still lodged in his arm.

"It wasn't that I was hanging out with bad company, I *was* bad company," he told me about his younger years, the same well-practiced testimony he gave nearly every time I would hear him preach. "I was the one your mama told you to stay away from. I was a drug taker, I was a drug dealer. I started smoking pot when I was in the military, in San Diego, and just moved on, started tripping on LSD, snorting cocaine.

"So I was down in San Antonio, Texas, with a couple friends. I'd gone there to buy some marijuana in a deal. I was gonna bring it home to Indiana and sell it and all. And the deal went bad. It was my fault, I didn't use my head. We were in the car, and the guy was there in the backseat, and he shot all three of us. Shot me right through the back, shot another guy in the head, shot the other guy in the stomach. I still got lead in my right arm. Went right through my back and lodged in my arm. You can feel it. It's just a little old .25 automatic slug, but you can still feel it. That was in March of '74. And in January of '75 I got saved."

"Just like that?" I asked. "Where?"

"Out in California. It was part of that whole Jesus Movement of the late sixties, saving the hippies and all that. I got saved at a little church there on Sunset Boulevard. And then I came back to Indiana and started witnessing in jails, and I did that for about nine years. And then I met Brother H. Richard Hall at a meeting of his in Kentucky."

H. Richard Hall's memory looms large in these parts. A classic

Pentecostal tent revivalist from the North Carolina hills, Hall had the ability to discern and heal the physical and psychological pain deep within the human complexity. He was a known ascetic who cut his own hair, pulled his own teeth, slept in his car and rarely changed clothes. And during the sixties and seventies, he nurtured a generation of way-ward young Southern men like Ferree, men with wild spirits and wandering eyes, turning their hearts to God and passing along the tradition of itinerant evangelism that runs as deep here as the coal in the mines.

"Brother Hall was one of the most incredible men I've ever met in my life," said Ferree, who still seems to ruminate on his mentor's passing in 2002 at the age of eighty-one, as if it happened yesterday. Ferree gave his life to Hall's vision; Hall gave him a voice and a vocation, introduced him to the Reason.

"I joined up with him, traveling around everywhere with the tent," Ferree said, recalling those gypsy years on the sawdust circuit. "Used to take my family, with the kids, and travel in an old school bus, sleep in it. And I did that for well near twenty years."

Hall, for his part, was an acolyte of William Branham, a celebrated preacher from Appalachian Kentucky who was said to have started the faith-healing movement after he was visited by a two-hundred-pound angel in 1946 and given the gift of reading people's hearts and discerning their sicknesses with vibrations in his left hand.

The blind soon saw, the crippled walked. Whether it was supernatural intervention or the power of thought, people were miraculously healed and Branham's fame spread. Followers claimed they could see a halo around his head, and when he conducted healing services some said his left hand would transmogrify, turning red and swelling to twice its normal size. He filled five-thousand-seat tents and packed auditoriums in major cities. At a revival in Jonesboro, Arkansas, in 1947, he was said to have attracted more than twenty thousand people from twenty-five states and Mexico, and more than half a million during a revival trip to South Africa in 1951. Also a seer, Branham predicted that California would sink into the sea.

Branham was killed by a drunk driver in the Texas Panhandle in 1965. Some believed he was a prophet, some that he was Elijah himself, prophesied to precede the Second Coming of the Lord. It was four months before Branham's embalmed body was laid to rest, his followers having kept him aboveground in expectation of his imminent resurrection.

Though Hall apparently had an ability to augur illness, he did not inherit the divining hand of Branham. And while Branham drew tens of thousands, Hall drew thousands. And to that end, Brother Ferree, a modern preacher with no supernatural gift of divination, may draw a hundred people to his revivals.

"I think that a lot of city people look at the tent revival as kind of outdated, kind of an *Elmer Gantry* thing, from a bygone age," he said. "Truth is, the tent ministry still works and it still does a lot of good, especially with mountain people, poor people and unchurched people."

Ferree preached to the backbone of the country, the sinking middle class; people who worked or used to work, people who lived by the Ten Commandments, or tried to. People who used to work in toilet factories and now worked at McDonald's and would just as soon die as file for bankruptcy or cheat on their bills. Times were hard financially and spiritually around here and Ferree, whatever his lack of education, was a steadying influence. It was times like these that people wanted a healthy dose of faith, not a stinking pail of intellectualism.

"A lot of independent preachers haven't been schooled in no Bible college, they don't talk too good, they don't speak all that well in grammar. You can listen to me, and I don't talk too good. People are gonna come because they like *the preacher.* I preach it hard and straight, but not everybody likes that. Some people like blues, some people don't; some people like rock 'n' roll, some people don't. But if you're anointed, people will come to hear you. I tell you, I've had preachers come in Armani suits and they couldn't move nobody. And then I've had boys that crawl down out of the mountains in their dirty overalls and people just go to tears when they open their mouth."

I leaned in to him and asked, "Okay, people up here don't like intellectuals. But what if it isn't true? What happens if you get to the other side of life's door and there is no Jesus there?"

He thought awhile. "What does it matter?" He repeated, "What does it matter, if I went around this world trying to help people. Help them have a better life. Love your neighbor. If it ain't true, what would it hurt to live in His word? Not a bit."

My belief exactly, I told him.

I don't know what possessed me, but as we rolled along in the Cadillac, I took his electric shaver off the front seat and shaved a spot of his jaw that he had missed. He smiled and kept on driving. When we got to the Knoxville radio station, he made me wait in the parking lot while he recorded his commercial.

When not on the road, Ferree ministered in Cleveland in a humble little church called the Full Gospel House of Prayer. It sat next to a tire repair shop, and when I got there Ferree was sitting in his Caddy, his shirt wet in the armpits, deep into the third hour of his concentration, as he did before every sermon.

I stood on the church porch in the shade with a man from Alabama waiting for services to begin. I'll call him Howard the Doubter. Howard told me he would never stand and give testimony in church, so ashamed was he of his life. He had just had a liver transplant, he told me, having ruined the old one with drugs. I told him a story.

My freshman year at college, a group of student evangelists had invited me to a Bible study. The Bible study was only about Acts, how the believers of Christ fell into rapture, filled with the Holy Ghost, on the Pentecost—the fiftieth day after Passover. They babbled in tongues—it was that part of the Bible. This was news to us few Catholics and Lutheran students they had managed to round up, to be able to speak in tongues. Imagine a dozen young car salesmen, their hair parted on the side and slicked down, their hands on your head, trying to bring on the tongues. Bring on the Ghost! They asked no questions about us, our religious journey, the troubles in our souls. It was a corrupt and loathsome moment. They laid them on. I freaked out. I wanted to go home.

So Glory Be! I got the tongues.

Shala hala mach al lala hasteesee!

It sounded like Arabic, I think. It was a fake. My lying miracle. I wanted to go home and never come back. I felt like I had been molested. I now have trouble with intimate spiritual relationship with charismatic Christians. That's the truth. Jesus said, after all, never to make a show of your prayers, go into a room and do it privately without hypocrisy.

"My cousin had the same experience and never went back," Howard the Doubter told me. I felt better and less nervous to be there.

A man with hair the color of cigarette ashes, a preacher from Alabama, was standing with us on the porch. He too had heard of such experiences. "It happens all the time and it's called spiritual embezzlement," he said.

I sat behind Howard in church. The service began with music, natural and clean. There was no looking over at one another for clues. These folks were just sinners working it out, out of work, out of time, out of patience and prospects. They wore cheap suits and floral-print dresses. The gave hosannas and rose to their feet and stared up into the heating duct than ran across the nave of the cinderblock church as though Jesus Himself may have been up in there. And why not? He could be anywhere and everywhere or nowhere for all Howard and I knew, standing there with our hands clasped behind our backs.

Ferree, a strong, severe, loquacious speaker, looked upon the congregation without really looking at anyone.

"Now, we got liberals out there who might look down upon us," he said in a not-so-veiled reference to me. "We got liberals who hate what we say in the pulpit. It don't fit their worldly concerns. But they die and the church lives on. Who's laughing? I'm not afraid of the Scripture, hallelujah."

He did a peculiar pony high-step. The Ghost was working on him now.

"Love God. Love each other. That's the Gospel."

"Yes Amen, I believe that!"

"Shaba itay! Lemme introduce Brother Johnny. Now, the old saying is a preacher should never allow another preacher into his pulpit be-cause the sheep might jump the fence, but ole Brother Johnny, he's all right. He's deep in Jesus Christ. Amen!"

More singing, more preaching about worries of your worldly pos-sessions, looks, status. The music had a narcotic effect. I drifted off, began thinking about *my* covenant. Why do I treat my wife so badly at times? Like dirt sometimes, when I promised she would become half of me and I half of her. Why would I treat myself so poorly? I won-dered. Because that's how I felt about myself sometimes, deep down. Like dirt.

It was a revelation. Not an answer but a new plateau to walk from. I slapped Howard the Doubter on the back. And just there, at this mo-ment, Brother Mike asked the congregation to put their hands on one another.

"Shaba itay!"

I went to put my hands on him, Brother Mike Ferree himself, the farmer's son from southern Indiana. I wanted to thank him, give him a brotherly squeeze, a silent apology. When I did he shoved me with a hand and a forearm into the pews, into the arms of some automaton, and told him to pray for me. The preacher had body-checked me like a hockey player. The automaton was sweating and smelled stale, he was bald with dandruff and overweight. He never looked me in the eye. He just repeated, "Praise Jesus, thank you, Jesus. Praise Jesus, thank you, Jesus."

I felt burning, rejected, punked out. I felt the sting of something deep and nameless and childlike. Something way back in my life. I felt unwelcome in the house of God. An object of suspicion. An outcast.

I went outside, tears of anger steaming in my eyes. I was told this would happen. The local reverend who told me about the hillbillies who shot up the Catholic woman's trailer also told me to pick a parable from the Bible. I picked the story of the Good Samaritan, which in its end means love your neighbor. One of Jesus' basics. The reverend said turn that parable on its head and think about the suspicion the modern man has for the stranger, even if the stranger had good intentions. These hill people would be suspicious, he warned me. Strangers are welcome here only to a point. Tell them about my doubts or that I was planning to move here and I would see it, the reverend advised me.

I told Ferree of my spiritual journey—a Christian without Christ—and he was doubtful of me. I was false in his mind. I thought about what he'd said about the flock jumping the fence to another preacher's church and I thought about collecting chess pieces. Bad chess players collect the pawns, because the rook is too hard to take. I was in the parking lot blubbering, carrying on, when Johnny, the visiting preacher, stalked out of the church. He came toward me with a belligerent stride and I got a flashback of all those drunken brawls I'd had in the parking lots of cheap Michigan bars. I was ready to slug him. It was dark and the bugs swarmed around the streetlights.

"You got an agenda to make us look bad," he said with a sneer. "You calling Brother Mike a fake? I think you're a fake."

I said, "You don't even know me, man. What kind of preacher are you? You even going to ask me what I'm feeling?" My voice was high and strained and immature. I was surprised by it.

I came for knowledge, I told him. I was invited to service and all I got was a push in the pews. "Try to be Christlike and love the stranger. Drop the suspicion, man." I was working now. I was dropping the Samaritan parable on him.

"You should do the same," he said, calm now, surprised as I was by my emotions. "You should talk to Brother Mike."

He got me right where I lived. Do the same. I said I would.

"Brother Johnny," I asked, "would you keep our conversation confidential? Would you keep my feelings private as a minister?"

He promised he would before going inside and telling Ferree all about it.

I waited in the parking lot until church was let out. It was late, the cicadas were screaming again.

I stepped into the church after the last worshipper departed. It was just me and Brother Mike and some cheap track lighting.

"I'm out of here," I said. Out of the circle of trust that I had never been in.

"You're an arrogant Hollywood *New York Times* leftist who came here to make me look stupid," he said with a face of soured milk.

He reminded me of my first stepfather. Tall, rigorous, strange deep-set eyes with large blue irises and constricted pupils shrouded by glasses. This was one of the more ridiculous moments of my life, I was thinking.

He surmised that I came here to mock the poor Southern white, the Christian, the only people in America who aren't allowed to have a culture. He leaned in to me and said, "You're from us people, I can tell."

I was getting something here that his flock craved yet never received. Personal time, me and Daddy. No preaching, no self-righteousness, no titles. I thought then, We are two flawed men, stooped and burdened with bigotry, poor English, vainglory. I suppose that, like the child, I got attention from the father that I wanted. Me, the boy-man. He, the surrogate father who called himself brother. He was disturbed by me, and said as much. I had taken him out of his control. In his world, he controlled the message. He controlled the group. And here I was, asking messed-up questions and carrying on in the parking lot.

"What was that all about?" he asked about my tears.

"Something from childhood, I guess." It was all I could summon.

He pulled up his shirt and undershirt from his trousers and showed me the stretch marks from the early years of alcohol abuse. He drank so much, he said, his skin ripped like an overfilled balloon. He pointed out the bullet still in his arm. I smiled crazily. I was entertained now.

"You're from these people," he repeated.

"Yeah, I'm from these people," I told him. "I know alcoholics and reprobates. Drugs and death. These are my people. Simple, insular, clannish, damaged. I'm not here to mock you. I'm here to show that our people count for something."

I laughed. I laughed at the whole thing. I laughed at my plywood façade. Maybe I'd outgrown my people; maybe they didn't need me. As I saw it, our people hurt each other as sport, our ever-human condition. We loved hard and hurt hard and we were perpetually saying we're sorry.

The perfidy between reporter and subject was laid bare once again.

"I don't need you," he said in his big cheap suit.

"I don't need you either, Brother."

"We're a lot alike, Charlie."

"Yes, we are, Mike."

"If I offended you, I'm sorry, Charlie. And I hardly say that even to my wife."

"I'm sorry too, and I find myself saying that too much to my wife."

Sorry? Neither of us really was.

The next morning I went deep into the backwoods to see Brother Junior. People there still lived in wooden shacks and cinderblock A-frames with corrugated steel roofs rusting in the humidity, every last one with a satellite TV dish mounted on the roof. The yards were square rows of tomatoes and corn.

Brother Junior lived off a ruinous road in an old powder-blue trailer on an acre. He added a slat-board porch with cardboard nailed into the ceiling. Miss Lilly kept an immaculate home. Their main possession was a large television with satellite hookup in the living room.

I imagined the grandchild, Stephen, the big, hard boy with a canned-ham head who couldn't keep his gum in his mouth, sitting in this trailer in the middle of the hills with flickering images of *Will & Grace* or *Seinfeld* running through his head, detached from the world and his grandparents. He was nine and large and said that his dream when he grew up was to lie around the house. With his hand buried in a bag of Doritos, I imagined.

And this was the Christians' fear. It wasn't that his people were trying to take over the world, Brother Junior told me, but rather the world was trying to take over his people. The liberals and atheists wanted to water it all down to nothing. Beaming images of decadence and homosexuality and godlessness into their living rooms and infecting their children. The little boy in the cotton patch knew more about the comings and goings of an Upper West Side Jew than he did of the people in his own Southern hollow, this cotton patch.

"Television ain't no sin," Brother Junior told me. "I ain't no old prune sitting in the corner. God put me in this world to live. But eventually a man's got to make up his mind. Is he living for this world or's he living for the next? Me, I'm livin' for the next and I'm trying to teach my grandsons that."

He talked about the mansion of gold that awaited him in the next world.

"What's a country boy going to do with a mansion anyway?" I asked him.

"Well, I ain't gonna be a country boy up there, I'm going to be as He is."

"Are there going to be colored people living in the neighborhood?"

"Only gonna be but one race up there. God made us all. We all God's children. Now, if you ain't Christian, you ain't gonna make it."

He showed me his serpent, Mark. He fed it fresh rats but killed the rats first because he couldn't stand to hear the rats screaming. "I know how that poison feels, so I kill 'em first."

He was a decent man. The best Christian I'd met in a long time. I'd have him for a neighbor anytime.

Miss Lilly made a lunch of soda pop and sandwiches of white bread and cheese spread and she gossiped on about the fat little boy's messed-up parents and how they had to take him in to save him from the abuse. It was a very American accounting of a child's life.

Afterward, I gave Brother Junior a wooden snake I'd bought at the nearby gas station. He laughed and then showed me the "trick" to handling a poisonous serpent. Hold it in the middle, never near the head, because at the head it could turn on you and bite.

"Never take it by the tail neither," he said. "Now, Moses, he threw his staff to the ground and it turned to a serpent. The Lord told him to take it up by the tail. Now, Moses got a revelation, but that's not the best way to do it."

I drove a few hours north to Morristown, Tennessee, to Brother Fer- ree's tent revival. Out the windows it was the same strip development, same fast-food chains, same gas stations. The secular smashed up against the religious. A church, a chicken shack, a Chevron with a special on Bud Lite, the green-topped Appalachian Mountains always hunkered in the distance. I was feeling sick, my eyes falling into my cheeks. I didn't think I had the energy for a good old-fashioned tent revival. The stuff with the shouting and music and healing by the roadside, a uniquely American thing, dying because of television and the mall and air-conditioning and disbelief and boredom.

I pulled up and parked in the lot and had a smoke way back because smoking is a sin, although I cannot find where it says that in the Bible. I can find where it says that it is not a sin to drink alcohol. In fact, Paul instructs us not to drink only water but also a little wine for our health. But that's just details. Pentecostalism is as much a culture as a religion.

Brother Ferree came strolling out of the port-a-john. I turned and hid the cigarette.

The crowd began to arrive, the tent was half full. The music rolled and the testifying began. It was the same stuff I'd been hearing all week: morose tales of absolution and deliverance from drugs, a gun that failed to fire, attempted homicide of a wayward woman, a tumor that miraculously disappeared, the anguish of a stillborn baby still alive nearly two decades later. . . . Why did it seem no happy people ever saw the light? Why was the journey a two-step: a life of destitution and then instant deliverance, as if it were a bulb that went on with a switch? I couldn't find the switch. Here, God was not an intellectual journey but a precipice.

How did you get from here to there? Just accepting Jesus with my lips had not worked for me. It hadn't worked for one of the preacher's sons, who told me later outside the tent, "I don't believe this crap. I wanna go to Iraq and kill people."

I advised him to stay out of trouble and graduate from high school and then he could go to Iraq and kill all the Muslims he liked. I figured I was doing his father a favor. His mother saw him sitting when he should have been praising, she saw him talking to me and threw him a dagger look and he slunk back, defeated.

The tent was circuslike, blue stripes, two poles, lit by ten household lampposts. It was easily a hundred degrees and, along with the mosquitoes, rapture was at a maximum.

Ferree took the pulpit: same suit, same cadence. He started into stuff about actors and hypocrites and gave reasons why he never let people of the congregation lay hands on him. "I'd never let a drunk touch me. You can't just lay your hands on me. That's my choice."

He was talking to me again. I tuned out.

After the sermon he granted me an audience. He informed me that I wasn't a Christian. I'm Catholic, I argued.

"You're not a *true* Christian because you haven't been born again," he said.

"That's what Confirmation is," I said. "But going through rituals doesn't mean anything unless you believe."

"Then you're a blasphemer."

I let that go, but it was no way to run a modern public relations campaign for Jesus. Instead, I asked him what happened between us at his church. He refused to talk about it. I apologized again. I told him that I had realized things about life: my hang-ups, my marriage, my stepfather.

"Well, if that's what really happened, then I'm glad."

"Why do you say *if* that way?"

"People say a lot of things."

"Yeah, but when people tell you they've found Jesus and give some story, you say, 'Amen, brother,' and hug them. Those are just words too. Why not an amen for me, Mike?"

"This conversation is over."

"No, wait a minute," I said. "I'm leaving. God bless you."

I checked into a hotel in Virginia. I feel lonely in hotels. The same cheap bedspread, same print of a duck pond, mirrors set to reveal your flaws, the stark lighting. I feel choked by the sameness. There are no surprises in a hotel, nothing original. It's so completely American that it seems un-American. In this hotel they were conducting a "Miss Tiny" beauty contest. The hotel was built to look like an Italian palazzo; but the carpets smelled and the walls were buckling. Milling about the lobby were overfed mothers with faces like prize melons. They were chastising their little dumplings for staining their Louis Vuitton power suits or their tiny chiffon wedding gowns. Tiny beauty queens. One day they would grow into debutantes and sorority whores! Eleven years old was too young for a girl to show off her hips and budding nipples. Their hair was done up in curlers and they were balancing on wobbly heels.

The elevator arrived. Two-Ton Sissy and her beautiful Miss Tiny, who looked exhausted, got in. We got off at the same floor. We walked the same direction down the corridor. Our rooms abutted. I got into my room and poured a bourbon and water and climbed into a hot shower. I could hear Sissy through the wall, admonishing Miss Tiny.

"Okay, we'll do runway now. Do you really want it? If you really want it, then you will go out there and take it."

It sounded sinister and I thought the Pentecostals might have something here. If what was on the other side of this shower wall was the material world, who the hell wanted it?

I toweled off, put on some porn and fell asleep.

Miami, Florida

The value of a racing horse is $600 for its hide and meat plus whatever a fool will pay.

—MIKE O'FARRELL, breeder

There are some things a man will not publicly admit: that he's dumb, that he's down or that he's dying. Generally, he does not need to say it. It can be smelled on his breath, seen on his unpolished shoes, read in his lined and papery skin. This is the sort of man who is a habitué of the horse track.

Most of these men are well beyond retirement age, and if the American horse track can be said to be God's waiting room, then the track diner, with its shabby carpet and drab walls, is His shoe closet. The joint reeks of arthritis rub and thin coffee. They start arriving around eleven-thirty to watch the horses run, but mostly they never go outside to watch the horses run.

They watch inside on television sets, simulcast races from all around the country. They wager on horses in California they've never seen before. By the end of the day they're sitting in a puddle of useless tickets, holding their skulls in their hands. It's like an infection. This is where your Social Security taxes go.

"I come here because what else am I gonna do," says Danny Foyes, a seventy-one-year-old Brooklyn-to-Miami transplant, who looks like a seventy-one-year-old Brooklyn-to-Miami transplant ought: trim, flat-rumped, tanned, a mâché of silver hair slicked with tonic. "Us guys, we grew up with the horses. It's what men were supposed to do when we were young. Nowadays, men don't really do it, except your geriatric crowd and the Jamaicans, of course. It sounds a little womanish, but you know . . . these guys are like my family. That's sad to hear myself say it."

The Calder Race Course is located in the no-man's-land of Miami, about a half hour's drive northwest from downtown. The track is not among the country's best, like Del Mar and Saratoga and Churchill Downs. It squats in a concrete patch, near the professional football stadium, surrounded by strip development, ribbons of freeway and concrete bungalows. Opened in 1971, Calder has seen better days. Battered by the recent hurricanes, the tote board on the infield is obliterated, the corrugated roofs of the stables have been torn away, the quarter pole is cockeyed and the signage on the grandstand is torn and now reads, "Caller."

In the track's commissary, Blinkers, you can usually find Danny and the rest of the usual crowd: Doc, the retired veterinarian; Johnson the ex-con; the Captain, a small Greek with deep pockets; Gas Can Carl, who pulls an oxygen tank along like a dance partner; and Norm, a man who sits and smiles all day, loser after loser, like he deserves the punishment. Nothing should be taken as advice, truth or well meaning. These men tell stories, so many stories, they can't keep them straight. Sometimes they tell each other's stories like they were their own.

This one from Johnson explaining why he walks with a limp when it gets cold, which of course it never does in Miami: "I was in a West Virginia whorehouse about forty years ago. I'm in the back. I got my clothes off when the madam screams, 'Grand jury,' which means it's the cops, it's a raid. So I grab up my clothes and jump out the window. How'm I supposed to know I'm on the second floor?"

Dozens of them, holding on, limping around, dragging. It must be the beauty of the horses.

"Beauty of the horses, yeah, you get over that in five minutes," Danny says. "You come for the action, you come to throw your money away."

Some stand in line listlessly, like they don't even really want to bet at all. But there they are. Then they watch the race on the simulcast screens and then they watch the rerun of the race on the simulcast screens and they will scream louder at the replay of the race than they did during the actual race, as if screaming is going to change the outcome. As though the results might magically change to 1–7–4 from 1–7–2.

"If I had not bet the 4, but the 2 . . ."

Danny rolls his eyes. "The whole damned track is based on one word. If . . . If I woulda boxed it. If I'd picked the 2. If . . . If you hadn't come to the track you never woulda lost your money, that's what I tell them. Dumb dopes. It's like watching a group of priests.

"Watch the faces around here, they're like votive candles," Danny says. He's really going now, his eyes are popping, his hands are working like a brush man at Grand Central Station. "As the race is running, their faces are flickering. 'Please, God, 7–4. Please, God. The Christmas presents.' It's like a fucking seminary around here. I'm not kidding, the faces are like a church candle. And then the horse loses. And then, like the horse, these fucking guys break down and whimper, limp away with bruised haunches where they been beating themselves. And their faces have melted like candles. Just a puddle. 'Oh, God, the Christmas presents.' Horse players are only happy when they're winning. And, of course, they're hardly ever winning."

Some never bet on a race at all. Some just come to sleep. Some come for the free electricity, plugging their motorized wheelchairs into the electrical sockets and shaking in the corner, spilling coffee all over themselves.

Some of these men are still married, most are divorced, some gave up women years ago in favor of the ponies and the life of general self-absorption. Those who are married complain of the constant henpecking from their wives, women with better sense, who wonder why their men simply don't take the $60 they will most certainly lose today, wrap it in a rubber band and throw it over the gates, because by the end of day, they will have nothing to show for their $60. And the wife has a point: $60 a day, five days a week, and you're starting to talk some real money here.

Horse racing, along with boxing and baseball, was once a top spectator sport in the country and the only way to legally wager in the United States (except for Vegas) when Danny was a young man. On any given weekend, tens of thousands of people would pack the grandstands of the nation's tracks—dressed in hats and ties and heels and pearls. The track was a legitimate place to be.

But attitudes and habits changed. In the seventies the government decided to get into the numbers racket, and now all but a few states conduct lotteries. In the eighties and nineties came the casinos and then came the Internet. People gamble in America like never before, to the tune of nearly $75 billion a year, or the gross national product of Egypt. That's the legal bets. Add in illegal sports betting and online gambling like poker, and you could be talking nearly half a trillion dollars, the gross national product of the Netherlands. Horse wagering accounts for just $15 billion of that take, slightly down from last year. The track is dying. You don't have to go to the track to bet on a horse anymore, which cuts into the track's piece. Instead, you can bet on any race in the country via the Internet and in between races look at pictures of naked women. A lot of men do.

But for my money, the track is a much better place to waste your money than the casino. There is a certain camaraderie at the horse track. There is a history. They've got their stories. You can't get that at a casino, watching Grandma staring stupidly at a slot machine as she blows her retirement. Who wants to watch that? The humanity of the thing has been sucked dry from gambling such as that.

There aren't too many women who come to the track anymore. Just the occasional hooker on the arm of a fat guy with some money, some gals out for a weekend or the crazy old lady who puts her lipstick on like a clown. Sometimes, though rarely, a man will bring his wife.

"The wife." Danny clucks while rolling his eyes. "She don't want me coming here. So I got an idea. I bring her down and buy her a fifty-dollar ticket on a horse that can't lose. The jockey can't lose. The thing's going off at 2-to-5. Can't lose. It's perfect. She's gonna win, be happy, see my point of view. Lay off a little bit. So I get her the ticket.

"The gate opens up and the jock falls off the goddamned horse. Of course, the horse keeps running. Horses are pack animals. They keep running. Well, the horse, it finishes first, but he don't got no jock on his ass so it don't count. That's kind of a rule, you gotta have a jockey on the damn thing. But my wife, she don't know that. She's going crazy.

"'Where do I cash the ticket?' she asks me.

"'Just forget it,' I told her. I haven't brought her since."

Danny worked his whole life, mostly as a Chrysler mechanic, save for that stretch when he was a maître d'hotel at a fancy restaurant. "I didn't know nothing except I like lobsters. The manager comes around, says he don't know what's happening with all the lobsters. 'We're going through a lot of lobsters,' he says. I was eatin' 'em for lunch, that's what was happening to all the lobsters. I love d'ose things."

He saved his money, raised a family, has grandchildren and still loves his wife, you can just tell, is all. "Ahhh. She's a good woman," he says with a sigh at the table where he always sits to study his racing program.

"Still beautiful. I hope she sends me a postcard from heaven to wherever I'll end up.

"You think they got animals running circles in heaven that you could drop a couple a bucks on? That would be nice."

Yes, that would be nice.

Now, when he comes home from the track, Danny sometimes lies. He gives her a $50 note and tells her he won. She doesn't believe him, but it cuts down on the henpecking.

Danny and I spend a few afternoons gambling. His shirt is always tucked in and he wins occasionally. I win even less. Johnson, the whoring ex-con, seems to do best of all. Always sitting there with his bifocals and his tight little smirk. "There is one way to win and a thousand ways to lose. . . ."

He makes enough money to buy the *good* coffee. Johnson is irritating, but he's right. The best Danny and I do, after an hour of calculating and confabulating over the *bad* coffee, is to box a trifecta—the top three finishers in no particular order—$10 each. But we mess around too much and miss the post time. The window attendant waves us off.

"No bets."

A good thing too. We picked wrong. All things considered, a $10 win.

Far away from the grandstands where the respectable people gamble is the backstretch. I wander around there seeing if I can pick up an inside tip.

The backstretch is a secret neighborhood behind the racecourse. It is where the horses are stabled, but it is also home to grooms, exercise riders and hotwalkers, those who take care of the horses. It is something straight out of Steinbeck, a Tobacco Road, a Cannery Row, a place of illegal immigrants, desperadoes, drunks and gamblers. The rooms are cement and cold. Lightbulbs dangling from sockets. Some men sleep in the feed stalls. The showers leak, used toilet paper is piled high on the bathroom floors.

A crumby named Bill, an old white guy commenting on the cinderblock wall topped with concertina wire that surrounds the track:
"They say the wall is to keep people out, but it's really to keep people in."

There is a race war simmering at the track. The front side, the business side, is where the white people work, and they have money. In the
back side it's brown. Latin. Broken windows, moldy showers, men
drinking and carrying on at all hours, working like burros seven days a
week including Christmas, a lonely time for Hispanics who are very
connected to their families. Eating Burger King and drinking malt
liquor, that's how they spend the Navidad.

No, brown people are to stay on the back side, says an exercise rider
from Venezuela who dates a white woman in the front office. "They
don't want to see us wandering around in our shitty boots and brown
skin looking at women. We're men, we're lonely," he says. "There's a
lot of racism here and in this country, and there are so many Spanish, a
day is coming when there's going to be hell to pay. A man can only
take so much." A Dominican named Ricardo has been cleaning the
toilets for thirty-seven years. He speaks no English. Why? "¿Porqué?
Porque, yo no tengo que." "Why? Because I don't have to."

Eddie Plesa, Jr., is a horse trainer of Italian extraction. It was his
people who used to be the Mexicans in this country, back when his
grandfather came, back when the newspapers ran headlines like, "Italian Kills Man."

The Hispanic tidal wave grates on Eddie, however. So many Spanish speakers have arrived in South Florida, they've become a large and
quite separate culture. "They don't want to speak English. They have a
sense of entitlement. They don't want to blend in."

Eddie, like many European and African-Americans, moved out of
his neighborhood as so many Latinos moved in. He doesn't like the
way things are going.

Nevertheless, he employs them. "You can't find an American to do
these jobs," he says.

Most of the jockeys come from Latin America: Chile, Peru, Mexico,

Puerto Rico. Owing to the rural nature of Latin America and the scourge of the hamburger that has swept the United States and made everybody fat, the jocks are mostly Latinos.

Having to make a weight usually around 118 pounds with riding equipment, the jockeys come in to work in the morning and sit in a hot box for an hour, or two or five, sweating off the poundage.

As a man gets older, his body wants to put on weight. To combat this, jockeys starve themselves; they take pills, diuretic cocktails, sleep in scuba suits, do roadwork. Some take Lasix, a drug given to horses with bleeding lungs. In humans, Lasix will cause a man to urinate uncontrollably, as much as two pounds an hour. This, in the business, is known as pissing like a racehorse. Jockeys suffer boils, loose teeth, sallow skin, twitches, dizziness, unfocused eyes, hair loss. Their bodies begin to eat themselves, since they give themselves little else to eat. This, of course, is the objective. It gets so bad sometimes, a man can't fuck, swallow or sleep. Just by sleeping a person loses two pounds through metabolism and respiration. A jockey's breath may be perpetually sour, tasting like ashes and tin, his mouth frothing like a dog at a salt lick.

After the hot box, the jockeys shower and fastidiously attend to their hair, giving their manes three dozen strokes with a brush before putting on a sleeveless shirt and silk knickers and standing out front of the jockey room, letting women get a look at their hair and muscles and sinew and bone. Yes, there are jockey groupies. And this despite the fact that jockeys, as a rule, shop in the children's department.

Pound for pound, jockeys are perhaps the greatest athletes in the world. They balance on stirrups three-quarters of an inch thick, on thousand-pound animals running forty miles an hour, covering twenty-eight feet per stride. All have suffered broken bones, been kicked, smothered and knocked unconscious. Two have died this year.

There is one jockey, Josue Arce, whose ears are so large, one wonders how he wins at all—surely the wind resistance from them slows him down. Consider that years ago they put the jocks in aerodynamic silks; the idea was to lessen wind resistance, which is interesting, since no one factored in the way a jockey rides, some squatting low behind the horse's head, others standing high above it. "So the ears are no more ridiculous a thought than the aerodynamic silks," Plesa, Jr., says.

When it's time to ride, the race is announced in the jocks' room, and they are escorted along with the horses directly to the paddock, the area next to the track where the horses are paraded around before the race. Here, some of the more ambitious gamblers surround them, hoping to glean a little something, inspecting the beasts' coats, their carriage, whether they appear bothered or agitated or what to make of that shit the animal just discharged, auguring the steaming pile as though it were tea leaves.

"He's lighter, mon," surmises one Jamaican. "He's really gonna run, I'm telling you."

"What are you talking about?" says the other Jamaican. "He's spent."

This is the conversation of the track.

The clerk of scales, the man responsible for weighing the jockeys, is Victor Sanchez, fifty-eight, himself a former jockey raised in New York City, and the snappiest dresser at Calder. Pinks and greens and purples. Three hundred ties, a couple dozen pairs of loafers, a rack of good suits and fedoras. It's like he stepped out of an old photograph. His assistant is Jesus Miranda, also a former jockey, who won three races in one day and has the photograph pinned above his desk to prove it. Below the photograph on his desk is a sack of hamburgers and french fries, the smell enveloping the locker room and discernible above the stench of liniment. The jocks salivate, curse Miranda, give intimate details about his mother, question his sexuality. Miranda only laughs a light little laugh, his metal braces shining noticeably, the outcome of years of bad diet and regurgitating french fries. He follows the little men into the hot box, offering them fried chicken from a bucket.

Angel Cordero hangs around the jockey room occasionally. He is a living legend. He won more than seven thousand races. He won the

Kentucky Derby. They all wanted to hang around the little big man during the good times. This included anybody who had anything to do with horses. Cordero was gold and then he was old and then he was wet laundry. All of a sudden nobody wanted to know him. And then his wife died in a car accident and the little big man was a little sad man. Javier Velasquez, the jockey, took him on as an agent at twenty-five percent. It was the right thing to do.

And that's what the track and horse racing is all about—money gained, money squandered; reputations won and lost, but mostly it's loss . . . a never-ending ride on a wheel of fate that seems to be weighted at the bottom.

Peewee Sassin, the assistant track secretary at Calder, says that despite conventional thought around the track, he has enough money to retire . . . provided he dies tomorrow.

Peewee, fifty-eight, is, as his name implies, a small man, with a fluted head, thin at the top and round in the nose and cheeks, like a wet hanging sandbag. He was perhaps, by his own description, one of the worst jockeys ever to mount a horse. He raced primarily in Detroit and won seventeen races in eleven years. "My best year, my agent got two hundred and thirty-seven dollars."

It was getting late into one particular season and Peewee had yet to win. The boys in the jock room decided to give him an early Christmas present. It was decided that Peewee was going to be handed a victory.

"'Peewee,' they tells me, 'just get up to the front and run.'"

"So I go out front and stay there and then we're coming around the final eighth pole and I'm in the lead.

"What can I say? I got hypnotized up there. I was staring at the harrows. It was so quiet and beauty-ful. The air was so fresh and the grandstand just passing me by."

The solitude was shattered by the sound of pounding hooves and the cursing of the jockeys as they mowed past Peewee.

"'Peewee, you dumb son of a bitch,' they was yelling.'"

Did he win the race?

"Naw. I couldn't even win a fix."

There were plenty of great jockeys in the mid-twentieth century. Eddie Plesa was not one of them. He could have been, but the darker side of his nature beat him to the history books. Though Plesa, seventy-eight, won six races in a single day in 1946, he was never invited to take a mount in the Kentucky Derby because he was rotten, crooked and for sale. He admits that.

"I ain't sorry for anything I done," he tells me in front of his son Eddie, Jr.'s stables. "Back then you got ten dollars for a ride, twenty-five for a win. It ain't like today."

If the son can be called White Hat Eddie for his clean and reputable manner, then the father must be known as Black Hat Eddie.

If proof of this is needed, then consider that among Black Hat Eddie's acquaintances, he counted one Sam "Golf Bag" Hunt, a hit man for Al Capone who earned the name because he carried his shotgun in a golf bag. Golf Bag's first victim survived the shooting and was forevermore known as "Hunt's Hole in One."

"I think he was involved in the St. Valentine's Day Massacre," Eddie recalls about his pal Golf Bag. "Anyways, he was a hell of a nice guy."

Eddie got his start at age thirteen when he jumped a freight train loaded with horses in Omaha, Nebraska. The horses made their way to Fairmont Park in St. Louis and Eddie made his way with them. He signed a five-year contract soon after as a bug boy, or apprentice jockey.

"They treated you like a whore back then," Eddie says. He got leased out to a trainer in Chicago for a month, and then another in New Orleans for forty-five days. He was fourteen at this point and hungry. That's when a wiseguy offered him $1,500 to hold back a horse. That was enough money for a Cadillac in those days.

"I didn't even know how to hold a horse. All I know is that he wants me to make sure the horse don't win."

The kid got the big idea to bang the horse into the starting gate as it opened and then rear back on the reins, causing the horse to stumble and get out last. Which it did. But the horse liked to run. And in the

final stretch, the horse had caught up to the pack and was threatening
to take the lead, so little Eddie decided to run the beast into the ass of
a horse ahead of him and then pull back on the reins again. That way it
looked nice and copacetic. But the horse didn't cooperate. It ducked
to the rails and took the lead on its own, at which point the kid jerked
back on the reins in plain view of everyone.

After the race, he was called into the steward's office. The officials
wanted to know who had paid him off.

"I was fourteen years old, I could cry at the drop of a hat. So I'm
blubbering like, 'I don't know what you're talking about.' Anyways,
they stripped me of my license to ride."

That was the first time, but not last time, he was stripped of his
privilege to ride.

The wiseguys who paid him to throw the race gathered him up and
squirreled him away in a fancy hotel in New Orleans and paid the
whole nut before eventually shipping him out to Arkansas. A month
and a half later, he was reinstated. "A man fixed it," he says.

The next time Eddie was suspended, the case made it all the way to
the U.S. Supreme Court, but it had nothing to do with cheating in a
race, per se. As it happened, Eddie was involved with cheating book-
makers on the West Coast. In the days before satellites and simulcast,
there was a way to swindle the bookies, something known as past-
posting. That is, getting a bet placed with a West Coast bookmaker
concerning an East Coast race that had just been run. The window of
opportunity between a New York race and a phone call to the West
was usually about three minutes. Eddie was in cahoots with a gang of
coconspirators who had in their possession a military transmitter in
Orange, New Jersey. The boys in Orange would radio the results from
Belmont to Seattle. Eddie, or an employee, would have the wire running up his arm and a receiver taped inside his glove. The boys in New
Jersey were arrested in a parking garage, and two hours later, the
whereabouts of Eddie and two associates were triangulated to an
apartment room in Seattle.

The federal agent who arrested the men in New Jersey had no warrant, but the U.S. Supreme Court ruled that though the evidence could not be used in federal court, it could be in state court.

The saga made national headlines, as Eddie Plesa was the first jockey or track official ever charged in a horse-fixing scheme.

He was reinstated in 1951 and won fifty-four races in twenty-seven days. It didn't last long. He was suspended in 1952 for taking a whip from another jockey.

Could he have been among the greatest jockeys of all time? I ask him.

"I don't know," he says. "I was up and down like a washwoman's ass on Monday."

Up and down, up and down, but it's mostly down. Especially if you're trying to do it legit. Picking horses requires a combination of conceit, self-denial and intelligence. One of the basics to keep in mind is that the trainers try to find advantageous races for their horses to win and that most horses are stabled at the track for the duration of their racing season. Therefore, you should realize that most of the regulars have seen the horses race before and have some understanding of their worth.

The track takes a percentage of the money wagered on a race and therefore it has no interest in its outcome. There is no fix there. When you bet, you do not bet against the track, you bet against the other gamblers at the track. This is known as parimutuel, French meaning betting between ourselves. People are not dumb with their money. Money is more important in America than almost anything else. Watch the tote board to see where the money is going. A horse listed at 15-to-1 in the morning that comes down to 5-to-1 is better than a horse moving in the other direction. People know things here.

The track tries to match horses of similar ability to keep things interesting. So watch for a horse moving up or down in class. Even if a horse has a good record, it may not be much if it has built a career against dogs.

Picking the favorite never yields money, and so there are exotic ways to gamble. An exacta, for instance, is picking the first- and second-place horses in order and pays bigger odds. A trifecta is picking the first three and pays bigger odds still; a superfecta, the top four. This pays astronomical amounts and requires knowledge about the horses. If this is too much for you, here are some other, easier methods, mostly for picking losers:

1. Always pick a filly in the mud. Mothers, some believe, make better mudders.
2. Choose gray coats on a gray day.
3. The Muldoon. Bet on two horses with similar names in the same race, such as Joe's Pride and Hungry Joe.
4. Charming names. Choose something like It's a Wonderful Life near Christmastime.
5. In Between the Sheets. Take the horses' names in a particular race, append ". . . in between the sheets" to each and choose the most lascivious-sounding one. For instance, Mike's Missile . . . in between the sheets, may be a good bet.
6. The Chinese Star. Scratch out any horse listed at over 10-to-1 in the program. Start with the favored horse and count through the list until you reach the seventeenth name. That is your favorite. Then continue from there to count until twenty-one. This is your second favorite. According to the Chinese, these numbers have power, with seventeen having more power than twenty-one.

"Watch out for the tout," Danny instructs me. The tout is a guy who will whisper in your ear, "Psssst, buddy, I got a little bird from the jock room who tells me the 5 horse can't lose. Can't lose. And listen, I'm a little short. If you could put five on it for me, I'd appreciate it."

And the tout tries to scam up five or six suckers like this: "Hey, buddy, I heard it from a little bird in the jock room who tells me the 3 horse can't lose. If you could put five on it for me, I'd appreciate it . . . Hey, buddy, I heard it from a little bird in the jock room who tells me the 2 horse . . ."

"Stay away from this guy," Danny says. "If you get a tip, the best thing to do is write it down, crumple it into a ball and flush it down the toilet."

I got such a can't-miss tip from a little bird inside the jock room. This guy was a jockey's valet. He was a white guy with a mullet. His boss was riding the 3 horse in the fourth race. He told me to bet two bucks across the board: win, place and show, which costs six dollars. The horse was going off at 30-to-1.

"Can't miss," the mullet told me, and I believed him because he was a nice little bird. I should have listened to Danny.

I watched as the filly stumbled out of the gate and finished last. The point of this story: never take a tip from a guy who works for tips.

If you can't figure the horses for yourself, then most tracks employ a fortune-teller to help you. His picks are listed in the day's racing program. Calder, I am told by some horse writers, has had its share of luminaries.

Bobby Slater was the former track handicapper whose clothes went in and out of style six or seven times before you were ever born. He wore plaids with spots, and that sort of thing. He was a Runyonesque character who would greet the secretaries with something like, "Morning, dolls." He drank two martinis a day and succumbed at the age of ninety. Even though he's dead, they still send notes around the country from Calder on Bobby's letterhead asking, for instance, that someone at Hollywood Park put $10 down for him on the 4 horse in the second race on the third of the month.

Bobby had a friend at the track called Harry the Horse. It wasn't like the name implied, however. Harry was less like a horse and more like a gofer, fetching papers and such around the track. In the Sport of Kings, the Horse was the king of the one-liners. "I'm so old," Harry once said, "when I was born, the Dead Sea wasn't even sick."

Harry the Horse went to see Bobby Slater in the hospital. When he came back to the track, the secretaries wanted to know how he was doing.

"He took a turn for the nurse," Harry said.

Bobby Slater came from Cincinnati and died in Miami. It is said that Bobby the bad dresser was laid out in a good suit, though this cannot be confirmed, as the casket at his service was closed. This is a shame because there is a photograph of Bobby still hanging at Calder. And if the story of the good suit is true, then Bobby Slater looked better dead than he ever did alive.

The current handicapper at the Calder track is Ron Nicoletti. This passage shall be known as "How to Become a Handicapper: or, the Short Beautiful Life of Ron Nicoletti."

Ron Nicoletti wasn't always a handicapper. Raised in Brooklyn, he made mounds of money in the seventies designing casual wear for leading lights such as Mick Jagger and Elton John. He had a shop in New York City.

He almost had a date with Lauren Hutton the actress, but he got into a car accident on the way to the date. "It never happened," he cracks.

He palled around with Sissy Spacek the actress, before Sissy Spacek became Sissy Spacek the actress. "Just good friends, nothing else," he says.

It's not as though he has never sealed the deal, however. Whenever a certain pop song plays in his office at the track, Nicoletti will swing his girth around in his swivel chair, throw a thumb toward the radio and proclaim proudly, "I nailed her."

Nicoletti once lived across the street from the designer Oleg Cassini in New York. The building housing Oleg Cassini caught on fire, so it seemed. Nicoletti ran to the rescue. The following is an excerpt from a small Gramercy Park newspaper, 1972:

"Then I got to the third floor and there was a woman screaming, she didn't speak English. There were flames coming from the top window where she was."

It was at this point that Nicoletti was overcome by smoke and passed out, falling down a flight of stairs in the process before being carried to safety.

"Turned out to be a grease fire," Nicoletti says without embarrassment. "Someone burning their dinner."

He eventually retired to the islands with his money, drank a lot of rum and grew bored. He came back to the States taking a job giving race results over the telephone. The rest is small cheap detail. This, in a nutshell, is how one becomes a handicapper. It is apparently not a bad living. Nicoletti has grown into his body and his mid-fifties, cut his Afro and settled down as a decent family man. He bicycles around in tight shorts.

His top four picks for every race appear in the day's racing program. Nicoletti claims to pick the winner thirty-two percent of the time. Usually it's the favorite.

"I don't pick the favorites," Nicoletti says without modesty. "I make the favorites."

There is a slate of big-purse races today; some good, unseen horses have come down from New York. I have challenged Nicoletti to a wager. It goes: Each man starts with $100. Bet any way you like, any configuration, any amount on any number of races of your choosing. If you don't like any race, don't bet on any. At the end of the day, the man with the most money takes all.

Now, Nicoletti is a big deal. The truth is, he is a pretty decent handicapper. He's so good, he's even got a simulcast show from the paddock. And when he's there bloviating, I make sure I'm there to razz him. As he's laying out his picks before race number one, I'm shouting from behind the hedgerow.

"Hey, Nicoletti! Stick to picking your nose. Nicolettiiiiiiii! You better call a priest, 'cause I'm gonna murder you, ya bum. Hey, Nicoletti! Your nose runs faster than your picks!"

I got him flustered, I can tell.

"Who is this guy?" Nicoletti stammers like a real Brooklynite.

After a couple of races I'm yelling something like, "Yo! Nicorino! Go back to stitching panties!"

Another race: "Nicoletti! If you grew a mustache, you'd look like your grandmama."

Another: "Nicky, baby! What? You sweating gravy over there."

"Tricky Nicky! It's a crime what you're doing. It's immoral."

"Hey Nickel-and-Dime-o-letti. You smell that? You smell something burning? I'm on fire!"

Truth is, I'm dying. I won't give you the specifics, I can't, I threw my racing form in the garbage can. Suffice it to say, it was loser after loser after loser. I enlisted Danny's help and Danny's money. We pooled dough on exotic bets—the trifecta, the superfecta, the wheel. Nothing. Danny's looking morose. I'm feeling sick. I'm down seventy-eight bucks, but what's worse, my ego feels like a rumpled paper bag. I've smoked two packs of heavy cigarettes. I'm on the beer now. Danny's on the beer now, and he doesn't drink beer.

Post-time for the last race is in seven minutes, when I bump into Nicoletti. He's had some winners, he says. Not having a bad day. He's only down eighty bucks.

"Eighty! Ha!" I'm winning. I'm beating Nicoletti by two bucks. It's all down to the last race. All's he's got to do is lose.

You guessed it. Nicoletti picks the favorite. Nice and safe.

Me, I've got a hunch.

The favorite wins. Mine comes in second. I throw my ticket to the wind and then the announcer calls a stewards' inquiry. Something illegal may have happened out there, somebody has challenged. The results are not official. It may be that I won . . .

But I can't find my stub, I'm picking around the ground like a pigeon in a rice pile. And then it's announced, the result is official. I've lost twice on the same race. Nicoletti's laughing at me. And I walk away and Danny's got an arm for me and says, "That's okay, kid. It happens to the best of 'em."

"If Nicoletti is so good, then why's the bum handicapping for a living?"

That's what I'd like to know.

ACKNOWLEDGMENTS

I would like to thank Arthur Sulzberger Jr., publisher of *The New York Times,* for his open mind and encouragement. This book would not have come to be without his television channel and a series of films I made there. I owe a great deal to Bill Smee and Lawrie Mifflin for making that project roll. My friend and director Alex Cooke, thank you for your vision and guts. Jonathan Stack and David McIlvride, thanks for your patience. Rolf Cutts, too, was a mentor. Eddie Keating lent his imagination and philosophy to these pages. Michael Wallis, professor of Route 66, and his book, *Pretty Boy,* were instructive as were the books *Son of the Morning Star,* by Evan S. Connell, and *Salvation on Sand Mountain,* by Dennis Covington. The Detroit Homicide Bureau and the Amarillo Dusters were exceedingly gracious about access. Guennadi Tregroub and Gamal Maltese taught me much about the art and history of the circus; Don Super about horses and marksmanship and the Old West and Mike Lentz about bull riding. My love to Amy for her advice and lonesomeness and for feeding the animals while I was gone. I want to properly thank my mother Evangeline for my life. I am deeply indebted to Todd Schindler for his hard work, his talented eye, and his gifted ear. A real friend. To those people whose names and stories appear in these pages: there is no finer art than life.